THE RISE OF THE AMERICAN COMICS ARTIST

The Rise of the
American Comics Artist

CREATORS AND CONTEXTS

Edited by PAUL WILLIAMS and JAMES LYONS

UNIVERSITY PRESS OF MISSISSIPPI / JACKSON

www.upress.state.ms.us

The University Press of Mississippi is a member
of the Association of American University Presses.

First printing 2010

∞

Library of Congress Cataloging-in-Publication Data

The rise of the American comics artist : creators and contexts /
edited by Paul Williams and James Lyons.
     p. cm.
   Includes index.
   ISBN 978-1-60473-791-2 (cloth : alk. paper) — ISBN 978-1-
60473-792-9 (pbk. : alk. paper) 1. Comic books, strips, etc.—
United States—History—20th century. 2. Cartoonists—United
States—Biography. I. Williams, Paul, 1979– II. Lyons, James,
1972– III. Title: Creators and contexts.
   NC1426.R57 2011
   741.5'97309048—dc22   2010016183

British Library Cataloging-in-Publication Data available

Contents

III: Artists or Employees?

IV: Creative Difference: Comics Creators and Identity Politics

V: Authorizing Comics: How Creators Frame the Reception of Comic Texts

Acknowledgments

We would like to express our gratitude to Seetha Srinivasan and Walter Biggins at the University Press of Mississippi for their enthusiasm, encouragement, and support—and our anonymous readers for helping to guide and hone our ideas for the book. Thanks also to Max Stites for taking the time to read the manuscript. It has benefited greatly from the generosity of Joe Sacco and Chris Ware, who have allowed us permission to reproduce their work, and from the invaluable insights of Jeff Smith, Jim Woodring, and Scott McCloud. Thanks to them, and the numerous other comics creators who continue to entertain, educate, and inspire us.

Introduction: In the Year 3794

—PAUL WILLIAMS AND JAMES LYONS

Comics will be the culture of the year 3794
—Salvador Dali (Qtd. in Gravett 2007, 14)

Salvador Dali's prediction invites one to hypothesize what the world of 3794 will look like—and whether any of its social coordinates will correlate to the ones we recognize at the start of the twenty-first century. Not so long ago, admirers of the medium's possibilities might have asked whether there could be any similarity between an Anglophone world that considers comics as culture and the one in which they currently lived. Over a thousand years in the future—that would sound about right for the kind of radical cultural reestimation that would have to take place before comics could escape the stereotypes and prejudices surrounding their production and consumption.

This is no longer the case: comics have jumped closer to the promise of Dali's 3794 in unprecedented ways. If comics are not often considered "culture" in the way some members of the population consider ballet and legitimate theater to be "culture," the current position they occupy in hierarchies of taste place comics as both high art and mass medium. This transformation is of course complexly related to the industrial, cultural, and academic institutions that have reshaped comics' production and reception.

As *The Rise of the American Comics Artist* demonstrates, one way to make sense of this process is to see the comics creator as the prism through which to explore recent changes in the medium. Crucially, shifts in the perception of the people creating comics have been the corollary of such changes, as well as contributing to them. As its subtitle suggests, this book employs the systems and structures of the comics industry to scrutinize the role of the creator critically, whether those contexts are institutional or cultural, economic or generic, ethical or aesthetic. While existing scholarship has addressed how comics is a creator's medium shaped by the styles, stories, and characters of individual writers and artists (see Sabin 1996; also Hatfield 2005; Raeburn 2004; Witek 1989), *The Rise of the American Comics Artist* is the first book to offer a detailed survey of the distinctive ways in which the dynamics of comics creativity has been reconfigured in contemporary culture.

The book is organized into five sections, each of which centers on a major way that creators have been understood: as powerful brands able to position comic texts according to the perceived logic of the market; as allegorists and interpreters of international political events; as (simultaneously) artists aloof from the concerns of financial reward and workers for hire; as political actors involved in the arena of representing gender, sexuality, and ethnicity; and finally as literary authors—with consequent implications for how reviewers and critics have analyzed the texts they produce. In each section the creators and texts symbolizing that particular conceptual node undergo critical attention, and each section references the scholarship relevant to its subject, inviting the reader to see what others have written regarding the study of contemporary comics. The creative and commercial decisions made by comics practitioners offer further opportunities for study, and several sections conclude with interviews with landmark creators from the period covered. These interviews correlate with the concerns of that section, illuminating creativity in ways that offer a productive tension with the preceding scholarship.

The historical period covered by this collection begins in the late 1980s, when ambitions for the medium were raised, and voices within and outside the comics industry proclaimed that the successes of Art Spiegelman's *Maus* (first published in collected editions in 1986 and 1991), Alan Moore and Dave Gibbons's *Watchmen* (1987), and Frank Miller's *Batman: The Dark Knight Returns* (1986) would propel comics towards new audiences. Few readers would disagree that the material form of comics has evolved since then, or that the type of narratives being written and drawn has expanded the vocabulary of the medium. *The Rise of the American Comics Artist* continues the process of mapping out how the position of comics has changed, especially in the eyes of reviewers and critics, whether found in universities or newspaper offices or in feminist discussion groups.

Certain articles about comics still perpetuate stereotypes, assuming the medium remains the preserve of awkward pubescent males, as this example from *The Times* (London) demonstrates: "COMICS. Cheap, flimsy, disposable. Scattered next to dirty socks on teenage bedroom floors" (Greenwood 2004, 15). Usually those stereotypes are introduced to disarm a potentially dismissive reaction by preempting reader skepticism. Nonetheless, this confirms the premise that consumption of comics cannot take place without apology.

British journalist Charles Shaar Murray laments, "Must the graphic-novel wars be fought over and over again?" (Murray 2005, 25). The assumptions made in *The Times* are being superseded by the new convention of starting articles bemoaning the need to justify the medium (see Paul Gravett qtd. in Allfree 2003, 14–15; also Thompson 2002, 11; Ware 2006, 10). The editors hope *The Rise of the American Comics Artist* will advance the terms in which we think about the production and reception of comics without contrition.

The broad periodization of the last twenty years is imprecise, but only because this collection tracks a series of parallel impulses in the comics medium, related to each other insofar as each area represents a shift in the wider cultural contexts in which comics creators produce work and that work is read. The origins of these transformations in comics' cultural context cannot be isolated to a single historical moment, and these shifts are continuing in and around comics in the public sphere; it is hoped the future direction of these changes can be better ascertained by close analysis of the comics industry.

In this collection that scrutiny emerges from around the English-speaking world, and the perspectives offered in *The Rise of the American Comics Artist* are suitably international—because American comics have a global audience, the field of production is driven by many creators from outside North America, and the financial decisions influencing the majority of comics production are made by multinational corporations. There are good reasons to understand North American comics in a transnational context: the institutional transaction of texts, creators, and capital across national borders has contributed to observable productive tensions in the comic texts themselves. Ana Merino's chapter on the comics of the Hernandez brothers and Jessica Abel tracks the adjustments of personal identity that border crossings between the USA and Mexico entail (with those adjustments subject to local understandings of gender roles). After *Watchmen*'s success, Alan Moore was soon joined in the U.S. comic industry by fellow British writers Neil Gaiman and Grant Morrison, and in his chapter on this "Brit Invasion" Chris Murray suggests that their ironic distance from the superhero as a defining myth of American superpower facilitated their play with the conventions of the superhero tradition.

Stephen Weiner's "How the Graphic Novel Changed American Comics" highlights how the idea of the "graphic novel" has come to dominate contemporary discussion of the comic form. Appropriately this chapter begins this collection and cites many of the texts analyzed elsewhere. It has become common in histories of the medium to cite Will Eisner and his 1978 *A Contract with God* as the first graphic novel and the first instance of that term used to promote an extended-length comics narrative. While the paperback edition did feature this label on its cover, *A Contract with God* was neither the first graphic novel, nor was Eisner the first person to coin the phrase. Weiner suggests other contenders also credited for inaugurating the graphic novel—and for having literary ambitions. One figure seems to have a preeminent claim: Swiss writer/artist Rodolphe Töpffer created long-form books combining words and pictures in sequence in the early nineteenth century (published in the U.S. in the 1840s), and we know of no one preceding Töpffer in creating narratives told through sequential images and published in mass-produced books (Gaudreault and Marion 2005, 5–11).

Following the claim by notable comics historian R. C. Harvey, we contend the first use of the *term* "graphic novel"—used in reference to an extended-length comics narrative—was originally coined in November 1964 by Richard Kyle in a newsletter circulated to the Amateur Press Association. With Kyle's permission, the term was subsequently modified and used by Bill Spicer in his *Graphic Story Magazine* (originally titled *Fantasy Illustrated*). Harvey also argues that the first instance of an extended-length comics narrative *marketing itself* as a graphic novel "was the 1976 publication of *Beyond Time and Again*, by George Metzger, where the term 'graphic novel' appears on the title page and on the dust jacket flaps" (Qtd. in Arnold 2003).

So why has *A Contract with God* soaked up such acclaim for bringing the "graphic novel" into the English-speaking world? Partly because of Eisner's repeated success in creating innovative comics—from his earlier superhero comic *The Spirit* to his many graphic novels since *A Contract with God*. Another reason is that *A Contract with God* was published outside the standard comic distribution networks of the 1970s (Chute 2008, 453, 462 n.3). In 2003, *Time* magazine defended celebrating the 25th birthday of the graphic novel concurrently with *A Contract with God*'s 25th anniversary: "Eisner's book, published outside the comic book system and pretty clearly the first comix work deliberately aspiring to literary status, by having the term on the front cover, crystallized the concept of a 'graphic novel.' But the matter is clearly open to debate" (Arnold 2003). Leaving the debate open seems wise, and the two exceptional aspects of *A Contract with God* that *Time* cited could also be seen in the wordless woodcut books of the mid-twentieth century—one of the last of these to be published was Laurence Hyde's *Southern Cross* (1951). The woodcut books represent an important part of the history of sequential art in book form, not least in their influence on contemporary comics creators (the woodcut style has been revived by current artists such as Eric Drooker).

Eisner's claim to have invented the phrase "graphic novel" seems to be an honest mistake; certainly, he has been highly influential in establishing other terms with which scholars understand the language of comics. After Eisner, we may now talk about "comics" as the physical manifestation of the medium on the newsstands alongside "sequential art" to indicate the structural principles of this medium (Eisner 1999; McCloud 1994, 5–9)—although this too is contested (see Chute 2008, 454–55). Comics scholar Hillary Chute has labeled her area of study "graphic narratives," resisting the "novel" element of the term because it associates longer-length comics work with fiction. Further, as Charles Hatfield's seminal *Alternative Comics: An Emerging Literature* (2005) notes, using the term "graphic novel" risks obscuring the economic imperative of serialization which often precedes comic books being collected into the graphic novel form (154). Comics creator Joe Sacco, well known for his works of comic reportage, *Safe Area Goražde* (2000) and *Palestine* (1996), also questions the term "graphic novel" for "trying to make it sound like we're really grown-up. But we are what we are . . . Comics is comics. I don't feel ashamed—so I don't need another couple of words to make me feel like I'm doing something worthwhile" (Qtd. in Leith 2003, 2).

Part of the reason for the high sales of *Maus*, *The Dark Knight Returns*, and *Watchmen* in the late 1980s and early 1990s was their production and promotion as a material form that justified the label "graphic novel." In theory, discerning adult readers were more attracted to these square-bound texts printed on glossy paper stock marketed and sold like books, rather than the "newsstand" comics with their staples (see Wynne 2003, 16). Able to be laminated and distributed through book publishing channels in ways that the comic book format could not, the graphic novel made sequential art into a far more desirable and marketable product for libraries and bookshops.

While the final chapter of *Alternative Comics* expresses Hatfield's cautiousness at the graphic novel's pole position in comics studies, he ultimately accepts the usefulness of the term (2005, 152–63). In arguing for the literariness of comics since the late 1960s and hailing the recent period of maturity as a "confident and thorough exploration of the form's peculiar tensions, potentialities, and limits" (66), Hatfield confides he once toyed with the title *The Rise of the Graphic Novel* for his 2005 book (53). His position precedes one of the contentions mapped out here: the legitimization of comics has depended upon the increasing ubiquity of graphic novels and other long-form narratives (5–6). One reason for the need for this collection lies in the five years that have elapsed since *Alternative Comics*'s publication: creators mentioned briefly in Hatfield's book have reached levels of critical and public recognition previously seen only in the case of Art Spiegelman, and the field of comics studies has expanded in ways that deserve scholarly comment. Transformations in the field of North American comics Hatfield was beginning to discern can now be analyzed with fuller and greater complexity from this later chronological moment.

A more specific example of how this collection extends and augments Hatfield's insights is in the aforementioned commerce between graphic novels and traditional outlets for book publishing. In her chapter on the critical and financial success of the DC publishing imprint Vertigo, Julia Round argues that use of the graphic novel as a publishing form is pivotal to the legitimization of comics. Hatfield notes the lucrative distributional opportunities bookshops and libraries represent, but the intellectual focus of his study is literary form, theme, and characterization in the context of the publishing apertures the comic book allows. He does not explore in detail the implications of the changing materiality of comic texts or the political economy of the industry and its institutions, although *Alternative Comics* certainly indicates they are important aspects of the contemporary field of comics production (30–31).

As Round discusses, the high visibility of the Vertigo titles and the accumulating star status of their creators enticed many book publishers (Penguin, Gollancz, Mandarin, Boxtree) to enter the field of graphic novel publishing (Sabin 1996, 162–67). However, the sales of the three seminal graphic novels *Maus*, *Watchmen*, and *The Dark Knight Returns* were not repeated, media interest waned, and subsequently comics companies such as Marvel and the new entrants into the graphic novel field sidelined the idea of comics produced for an adult audience (Sabin 1996, 171; Lee 2002). In 2000, Roger Sabin estimated that comics shops in the U.S. and UK were now a third of the number that existed ten years prior (18). The late 1980s moment of the graphic novel's emergent visibility and its extensive publicizing (although not its invention) represents a pivotal shift in the position of comics within Anglophone culture more generally, and made the developments of the next twenty years possible, although it also sounds a note of caution against contemporary cheerleaders for comics' acceptance as cultural form. The historical moment this book takes as its starting point also had its publishing stars, its literary prizes, and its hopes that comics would become "just another" artistic medium. Dan Franklin of Jonathan Cape, the company responsible for publishing some of the medium's most notable recent successes (Daniel Clowes's *Ghost World* [2000], Marjane Satrapi's *Persepolis* [2003]) has cautioned, "I don't believe it's going to be a truly mass phenomenon . . . it's still difficult to get these books into the bookshops—they're still full of superheroes" (Qtd. in O'Keeffe 2005, 16).

Arguably one reason superheroes continue to be the dominant comics genre is because of the proliferation of comics source material being adapted into successful blockbuster Hollywood films. The profitable precedent of Tim Burton's *Batman* and advances in the verisimilitude of CGI visual effects has seen films based on the superheroics of Spider-Man, the X-Men, the Hulk, Daredevil, Ghost Rider, the Fantastic Four, Iron Man, and Superman—with further superhero films planned. Rather than solely targeting the typical superhero comic reader, the young-adult/teenage-male demographic, these films are produced for (and released during school vacations to attract) the lucrative family audiences that substantially boost profits. These films' source material, the superhero genre once nearly monopolized by Marvel Comics and DC Comics, has historically dominated perceptions of the American comics industry since the 1940s. However, exceptions such as *Sin City* (2005), *Ghost World* (2001), *American Splendor* (2003), *V for Vendetta* (2006), and *From Hell* (2001) demonstrate that Hollywood sees the potential for adaptation in numerous comics genres. Looking at press coverage, journalists repeatedly cite the adaptation of comics sources into Hollywood films as evidence they are a legitimate medium (O'Keeffe 2005, 16; Allfree 2003, 14–15; Thompson 2002, 11). Will comics become a permanent satellite of the entertainment industry, or will the medium suffer a finite shelf life? Regardless, the current prominence of comics at the movies is one more indication the medium of sequential art enjoys a new position in Anglophone culture (see Gordon, Jancovich, and McAllister 2007).

Section two of this collection explores the dialogue between comics and international political events. The nature of comics' cultural status means that these issues may be addressed in ways unavailable to novelists, journalists, and filmmakers working in traditional channels of information dissemination. In *Comics, Comix & Graphic Novels* (1996), Roger Sabin suggests comics are worthy of our attention precisely because their creators do not look to cultural recognition as the sole factor in measuring a successful product. Borrowing a phrase from Spiegelman, for Sabin the freedom that "flying under the critical radar" permits is one reason the field of contemporary comics is so varied, rich—and controversial (Sabin 1996, 9).

This freedom needs to be understood against a U.S. society where national unity was fetishized immediately after the terrorist attacks of 9/11, when questioning the righteousness of America's presence around the world led to vicious and hostile retorts. Graham Murphy's chapter regarding *Uncle Sam and the Freedom Fighters* (2006–2007) studies how its creators exploited the freedom of the comics medium to comment on the erosion of civil liberties within the United States. Murphy's chapter concentrates exclusively on superhero comics, historically the best-selling comics genre (and still largely so), but this collection discusses comics produced in a variety of genres and production forms, befitting the plurality of the medium in the twenty-first century. *The Rise of the American Comics Artist* illustrates the wealth of genres produced by North American comics creators, from documentary to romance, horror to political satire. This multiplicity is not new to the medium but they are being newly acknowledged. For instance, in the illustrated press of the late nineteenth century, sequential art often served as a means of reportage. In Joe Sacco's works, the comic creator's function as an eyewitness journalist is resurrected, as Andrea A. Lunsford and Adam Rosenblatt demonstrate in their chapter, returning to the relationship between international politics and observation in sequential art.

As in other media, certain comic texts assert their distance from more obviously commercial products in order to state their oppositional credentials. In section three, James Lyons explores how the cultural currency of nonconformity that alternative comics profess might reap the very financial rewards they mock. His chapter focuses on Shannon Wheeler's *Too Much Coffee Man*, where the transaction between profit, popularity, and providing an alternative to "mainstream" (superhero) comics was self-reflexively acknowledged in a comic text in which that tension was particularly tender. This section also relates how comics creators balance the imperatives of artistic self-justification and commercial survival. In his interview, Jim Woodring confirms that this balance is not an academic abstraction but a lived concern for the professional comics creator. David M. Ball's chapter, "Comics Against Themselves: Chris Ware's Graphic Narratives as Literature," takes as its subject the work Ware produced for *The New Yorker* magazine and explores the nature of that work with regard to a modernist aesthetic of fragmentation, the institutional maneuvers that sell comics, and Ware's witty, self-conscious representation of the relationship between comics-as-art and comics-as-a-popular-publishing-industry.

The presence of this polarity in 1960s and 1970s *comix* (a spelling primarily used to refer to countercultural comics) is one of the many legacies that era has bequeathed to contemporary creators. Prominent comix artist Robert Crumb depicted himself as "the long-suffering patient artist-saint" and "the status-quo booshwah businessman cartoonist" in "The Many Faces of R. Crumb" in *XYZ Comics* (1972) (Rpt. in Crumb and Poplaski 2005, 186; discussed in Hatfield 2005, 119–22). Two California printing presses, The Print Mint in Berkeley, and Rip Off Press in San Francisco, published comix whose characters and content were owned by their writers and artists, preceding the growing propensity for intellectual property rights to remain with comics creators (Skinn

2004, 128–36). Crumb used the back cover of *Zap* #0 (1968) to challenge the denigration of the medium (according to then prevailing cultural hierarchies) as literature's inferior: "Did your mother ever tear up YOUR comic books?... Were you given lectures about how comics were CHEAP TRASH put out by evil men? Do you feel a spark of GUILT every time you pick up a comic book? Do you feel like you ought to be reading a good book instead? Let ZAP comics wisk [sic] away all such foolish notions!" (Rpt. in Crumb and Poplaski 2005, 242). Crumb's defense of comics' cultural legitimacy has become something of a fragile orthodoxy. The underground's influence on contemporary North American comics culture is profound, and in addition to issues like creator rights and institutional respectability, one could add controversial sexual subject matter, formal experimentation, explicit commitment to leftist political agendas (especially those concerned with identity politics), and the use of comics as life-writing and self-expression (Hatfield 2005; Hatfield 2008, 139; see also Rosenkranz 2002).

Section four of *The Rise of the American Comics Artist* considers the politicization of the portrayal of identity that various collectives (such as the Civil Rights movement, the women's movement, and the Chicano movement) stressed in the 1960s, and Joe Sutliff Sanders, Paul Williams, and Ana Merino contribute chapters on the ways that comics creators have been placed, or have placed themselves, within political debates about affiliation and identity. Williams and Merino discuss the work of the Hernandez brothers and Jessica Abel, with the former contextualizing these creators within "contemporary women's comics" and the way different material contexts of production invoke particular reading communities. Merino's study looks closely at these creators' texts in order to understand the Hernandez brothers' legacy in Abel's work on the terrain of feminine Latin/o American identities. Sutliff Sanders's account of sexuality in contemporary comics situates its representation in antagonistic historic relation to preexisting trends, such as those generated by official sanctions (see Weiner's chapter in this volume) and the underground comix.

Connections between countercultural comix and contemporary comics culture are not only thematic but biographical: underground publisher Last Gasp's anthology *Weirdo* was first released in 1981 with Crumb as editor. *Weirdo* featured Crumb's work, as well as that of other comix creators such as Spain Rodriguez and Bill Griffith (creator of the popular character Zippy), before falling under the stewardship of Peter Bagge, an influential and successful figure in the contemporary comics field. *Weirdo* also published comics by the award-winning Joe Sacco, one of the most critically noted creators of the last twenty years. Griffith co-founded *Arcade: The Comix Revue* (1975–1976) with Art Spiegelman, an anthology that published their major contemporaries in the field, including Crumb, Spain, Kim Deitch, Robert Williams, Gilbert Shelton, and S. Clay Wilson. The comic series Spiegelman has edited have bridged the underground to the next generation of creators, his later anthology *Raw* (1980–1991) featuring comics by Chris Ware, Daniel Clowes, and Charles Burns, all prominent ambassadors of contemporary American comics (Skinn 2004, 52, 250).

The graphic novels of the 1980s were influenced by superhero comics from the late 1960s and early 1970s. Bradford W. Wright argues that attempts by Marvel and DC to respond to social and political currents at the end of the 1960s led to superhero comics that were self-referential, morally ambiguous, more thoroughly referencing political events, and populated with introspective and disenchanted characters. Though unable to survive financially through the traditional distribution outlets of the early 1970s, these themes would be reused and reworked by successful graphic novel creators in the 1980s onward, such as Frank Miller, Alan Moore, and Alex Ross (Wright 2008, 156).

Another aspect of the comics medium's new dimensions is the emergence of semi-regular reviews in the literature sections of the mainstream newspaper and magazine press, such as *The Independent* and *Guardian* in the UK and *Time* in the U.S. The final section of *The Rise of the American Comics Artist* notes how comics are accruing markers of institutional respectability such as these reviews, and asks how this affects the way we read comics. What does it mean to see the comics creator as a novelist and the comic text as a work of literature? The Pulitzer Prize that *Maus* won in 1992, along with healthy sales, marked Spiegelman's work as exemplary among his peers for its critical and commercial recognition (Sabin 1996, 188). His evolving reception by readers, academics, and journalists—and what that reveals about comics culture—is discussed by Ian Gordon and Andrew Loman.

Readers might wonder why this volume continues the academic criticism on *Maus*, a field that already includes Joseph Witek's *Comic Books as History* (1989), the essays by prominent *Maus* scholars collected in Deborah R. Geis's *Considering Maus: Approaches to Art Spiegelman's "Survivor's Tale" of the Holocaust* (2003), and essays by Chute (2006), Doherty (1996), Hirsch (1992–93), Huyssen (2000), Michaels (2006), and Young (1998) (see the Gordon and Loman chapters for further examples). Additional retrospective is warranted since the scholarship growing around creators such as Chris Ware suggests *Maus* was not an anomaly. As Loman demonstrates, the institutional form of the literary anthology has widened the gap between Spiegelman and the comics industry, but previously unexplored aspects of *Maus* come into relief when it is studied in the context of American comics history. Gordon also reflects on the evolution of Spiegelman studies and considers the development of the language of comics scholarship more generally—reflecting on his own response to early comics scholarship in light of the recent development of the field. Spiegelman is one of a few comics creators analyzed more than once in this collection, albeit with distinct interpretative frames. While reflecting the multiple methodological approaches that comics scholarship has adopted, a polyphony that some writers celebrate as comics' "antidisciplinary" character (Hatfield 2008), this volume acknowledges that certain creators and texts enjoy a disproportionate amount of press. Discussion of key issues in the field requires an extended focus on their significance.

Journalists have seized upon three markers of legitimacy: the "exhibition," the "literary society," and most important, the "prize" (see Leith 2003, 2; Thompson 2001, 12; Thompson 2003, 16). These events are taken as examples of an institutionalized level of connoisseurship and critical recognition. By encouraging certain types of comics (financially, in the case of £10,000 prizes) and discouraging others (those texts that are simply not chosen for exhibitions, for example), the medium is tentatively "regulated" and monitored by judges and curators. Perhaps most notable of all was Chris Ware winning the *Guardian* First Book Award for the graphic novel *Jimmy Corrigan: The Smartest Kid on Earth*. Ware's prize is repeatedly invoked, often to persuade one that comics have "come of age" (Greenwood 2004, 15 and Campbell-Johnston 2005, 19; see also Leith 2003, 2; Thompson 2002, 11; Lee 2002; Jamieson 2003, 8; Rowson 2004, 31; Dewan 2004, 17).

That recurrent metaphor fixes on the medium as emerging from its puberty, having learned from the mistakes of youth, progressing from an (undesirably long) childhood of bullying to an adulthood of acceptance. For this personification of comics to seem teleological, it has to elide the earlier, presumptuous celebrations of the medium's rites of passage. Crumb's work, for instance, has been exhibited since the early 1970s (Crumb and Poplaski 2005, 334–37), and Pulitzer-winner Spiegelman could be forgiven for being puzzled at the British newspaper reviews hailing *Jimmy Corrigan* as "the first comic to win a leading literary prize" (Gatti 2005, 4; Allfree 2003, 14). Do such attempts to tie the medium to legitimate artistic and literary bonafides reveal comics' insecurity? (Gaudreault and Marion 2005, 12). Paul Williams will interpret the critical respect accrued by *Jimmy Corrigan* as the result of the successful presentation of Ware's literary credentials and that graphic novel's ability to fit the context of the Great American Novel—with its attendant cultural capital.

Over the last twenty years, the medium of comics has reached new audiences through different print and electronic forms, fostering genres that are newly understood in the public's broad perception of what comics are. Through an exploration of the changing function, construction, and actions of the comics creator, *The Rise of the American Comics Artist* has recorded those changes and what they mean for the medium. These circumstances have produced a North American comics culture creating some of the most striking works in the (admittedly short) memory of comics; we hope the following essays match the comic texts they discuss for their originality and insight.

WORKS CITED

Allfree, Claire. 2003. Visual Arts: The New Superheroes. *The Independent*, 24 June, 14–15 [Features].

Arnold, Andrew D. 2003. A Graphic Literature Library. *Time.com*. http://www.time.com/time/columnist/arnold/article/0,9565,547796,00.html [accessed 1 Apr. 2009].

Campbell-Johnston, Rachel. 2005. Who can Rescue the Movie World? Is it Real? Is it a Drawing? Yes, it's . . . *The Times*, 19 May, 19 [Features].

Chute, Hillary. 2006. "The Shadow of a Past Time": History and Graphic Representation in *Maus. Twentieth Century Literature* 52(2): 199–230.

———. 2008. Comics as Literature? Reading Graphic Narrative. *PMLA* 123(2): 452–65.

Clowes, Daniel. 2000. *Ghost World*. London: Jonathan Cape.

Crumb, R., and Peter Poplaski. 2005. *The R. Crumb Handbook*. London: M. Q. Publications.

Dewan, Ted. 2004. Welcome to the Strip Club. *The Times Educational Supplement*, 18 June, 17.

Doherty, Thomas. 1996. Art Spiegelman's *Maus*: Graphic Art and the Holocaust. *American Literature: A Journal of Literary History, Criticism, and Bibliography* 68(1): 69–84.

Eisner, Will. 1996. *A Contract with God*. New York: DC Comics. Originally published in 1978.

———. 1999. *Comics & Sequential Art*. Tamarac, FL: Poorhouse Press. Originally published in 1985.

Gatti, Tom. 2005. Lives in Graphic Detail. *The Times*, 3 Sept., 4 [Features].

Gaudreault, André, and Philippe Marion. 2005. A Medium is Always Born Twice . . . *Early Popular Visual Culture* 3(1): 3–15.

Geis, Deborah R., ed. 2003. *Considering Maus: Approaches to Art Spiegelman's "Survivor's Tale" of the Holocaust*. Tuscaloosa, AL: University of Alabama Press.

Gibbons, Fiachra. 2001. Graphic Novel wins Guardian Book Award. *Guardian*, 7 Dec., 9.

Gordon, Ian, Mark Jancovich, and Matthew P. McAllister, eds. 2007. *Film and Comic Books*. Jackson, MS: University Press of Mississippi.

Gravett, Paul. 2007. The Strip: Cult Fiction. *Art Review* 11: 44.

Greenwood, Phoebe. 2004. Stars and Strips. *The Times*, 8 June, 15 [Features, Times2 section].

Hatfield, Charles. 2005. *Alternative Comics: An Emerging Literature*. Jackson, MS: University Press of Mississippi.

———. 2008. How to Read A . . . *English Language Notes* 46(2): 129–149.

Hirsch, Marianne. 1992–93. Family Pictures: *Maus*, Mourning, and Post-Memory. *Discourse: Journal for Theoretical Studies in Media and Culture* 15(2): 3–29.

Huyssen, Andreas. 2000. Of Mice and Mimesis: Reading Spiegelman with Adorno. *New German Critique: An Interdisciplinary Journal of German Studies* 81: 65–82.

Hyde, Laurence. 2007. *Southern Cross*. In *Graphic Witness*, ed. George A. Walker, 291–412. Buffalo, NY: Firefly Books. Originally published in 1951.

Jamieson, Teddy. 2003. Outstripping the Best. *The Herald*, 22 Nov., 8.

Lee, Stewart. 2002. Draw Attention. *Sunday Times*, 6 Jan., n.p. [Features section].

Leith, Sam. 2003. Comic Boom. *The Daily Telegraph*, 8 Nov., 2.

McCloud, Scott. 1994. *Understanding Comics: The Invisible Art*. New York: HarperPerennial. Originally published in 1993.

Michaels, Walter Benn. 2006. Plots Against America: Neoliberalism and Antiracism. *American Literary History* 18(2): 288–302.

Miller, Frank, and Klaus Janson. 1986. *Batman: The Dark Knight Returns*. London: Titan Books.

Moore, Alan, and Dave Gibbons. 1987. *Watchmen*. London: Titan Books.

Murray, Charles Shaar. 2005. Tragedy in Comic Form. *The Independent*, 4 Feb., 25 [Features].

O'Keeffe, Alice. 2005. Strip Lit is Joining the Literary Elite. *The Observer*, 20 Nov., 16.

Raeburn, Daniel. 2004. *Chris Ware*. London: Laurence King Publishing.

Rivett, Miriam. [2000]. Technology into the Digital Realm. In *Below Critical Radar: Fanzines and Alternative Comics from 1976 to now*, ed. Roger Sabin and Teal Triggs, 65–80. Hove: Slab-O-Concrete Publications.

Rosenkranz, Patrick. 2002. *Rebel Visions: The Underground Comix Revolution: 1963–1975*. Seattle: Fantagraphics Books.

Rowson, Martin. 2004. He Who Draws, Whinges—Why Cartoonists Belong on the Outside. *Independent on Sunday*, 13 June, 31 [Features].

Sabin, Roger. 1996. *Comics, Comix & Graphic Novels*. London: Phaidon Press.

———. 2000. Strip Teasers. *The Observer*, 24 Dec., 18 [Review].

Sacco, Joe. 1996. *Palestine*. Seattle: Fantagraphics Books.

——— 2000. *Safe Area Goražde*. Seattle: Fantagraphics Books.

Satrapi, Marjane. 2003. *Persepolis*. London: Jonathan Cape.

Skinn, Dez. 2004. *Comix: The Underground Revolution*. London: Collins & Brown.

Spiegelman, Art. 1987. *Maus I: My Father Bleeds History*. Harmondsworth: Penguin. Originally published in 1986.

———. 1992. *Maus II: And There My Troubles Began*. Harmondsworth: Penguin. Originally published in 1991.

Thompson, David. 2001. Life, Jim, But Not as We Know It. *The Independent*, 5 June, 12 [Features].

———. 2002. From Mickey to Maus. *The Times*, 20 Sept., 11 [Features, Times2].

———. 2003. Slick on the Draw. *The Observer*, 22 June, 16 [Review].

Ware, Chris. 2000. *Jimmy Corrigan: The Smartest Kid on Earth*. New York: Pantheon Books.
———. 2006. Cartoon Special: Building Stories. *Independent on Sunday*, 1 Oct., 10 [Features].
Witek, Joseph. 1989. *Comic Books as History: The Narrative Art of Jack Jackson, Art Spiegelman, and Harvey Pekar*. Jackson, MS: University Press of Mississippi.
Wright, Bradford W. 2008. From Social Consciousness to Cosmic Awareness: Superhero Comic Books and the Culture of Self-Interrogation, 1968–1974. *English Language Notes* 46(2): 155–174.
Wynne, Frank. 2003. Out There. *The Times*, 21 June, 16 [Features Weekend].
Young, James E. 1998. The Holocaust as Vicarious Past: Art Spiegelman's *Maus* and the Afterimages of History. *Critical Inquiry* 24(3): 666–99.

I: Marketing Creators

CHAPTER ONE

How the Graphic Novel Changed American Comics

—STEPHEN WEINER

The American comic book landscape changed dramatically in the 1970s and 1980s primarily because of two factors: first, the creation of the "direct market," a system where publishers sold comic books directly to specialty comics stores, and second, challenges to the Comics Code Authority that regulated the newsstand comic book industry. This chapter will argue that these economic and institutional factors indirectly led to the creation of the graphic novel. In turn, after a series of unstable economic and material conditions, the graphic novel has become a fixture on library and bookshop shelves independent of the comics shops and newsstands.

What was the Comics Code Authority, and how did it work in tandem with the production, distribution, and reception of U.S. comics? The history surrounding the industry self-regulation that led to the creation of the Comics Code Authority is contested by historians and creators alike. In the barest terms: following allegations the comic book industry caused juvenile delinquency, several major comics publishers formed the Comics Magazine Association of America (CMAA) in 1954, an industry body established to govern the content of comic books. The majority of U.S. comics publishers agreed to submit proof copies of their titles to the CMAA, whose reviewers would recommend any changes in line with the CMAA code of acceptability. Once those changes were made and the comic met the CMAA's standards, it received the Comics Code Authority seal and was thus deemed fit to be distributed and sold on America's newsstands (Wright 2003, 172–73; Nyberg 1998).

An alternative comics sales model was exploited by "underground" comix beginning in the late 1960s, a movement explored thoroughly in Patrick

Rosenkranz's 2002 book *Rebel Visions: The Underground Comix Revolution: 1963–1975* (see also Skinn 2004). Associated with creators such as Robert Crumb, S. Clay Wilson, and Spain Rodriguez, underground comix offered political, sexual, and autobiographical narratives exploring countercultural themes including illegal drug-taking and "free love." They were not sold via the formal channels of distribution and retail the major publishers used at the time. Published by smaller presses such as Krupp Comic Works (later Kitchen Sink), The Print Mint, Last Gasp, and Rip Off Press, these comics would be exchanged for other comics and sold via mail order and from the "head shops" supplying a range of countercultural products: drug paraphernalia, psychedelic posters, and incense sticks, to name a handful. In bypassing the newsstands, underground comix could—and did—ignore the Comics Code Authority restrictions, and their contents were deliberately more controversial than the innocuous fare of traditional comics (Sabin 1996, 107).

Until the 1970s, the majority of comics were sold to newsstands and newsagents in bundles of mixed titles on the basis of sale-or-return: publishers agreed to buy back any unsold comics, a commercial system relatively successful during the boom sales years in the 1940s and 1950s when popular titles sold over 70 percent of their print run, but less so in the 1960s and 1970s when break-even sales of 30-40 percent were accepted. Bradford W. Wright estimates that three copies were being printed for every comic sold. Not only was this inefficient, but as a business model it was increasingly fragile when printing costs substantially inflated comic prices during the 1970s (Wright 2003, 258, 261). During the 1960s and 1970s, commercial opportunities had opened up by the sporadic avenues through which fans sold back issues of comic books to fellow fans. Certain comics became sought after because they contained popular characters or because they represented the work of desirable artists, and they began to be sold secondhand through comic "marts," conventions, and mail-order businesses (Sabin 1996, 157).

The direct market—selling comics to specialty comics stores at a greater discount than that offered to the newsstands on the proviso they could not be returned—was a financial solution to this distribution issue. The steady growth of stores specializing in selling comics (often in addition to action figures, T-shirts, posters, and other comics-related merchandise) from the late 1970s to the early 1990s was closely related to the rise of the direct market, and the two phenomena sustained each other symbiotically. By the mid-1980s, the direct market was the dominant mode of comics distribution and approximately 2,000 comics stores existed in the U.S. (Sabin 1993, 68). Retailers could order a specific numbers of copies of individual titles for their store, tailoring the comics they bought to the clientele they served, thus minimizing unnecessary expense. If issues on the shelves did pass out-of-date, rather than return them to the publishers, retailers stored them in special plastic bags and sold them as back issues. Publishers could offer greater reductions to the retailer on the direct market because they were saving costs by not printing comics that would be returned unsold. And there were additional advantages: store owners knew who their target market was—most were comics buyers themselves—and could promote their wares accordingly while feeding informed marketing information back to the publishers (Wright 2003, 261).

TOWARD THE GRAPHIC NOVEL

Adult readership of comics, significant in the 1940s, had not altogether disappeared after the imposition of the Comic Code Authority in 1954. Marvel Comics had demonstrated that older readers could be interested in superheroes—headlined by *Spider-Man*, Marvel's superheroes in the 1960s had personal problems as daunting as the supervillains they fought, but these stories were far tamer than the explicit narratives of the underground comix. DC Comics attempted to tell more adult stories in a *Green Lantern/Green Arrow* storyline written by Dennis O'Neil and drawn by Neal Adams in the late 1960s. In these issues Green Lantern was introduced to problems of race and poverty by Green Arrow; another subplot involved Green Arrow's teenage partner, Speedy, becoming a heroin addict. Any mention of drugs was forbidden by the Comics Code Authority, and these issues were published without the CCA approval, an indication of greater changes to come.

Following the *Green Lantern/Green Arrow* narrative, other creators and publishers experimented with content and how stories were delivered to the reading public. In 1974 superhero artist Gil Kane self-published a text-heavy fantasy called *Blackmark*—at the time, the idea of a series designed to be finite and self-contained went against the conventional publishing model of ongoing titles. Another early "graphic novel" (the term had yet to be popularized) was DC's *Manhunter*, by Archie Goodwin and Walt Simonson. Originally a 1940s superhero, Manhunter was angst-ridden and sarcastic in this updated version, and hell-bent on stopping the organization that had rescued him and increased his abilities. *Manhunter* appeared as a finite backup feature in *Detective Comics* in 1973 and 1974, and garnered six industry awards despite being only seven episodes in length. *Manhunter* was a superhero story for adults—it was collected in book form in the 1970s and later reprinted in the mid-1980s.

Precursors to what we now understand as the graphic novel were also appearing in the world of trade publishing. Little Brown had acquired the rights to publish an English-language version of Hergé's *Tintin*. The adventures of a boy reporter and his dog, *Tintin* had been a staple of the European comics market for decades. Sales were strong, perhaps because *Tintin* avoided the familiar genres and visual styles of American comics—and thus sidestepped pejorative assumptions about what a comic book should be. Other European books, such as *Asterix*, followed. The idea of comics being distributed and sold in book form had been advanced earlier in the twentieth century by artists such as Lynd Ward (*God's Man*) and Frans Masereel (*The City*), whose wordless "picture novels" were intended for an adult readership and published by trade houses rather than comic book publishers.

In 1978, veteran cartoonist Will Eisner produced *A Contract with God and Other Tenement Stories*, a collection of four interrelated stories about tenement life in the Bronx during the Great Depression. Known for his seminal work on the 1940s newspaper comic book insert *The Spirit*, Eisner believed the potential for comics readership was widely untapped. He used the term "graphic novel" while pitching his manuscript-length comic book to a mainstream publisher, apparently unaware of its previous usage (see the discussion of the term in the introduction). *A Contract with God* was sold in bookstores as opposed to comic book stores, although initial sales were disappointing. Other trade publishers were more successful: Knopf published Jules Feiffer's *Tantrum*, the story of a middle-aged man who refused to grow up, in 1979. Feiffer's existing popularity as a cartoonist and the accessibility of the artwork made this graphic novel a commercial success.

The biggest movement toward the graphic novel format came from comic book publishing. In 1980 Canadian writer/artist Dave Sim, whose *Cerebus* (co-drawn with Gerhard) had been successful in the alternative comics marketplace, began collecting the stories serialized in *Cerebus* into "phone books" (as he called them), selling these collections directly to comics stores. Comic book collections or graphic novels had many advantages as a format to introduce new readers to certain comic titles: they were more affordable than individual issues and readers did not have to make multiple trips to the stores to buy them.

While mainstream comics publishers still grappled with the concept of the graphic novel, they were slowly exploiting the market with more complex stories. Writer Alan Moore and artist Steve Bissette reinvented the horror comic

The Saga of the Swamp Thing for DC Comics—originally Swamp Thing mostly battled demons and werewolves, but in Moore and Bissette's hands the character became a plant who thought he was human, and the stories became meditations on sentience and the ethical responsibility of the human race towards the ecosystem. *The Saga of the Swamp Thing* was an enormous success, and eventually DC collected the best issues in a series of graphic novels.

Marvel also experimented with less juvenile content, and had newcomer Frank Miller eventually write *Daredevil* as well as draw it. Surveys of the direct market suggested that readers were still attracted to superheroes, but with a tone of realism; with many enemies from organized crime networks, *Daredevil* lent itself to realistic superhero drama (Wright 2003, 262; Sabin 1996, 160). The success of *The Saga of the Swamp Thing* and *Daredevil* gave Moore and Miller celebrity status among American readers, and DC gave both creators the opportunity to try longer, complete stories. They responded with narratives that would define the parameters of the graphic novel.

In Miller's *Batman: The Dark Knight Returns* (1986), Batman emerges from retirement at fifty to rescue a Gotham City-turned-war zone by its criminals and villains. Published in four high-gloss installments, Miller's Batman was a vigilante whose actions were publicly questioned, driven by profound childhood trauma, and barely more stable than the villains he fought—DC collected the issues into the graphic novel format in 1986. Meanwhile, Moore and artist Dave Gibbons produced *Watchmen*, a narrative unfolding around the murder of a government-sanctioned superhero in a world where other superheroes had been outlawed and Richard Nixon never resigned under threat of impeachment. *Watchmen* was published in twelve issues in 1986 and collected into the graphic novel format in 1987.

Also in 1986, Pantheon Books published the first volume of Art Spiegelman's *Maus*, arguably the most important American graphic novel (*Maus* and Spiegelman are discussed elsewhere in this volume by Ian Gordon and Andrew Loman). While *The Dark Knight Returns* and *Watchmen* came out of the superhero tradition, *Maus* was a product of the underground comix and has come to enjoy greater critical status than either of its peers. *Maus* told the story of Spiegelman's parents' survival in the concentration camps during World War II and the cartoonist's own trauma growing up with concentration camp survivors and their memories. The combined success of *Maus*, *Watchmen*, and *The Dark Knight Returns* attracted publicity and healthy sales, bringing new readers into comics and into the comics stores (Sabin 1993, 95).

Media attention created by the "Big Three" graphic novels diminished by the late 1980s, and graphic novel sales in the early 1990s were disappointing.

The recession in the American and British economies affected potential readers' abilities to buy graphic novels (relatively expensive compared to paperback books). Media coverage remained sympathetic but revisionist superheroes were no longer novelties, prejudice against comics for much of the reading public had not substantially dwindled, and bookstore chains like Waldenbooks and Dalton's found they simply were not selling enough units (Sabin 1993, 111–14, 177–78). The graphic novel had not buttressed its status in the publishing industry and the 1986–1987 cycle of sales and media attention seemed to have peaked.

"ALTERNATIVE COMICS" AND SELF-PUBLISHING

Many very small comics companies sprang up in the 1990s—often producing black and white "alternative" comics published by the cartoonists themselves. As the term suggests, these comics were identified as "alternative" because they (usually) provided readers with a different genre and range of characters compared to the DC and Marvel superheroes. Alternative comics tended to be black and white (less production costs), sold in smaller numbers through the comics shops and through the mail, and their contents remained the property of the creators, whereas the major companies largely retained copyright on the characters and material they published. The enormous print runs necessitated by the sale-or-return system servicing the newsstands was impossible for small publishers, but the growth of comics shops and the direct market made self-publishing and small press publications financially viable. Consequently, comics shops served as the major retail outlet for titles containing non-superhero narratives, marketed on the strength of their creators' reputations, and for those intended to be collected into graphic novels. They played an essential role in the rise of comics aimed at adult readers and the graphic novel itself.

A vocal figurehead of the self-publishing movement, Dave Sim's independent comic book *Cerebus* featured previews of new self-published titles within its pages and collaborations with other self-publishers. Advocates of self-publishing pointed to the total control it gave creators over publishing, distributing, and promoting their work, allowing writers and artists to publish comics that would otherwise go unseen. Other particularly notable examples of self-published books were *ElfQuest* by Wendy and Richard Pini, *Teenage Mutant Ninja Turtles* by Peter A. Laird and Kevin Eastman, *Bone* by

Jeff Smith, *Strangers in Paradise* by Terry Moore, and *Understanding Comics* by Scott McCloud. With the exception of the latter text, these books were initially published in periodical format, but later collected into book-sized volumes containing a complete "story arc," or storyline. In different ways they all contributed to the visibility of the comic outside its traditional readership and advanced the cause of the graphic novel.

Initially published in black and white, *ElfQuest* was reprinted in book form in color and found its way into bookstores in the early 1980s. At that time, it was also licensed to Marvel Comics for a reprint series, licensed again to DC Comics in the late 1990s—and each incarnation brought new readers. *ElfQuest* demonstrated that the graphic novel format was viable for a non-superhero genre series and that the bookstore was a potential sales point for graphic novels. *Bone*, written and drawn by Jeff Smith, was published by Smith's own imprint, Cartoon Books, in 1991. An epic fantasy with a heavy dose of humor, *Bone* was published bimonthly, and Cartoon Books began collecting *Bone* into the graphic novel format in 1993. Smith's ability to move between humor and drama caught readers' attention: the first *Bone* collection, *Out from Boneville*, sold 50,000 copies in 18 months.

Strangers in Paradise demonstrated Terry Moore's accomplishments as a writer as well as artist and was loaded with text—readers were periodically offered pages with narrative prose, poetry, and song lyrics in the middle of an issue. Along with this formal experimentation, *Strangers in Paradise*, like *Bone*, was a finite story with a clear beginning, middle, and end—as in a prose novel. Scott McCloud's 1993 book-length examination of the cartoon form, the non-fiction graphic novel, *Understanding Comics*, introduced novices to the ways comics worked, in addition to inspiring cartoonists to make more ambitious comics. To better demonstrate his concepts, McCloud wrote and illustrated *Understanding Comics* in comic book format. Originally released by Tundra Publishing, *Understanding Comics* exceeded its origins in the comic book specialty market, aided by good media coverage. Harper picked up *Understanding Comics* in 1994 and a partnership between trade publishing and comics publishing began.

One legacy of the small and self-publishers was the opening of the library field to graphic novels. The graphic novels produced by small publishers shared the accessibility that has often characterized comics distributed on the mass market, so that librarians could see their usefulness—particularly in drawing boys into libraries. They were also different enough to avoid the stigma from mainstream comics, going back to the 1950s when comic books were blamed for causing juvenile delinquency. Small publishers made full use of this partnership with libraries, because, unlike the big publishers, they needed every sale they could get.

SUGGESTED FOR MATURE READERS: DC, MARVEL, DARK HORSE, AND THE 1990S GRAPHIC NOVEL

DC Comics fully joined the fight for adult readers with their Vertigo imprint (as explored in chapters two and three of this collection). The most successful Vertigo title was *The Sandman*, a monthly horror and fantasy comic drawing on recognizable literary and popular culture traditions. The overarching *Sandman* narrative was divided into several story arcs that were later collected into a series of graphic novels. Different artists illustrated specific storylines, giving each a specific visual style.

The significance of the self-contained narrative as a statement of literary sophistication was exploited by a new publisher founded in 1986 by Mike Richardson: Dark Horse Comics. Dark Horse focused on publishing the "limited series," a story told in a finite number of issues publicized in advance and then collected into a graphic novel. Richardson planned to differentiate his product from Marvel and DC by attracting the best creators in order to generate new characters—one way to do this was allowing creators a share in the profits (earlier alternative comics publishers like Pacific had adopted this approach with some success—see Sabin 1996, 158). Dark Horse's line of creator-owned titles includes the notable commercial successes of Frank Miller's *Sin City* and Mike Mignola's *Hellboy* franchise.

Up to the mid-1990s, selling comics had not worked well in prose bookstores; comics retailers were forced to purchase single graphic novels in multiple numbers, and because they could not be returned, the risk attached to buying them increased. In the mid-1990s it became possible for retailers to order single copies of books published by DC Comics. This change allowed retailers to special-order books to meet customer demand without the risk of graphic novels going unsold and thus occupying shelf space better used for products with a faster turnover. In addition to the form offering a convenient package at a reasonable price (compared to individual comics), the graphic novel was financially more viable to retailers and as a result, more available to consumers.

This new system of ordering made it possible for bookstores and public libraries to order graphic novels directly from a vendor, whereas previously libraries had been forced to order graphic novels through a comic book shop. This now made it possible for public libraries to collect graphic novels. Drawn to the readability of the books, librarians promoted them heavily. Graphic novels circulated with alarming frequency, allowing librarians to help break the prejudice against comics that had persisted since the mid-1950s. These books infused the public library with a new energy and *hipness*—and as a result, graphic novel collections have become the fastest-growing print component of public library collections since 2002.

COOL COMICS

Cultural shifts took place alongside these economic changes. In the mid-1990s it seemed *everybody* loved comics, from filmmakers such as Kevin Smith, who used the comics industry as a backdrop for his film *Chasing Amy* (1996), to highbrow intellectuals like Norman Mailer and John Updike, who wrote a letter of complaint to the *Boston Globe* when *Spider-Man* was removed from the daily comics page. Graphic novels were in public libraries across the United States, articles about comics appeared in the arts coverage of the mainstream press, and universities began to offer courses on comics in their arts and comparative literature departments.

Following in the tradition of the underground comix and *Maus*, graphic novels pondering political events and social injustice without the scaffolding of superheroic violence grew in visibility. These included cartoonist-journalist Joe Sacco's *Palestine*, which examined the Israeli-Palestinian conflict, various semi-autobiographical works by Will Eisner, Dan Clowes's *Ghost World*, and Jason Lutes's *Jar of Fools*. Originally self-published, *Jar of Fools* was picked up by small publishing houses and became a critical hit, reviewed by *The New York Times Book Review* and novelist Sherman Alexie.

Reviewers promoted these graphic novels based on the interest of their subject matter—not whether they represented a more "grown up" approach to men in tights beating each other up. These "literary" or "art" graphic novels had little or no chance of a sequel, minimizing the possibility of spin-offs, but as a result these texts were even less beholden to the need to adjust their narratives to afford the possibility of the characters repeating their "adventures." Academic interest in comics was growing: in 1998 the University of Massachusetts sponsored "The Graphic Novel: A Twentieth Anniversary Conference on an Emerging Literary and Artistic Medium," a three-day symposium featuring cartoonist Will Eisner. The most widely recognized academic support of the burgeoning graphic novel format was the line of books published by the University Press of Mississippi, chaired by comics and Faulkner scholar M. Thomas Inge. These widening circles of interest in comics came to encompass the work of major prose novelists: Robert Myer's *Super-Folks* (1977) referred to comics and the comic industry, as did Jay Cantor's "novel in five panels" *Krazy Kat* (1988), using the early days of the industry as backbone, and Michael Chabon's *The Amazing Adventures of Kavalier & Clay* (2000) won a Pulitzer Prize in 2001.

Three of the twenty-first century's most feted graphic novels are Chris Ware's *Jimmy Corrigan: The Smartest Kid on Earth* (2000) (which won an American Book award, the Angoulême Festival's Prize for Best Comic Book, and the *Guardian* First Book Award); Marjane Satrapi's memoir, *Persepolis* (2003), recounting her experiences growing up in Iran and Europe; and Craig Thompson's autobiography about growing up in a repressive household, *Blankets* (2003), named a Best Book of the Year by *Library Journal*. The success of books such as *Blankets* and *Persepolis* with the non-traditional comics readership demonstrated there was indeed a bookstore market for graphic novels—but the major impetus for graphic novel sections in bookstores was the infusion of graphic novels from Japan, known by the Japanese term for comics, manga.

Unlike many American comics that used male power fantasies as the basis for their stories, manga was not dominated by a single genre or gender and enjoyed a unisex readership. In the U.S., however, the proliferation of largely male superhero comics made comics shops unattractive environments to female readers—"Women were certainly not welcome," as Roger Sabin summarizes (1996, 157). Manga had uncovered a female readership for the graphic novel and solidified the placement of graphic novel sections in bookstores.

Manga's growing popularity also allowed librarians to use graphic novels to entice reluctant readers inside the library doors and increasing their circulation. Meanwhile, the proliferation of graphic novel reviews continued—*Entertainment Weekly*, *Rolling Stone*, *The Boston Globe*, and finally *The New York Times Book Review*. *Watchmen* by Alan Moore and Dave Gibbons, one of the first graphic novels to break out of the comic book marketplace, was named one of the top 100 novels of the twentieth century by *Time* magazine in 2005.

American publishing houses soon established graphic novel imprints—some intent on capturing the manga reading public, while others hoped to duplicate Pantheon's success. Scholastic, the successful publisher of the *Harry Potter* novels, rereleased Jeff Smith's *Bone* in full color in a size similar to contemporary bestselling paperbacks, distributing it through school book fairs, library programs, bookstores, the comic book marketplace—and selling millions of units. Other children's divisions followed, emboldened by the popularity and modishness of the graphic novel format. By the end of 2006, almost every major trade publisher sponsored some kind of graphic novel imprint. When Gene Yang's graphic novel examination of ethnic, cultural, and mythic identity, *American Born Chinese* (2007), won the Printz prize (an annual award given by the American Library Association to the Best Book for Young Adults), it seemed an unremarkable recognition of excellence in the publishing field.

*This article is dedicated to Julian and Lily.

WORKS CITED

Nyberg, Amy Kiste. 1998. *Seal of Approval: The History of the Comics Code*. Jackson, MS: University Press of Mississippi.
Rosenkranz, Patrick. 2002. *Rebel Visions: The Underground Comix Revolution: 1963–1975*. Seattle: Fantagraphics Books.
Sabin, Roger. 1993. *Adult Comics: An Introduction*. London: Routledge.
———. 1996. *Comics, Comix & Graphic Novels*. London: Phaidon Press.
Sabin, Roger, and Teal Triggs. [2000]. Introduction. In *Below Critical Radar: Fanzines and Alternative Comics from 1976 to now*, ed. Roger Sabin and Teal Triggs, 1–14. Hove: Slab-O-Concrete Publications.
Skinn, Dez. 2004. *Comix: The Underground Revolution*. London: Collins & Brown.
Wright, Bradford W. 2003. *Comic Book Nation: The Transformation of Youth Culture in America*. Rev. ed. Baltimore: The John Hopkins University Press.

CHAPTER TWO

"Is this a book?" DC Vertigo and the Redefinition of Comics in the 1990s

—JULIA ROUND

Not only comics publishing but also perceptions of it have changed radically during this century, and the comic book has become a graphic novel, invoking notions of permanence, literariness, and artistry. In Chapter Three, Chris Murray considers the emergence of literary themes and allusions in DC Comics during the 1980s as a consequence of British writers crossing the Atlantic and entering the U.S. comics industry. This chapter offers a complementary examination of the technological changes and marketing innovations that contributed to the redefinition of comics at the end of the twentieth century, specifically with regard to the role of DC Vertigo and the rise of the graphic novel and trade paperback in the 1990s. It will draw on the expertise of Karen Berger, DC Senior Vice President and Executive Editor of the Vertigo imprint, and Steve White, Senior Editor at Titan Comics (who handle DC's reprints for the UK market).[1]

As the introduction outlined, Will Eisner's *A Contract with God* (1978) is often incorrectly cited as the first graphic novel: an adult-oriented novel-length comic marketed to a wider audience. Marvel claims its first graphic novel is *The Death of Captain Marvel* (1982), and the end of the twentieth century saw the rise of this form as mainstream comics began to "grow up." Although adult comics and longer formats had in fact been around for many years, this cultural perception of the emergence of the graphic novel has affected the ways in which today's comics are both marketed and received. For the purposes of this article the graphic novel (also known as a "prestige format" single issue) is defined as a "permanent" comic: it is often longer than the usual single-issue comic (with 20 to 24 story pages) and consists of new material printed on higher-quality paper. Trade paperbacks use the graphic novel form to collect and reprint single stories (either reprinting entire mini-series, or typically runs between four and twelve issues from longer, ongoing series).

This chapter will explore the graphic novel's evolution and specifically its use by the DC Vertigo imprint. It will examine the processes and effects of factors such as digital production and computerized printing, expensive and permanent binding, distribution via bookshops, pricing, franchising, and the repackaging and reissuing of previously published work. These elements have shaped the medium by bringing the graphic novel closer to the aesthetic of the literary text, while also maintaining the status quo of the comics market in some respects—by allowing for the production of collectors' editions, for instance. They sit alongside aspects external to the industry such as the redefinition of the audience and emergent intellectual property and copyright laws, which have also affected the ways in which comics are created, produced, and received.

A DIGITAL AESTHETIC

Traditionally, comics have been perceived as disposable, low-quality pulp fiction aimed at a child market. However, as the product of a publishing business the medium is shaped by its production values, and these have significantly evolved since the early days of comics publishing. Early comic strips in newspapers and magazines were limited by thickset black line-work, due both to the letterpress method of printing (in which inked plates "stamped" an image onto paper) and the poor quality of the paper used. In the 1950s this process gave way to offset printing, whereby comics were first laid out in pencil, then inked, colored, shot to film, and finally printed, allowing for more delicate lines. By the 1990s publishers such as DC had their own "in-house computer coloring department" (Gold 1990, 3), and, as Steve White confirms, "computerization [has] more or less brought everything in-house." Today the offset process still dominates, now via computer-to-plate production rather than the shot-to-film process (although entirely digital printing is now a possibility, at present it can produce only limited quantities).

DC launched its Vertigo imprint in 1993 using six popular series from the 1980s, all of which were reworkings of older DC supernatural or horror characters (*The Sandman, The Saga of the Swamp Thing,*[2] *Hellblazer, Animal Man,*

Shade: The Changing Man, and *Doom Patrol*). It was a conscious move away from superheroics—even in their gritty and realistic 1980s incarnation. For example, in the hands of writer Neil Gaiman *The Sandman* became a mythological epic, sharing little more than a name with Jack Kirby's earlier series. Alan Moore had already redefined the character of the Swamp Thing as a plant elemental with social concerns, rather than a freak creature of horror. Peter Milligan's rewrite of Steve Ditko's *Shade: The Changing Man* incorporated a hefty dose of surrealism, as did Grant Morrison's run on *Doom Patrol*. Morrison also revived Dave Wood's *Animal Man* as a metafictional commentary on alternate realities and under Jamie Delano's run, the character would later be recreated again as an "animal avatar" (a kind of animal god akin to Moore's redefinition of Swamp Thing). And *Hellblazer*'s antihero, John Constantine, had little to do with (super) heroics from the series' beginning.

These core titles were reconceived in the 1980s, not simply as "more realistic" superheroics, but instead as mythological, surreal, religious, and metafictional commentaries upon the comics medium and industry. Rather than continuing the trend for gritty vigilantes and superhero politics, Vertigo's content and style revolved around dark fantasy and sophisticated suspense. Vertigo was conceived as a home for comics "led by the ideas, by the writers really wanting to do something different in comic books," stresses Executive Editor Karen Berger. Along these lines, she also fought—and won—a battle *not* to include the DC bullet logo on the Vertigo covers, a "very very big deal." Similarly, many Vertigo titles used an innovative aesthetic Berger says was "very deliberate, we really just wanted to show different types of art styles too." In an industry often reluctant to take risks, she adds, "at the time it was a big noticeable deal."

Shatter (written by Peter Gillis, with art by Mike Saenz and Bert Monroy, and published by First Comics in 1984) was the first comic to feature entirely digitally created art. Produced on a 128k Apple Macintosh computer using MacPaint, it has an obvious computer aesthetic, as the maximum print level at the time was 72 dots per inch (a figure now in the thousands) that results in a dot-matrix printing effect. The use of technology is also emphasized by its content, which owes much to films such as *Blade Runner*. *Shatter* illustrates how the early days of computer-generated comics were not only limited by the tools available, but also by the preconceptions attached to the process and software. By contrast, John Totleben was one of the first artists to use collage and paint for his 1980s *The Saga of the Swamp Thing* covers and this type of aesthetic experimentation was embraced in the Vertigo stable.

The Sandman, whose covers declined to show the title character and instead featured Dave McKean's idiosyncratic and abstract artwork, is the best-known example of this process. McKean's materials range from pencil and ink, to collage and acrylic, to photography and Mac manipulation. Other artists embraced multimedia—for example Tom Taggart's *Doom Patrol* covers were sculpted in miniature, arranged in sets, and photographed. Subsequent Vertigo titles (such as Glenn Fabry's painted *Preacher* covers, or Gavin Wilson and Richard Bruning's computer-enhanced photographic covers for *Sandman Mystery Theatre*) also had a distinct look. Innovation extended to the interior pages as well—certain *Sandman stories* were penciled but not inked (such as *The Sandman* #70–72, "The Wake," printed directly from Michael Zulli's pencils)—others discarded conventions such as panels or speech balloons (*The Sandman* #74, "Exiles"). In *Animal Man*, Morrison often used the artist's penciled drafts alongside the finished artwork, visually reflecting the various layers of reality and metafictional nature of the story. In this way the Vertigo books were conceived and marketed to be both conceptually and visually different from mainstream superhero fare.

PERMANENCE AND PACKAGING

New coloring and digitization technology also allowed for the rerelease of older works around this time. While some might argue this process maintained the status quo of the comics audience by feeding the collectors' market, repackaging and reissuing also altered perceptions of comics by allowing for large, book-format bindings that brought them closer to the notion of a literary text. "Marvel Masterworks" (begun in 1987) and "DC Archive Editions" (1989) were hardcover, full-color collections of rare and classic series whose expensive, highbrow status was reinforced through marble-effect or silver dustjackets, full color restoration, and hardback binding. However, they were also priced beyond the reach of much of their audience. Black-and-white paperback lines ("Marvel Essentials" and DC's "Showcase Presents") were subsequently brought in as more affordable alternatives.

The process of reprinting and reissuing collections was adopted by Vertigo and the imprint quickly gained a reputation for using the trade paperback format as single issues were often reprinted and rereleased within collections. *The Sandman* trade paperbacks (featuring new covers by Dave McKean) began to be released as early as 1990 and in this way the format was established by the time of the Vertigo launch in 1993. The releases were dictated by market demands: for example, *The Sandman*'s second story arc, *The Doll's House*, was the first to be released as a trade paperback, due to the success of the massively popular *The Sandman* #8 ("The Sound of Her Wings"). As well as imbuing the Vertigo product with a sense of permanence, this process again allowed for a further redefinition of these comics' aesthetic, as the collections boasted high-quality glossy covers featuring new artwork. The process has continued; after a second generation of *The Sandman* trade paperbacks (with different covers), *The Absolute Sandman* began in 2006—each oversized leather-bound hardback reprinting twenty or so single issues, recolored using the latest technology.

Experiments in format (such as the alternate cover craze) abounded in the 1990s; however, the trade paperback was instead used by imprints such as Vertigo to redefine their product and collect a group of titles under a label with a clear identity and distinct aesthetic. Associated marketing also allowed different audiences to access it, as will now be seen.

LOCATION, LOCATION, LOCATION

The publication of comics by mainstream publishers and their appearance in bookstores are two of the most important developments affecting the medium's perception in recent years. Comics marketing was initially aligned most closely with that of magazines and other periodicals, and dog-eared copies were jammed into newsstand racks or sold at drugstores and grocery shops. But the concept of the specialty comics store did not become popular until the 1980s with the advent of direct distribution.

The direct distribution system was invented in the mid-1970s by New York comics retailer Phil Seuling. The exact start date is difficult to establish—Mark Shainblum gives it as 1976, but contemporaries of Seuling state that his company, Seagate Distribution, was dealing with DC and Marvel in this manner as early as 1973 (Hanley 2000). The direct distribution system provided an alternative to the existing sale-or-return policy practiced by newsstands and drugstores that purchased comics from periodical distribution companies. Direct market sellers bought their comics stock *directly* from publishers at a cheaper price, although they could not return unsold units. Direct distribution thus restored the industry's uncertain finances as it allowed the end-seller to make more money on titles sold, which led to the creation of more specialty stores—and the system dominated the market by the mid-1980s.

The specialty store encouraged a different kind of audience than the casual newsstand and drugstore reader. This in turn affected the creation and reception of comics—as they no longer ran the risk of returned units, publishers created titles aimed at more dedicated fans, and some of these books proved too obtuse to appeal to casual readers. And the stores themselves were often characterized as intimidating and consequently unattractive to the general public. This, together with speculative promotions (e.g., multiple alternate covers), led to the market crash in the mid-1990s. It became clear that false "collectors' hype" had artificially inflated prices, and a lack of new readers meant the industry was cannibalizing its own market.

Vertigo survived the crash, however, and indeed benefited from it. As Neil Gaiman comments: "We were selling 100,000 copies [of *The Sandman*] a month and we were down at number 70 or so, and the best-selling comic was selling in the millions. And then the bottom fell out of the industry and all of a sudden there we are still doing our 100,000 copies and we're now at number 25. And by the end of it, we were *still* doing 100,000 and we were at number one. We were beating *Batman* and *Superman*" (Savlov 1999).

In recent years comics have surpassed previous publishing and marketing limitations and are now being released by mainstream publishers and situated in high-street booksellers. Selling through retailers like Barnes & Noble might be said to bring comics closer to the notion of the literary text, and many book publishers are joining the trend. In August 2007, Tara Mulholland noted that Random House UK increased its output of graphic novels (published by imprint Jonathan Cape) threefold over the preceding twelve months, publishing nine new titles since 2006. In July 2007 Harper Collins UK launched its first graphic novel series (the *Agatha Christie Comic Strip Editions*), Bloomsbury published their first graphic novel for adults in 2009 (*Logicomix*), and other publishers such as Faber & Faber continue to sign up-and-coming graphic novelists (Mulholland 2007).

Genre limitations are much less apparent; for example, academic publishers Hill & Wang (a division of old-school company Farrar, Straus & Giroux) published a graphic novel adaptation of the "9/11 Commission Report" in 2006. This expansion of traditional prose publishers towards creating their own comics imprints should be noted, and Vertigo was again at the fore of this trend, mostly due to the popularity of its trade paperbacks. A recent deal between Vertigo and Random House Distribution has further contributed to this movement (and brought in "significant sales increases in just a few months") and Karen Berger says that Vertigo is now "perfectly poised to increase our presence in the large bookstore chains, as well as expanding our reach into independent stores and alternative bookselling arenas."

The graphic novel presence in bookstores has increased exponentially in recent years, with British retailer Waterstones reporting that their graphic novel sales increased by forty-one percent in the 2006/2007 financial year (Mulholland 2007). A London branch of Blackwells began stocking a half-shelf of graphic novels (six titles) in early 2005, which increased to thirty shelves in eight months—and to forty shelves by 2007 (Gravett 2006). Here, as at other companies, initial separatist issues have given way to acceptance. For example, Foyles bookshop initially categorized its graphic novels by publisher rather than author, with the caveat they would sometimes categorize "by personality [. . .] because people's purchases can be influenced by the popularity and status of an author" (Gravett 2006). This evidences a further movement towards aligning comics with "proper" books as yet another distinction is broken down.

Assigning a singular authorship to the graphic novel has privileged the notion of the comics creator. Pitches for new characters and unsolicited series ideas also stand in contrast to the production-line processes of early comics, and such new material is generally creator-owned. Neil Gaiman was given free rein to rewrite Kirby's version of *The Sandman* and, though DC retains copyright on the title, Gaiman has used his status to strike an agreement that, as such a radical reworking, his version will not be revived.

Changes in industry creative practices have also contributed to redefining the comic book as an individual work rather than a mass-produced cultural artifact. Writer and artist teams are assigned to a long-running series or company-owned character and their "run" is well publicized to promote the new treatment of the character, placing the emphasis on individuality and distinctiveness rather than continuity. For example, Jamie Delano killed off Buddy Baker in the first issue of his run on *Animal Man*. Similarly, Garth Ennis famously began his run on *Hellblazer* by giving lead character John Constantine terminal lung cancer. The migration of British creators to Vertigo (documented in Chapter Three) altered the industry's creative emphasis by the start of the 1990s, as Dave McKean comments: "We really just wanted to break it all apart, and remodel it in our image. We were very happy to do that and they were very happy to let us do that, because the books were selling very well" (McCabe 2004, 24). The high profiles of these writers and artists meant an entirely different sort of creative process was happening, compared to the anonymous assembly lines of comics history.

By using highly publicized British writers, Vertigo's production and marketing emphasizes the notion of a "star creator" (whether writer or artist) whose name sells the book. This produces a constructed concept of singular authorship that brings comics closer to the notion of literature. The marketing and genre-crossing allowed by this literary presence also creates a wider readership than was possible within the specialty stores, while dispensing with the overtones of disposability and casualness inherent to newsstands and drugstores.

A LITERARY STYLE

The value placed on individuality of style has led to a strong sense of creator recognition in today's comics. Steve White reflects on conversations with Tom DeFalco (writer and ex-Editor-in-Chief of Marvel Comics) concerning the formation of Image Comics in the early 1990s, when a group of superstar creators coordinated a mass exodus from Marvel Comics and set up their own company in order to retain ownership of their work. The prevailing wisdom of the industry at the time was that readers were more interested in the characters than the creators, but this theory was quickly proved wrong when the first issues of *Spawn* and *WildC.A.T.s* (new titles published by Image) sold record-breaking numbers. White comments further: "I used to follow creators, you know, you would pick up a book because it was drawn by an artist whose stuff you really liked, that kind of thing, so that logic never really rang true with me."

More recently, the star artist has given way to the star *writer*. Online forums have discussed "how the whole industry shifted from artist-driven (Lee, McFarlane, Miller et al.) to writer-driven (Ellis, Rucka, Straczynski, Bendis, Morrison, etc.)" and comment: "It was a change for the better" (Mayer 2004). Vertigo has certainly followed this route, as Karen Berger states: "It was totally writer-led." This new emphasis on narrative further redefined comics as literature. Fuller scripting may also have contributed to reemphasizing narrative elements in contemporary comics, such as Neil Gaiman's detailed panel descriptions, examples of which are reprinted in *The Sandman: Dream Country* trade paperback and *The Absolute Sandman* series. It was a scripting method Gaiman picked up from Alan Moore (Comic Book Rebels 2008).

Karen Berger explains "it was really Alan Moore who changed the perceptions of writers in comics [. . .] he really showed that you could do comics that were literary, but modern and popular, but could really stand next to a great work of fiction, of prose fiction, and that really changed everything. There was no going back after Alan did *Swamp Thing*"—which went on to be one of the core Vertigo titles, although Moore's run was long finished by this time. Other books such as Grant Morrison's *Animal Man* and *Doom Patrol* (although the latter was written by Rachel Pollack at the time of the Vertigo launch) picked up on the literary trend by breaking down the fourth wall and incorporating a heavy dose of metafictional commentary. For example, in *Doom Patrol* #21 ("Worlds in Collision") Robotman/Cliff Steele asks " . . . is this a *book* or is it *real*?"—ostensibly talking about an object in the comic (the "black book") but while looking out from the panel, directly at the reader. In *Animal Man* #5 ("The Coyote Gospel") Morrison juxtaposes various realities (cartoon, comic book, and "real life") and the final panel features an artist's hand and paintbrush. In *Animal Man* #26 (Morrison's final issue), Animal Man becomes aware he is living in a comic book and confronts his creator. Morrison would continue his exploration of coexistent realities and the notion of creator-as-god in subsequent Vertigo work such as *The Invisibles*.

The adoption of the graphic novel format, the move to bookstores, and a new self-awareness and literary style brought the scope and structure of the Vertigo comics closer to the notion of the literary text. Steve White comments that "there definitely seems to be an attitude among creators that they're writing for the trade paperback" and stories are now structured around "the bigger picture." Karen Berger also says that "Vertigo is seriously amping up its acquisitions of original graphic novels" and that in 2008 they will be dedicating two editors to this area. She emphasizes Vertigo's move away from genre work, citing memoirs such as Percy Carey and Ronald Wimberly's *Sentences* and Mat Johnson and Warren Pleece's *Incognegro* that, it is hoped, will follow comics like Marjane Satrapi's *Persepolis* in reaching out to a different audience.

Finally, the label itself has helped redefine the medium. Paul Gravett attributes much of the graphic novel's success to its rebranding and notes the "cachet" of this new label (Mulholland 2007). The new location of the bookstore emphasizes this redefinition, and both elements align to produce structural and aesthetic similarities that now associate books and comics more strongly than ever, as both content and appearance use a template that owes more to the "novel" than the "graphic." Of course, these changes are not without consequence and it might be argued that, with a novelistic plot and structure and a material product resembling a book, comics today are becoming unrecognizable. Steve White is certainly aware of this potential pitfall, hinting that if the public stops buying single issues, then companies may decide to produce graphic novels only and this "cuts out the middle man, the comic buyer." That said, he also notes the positive aspects of such an expansion, such as a new readership.

REDEFINING THE AUDIENCE

As a consequence of all these production and marketing changes, the comics audience is changing. At the beginning of the 1990s DC market research defined its average reader as "twenty-four and male and very literate" (Pearson and Uricchio 1991, 29), and it seems clear that an adult readership for comics has been perpetually present. Evidence of this might include propaganda comics for servicemen in the 1940s, underground comix in the 1960s, and publications such as Marvel's *Epic Illustrated* in the 1980s. However, the gender bias in the audience is less of a fallacy than its child readership, and the majority of comics readers are indeed male.

Karen Berger says one of her goals for Vertigo was to "get people who don't read comics to discover them, because that's what happened to me," and Vertigo has brought DC a substantial new readership as titles such as *Y: The Last Man*, *Preacher*, and, of course, *The Sandman* drew women into the comics mainstream. Karen Berger ascribes this not only to a move away from superheroics and the presence of strong female characters, but also to "the emotion and the love and passion" in titles such as *Preacher*. She concludes: "People don't think men respond to relationship stuff when they do." Certainly the imprints following Vertigo, such as DC's Minx (2007), are built on the same foundations. Minx is aimed at this expanding audience but, like Vertigo before it, without the restrictions of genre and style. Just as Vertigo moved away from the superhero mainstream, Minx is moving beyond the manga sensibility that originally inspired it. Headed by long-standing Vertigo editor Shelly Bond, its titles have the same formula of star writers (such as Mike Carey, who co-writes a title with his daughter Louise, *Confessions of a Blabbermouth*) and focus on well-written, literary stories that cover a wide range of subjects.

Fifteen years ago, comics conventions were a male-only zone.[3] Today the expanding popularity of science fiction and fantasy television (such as *Buffy the Vampire Slayer*) has seen a preponderance of gender-neutral merchandise in comics stores. This, together with the move to the bookstores and the variety of mainstream titles available, has resulted in an expanded audience, and the closed-front comics store is rapidly becoming a thing of the past. The fan culture that sustains this medium is more widely spread than ever—but has it also been redefined in the process?

INTELLECTUAL PROPERTY AND MULTIMEDIA

Fan culture has always shaped comics: the initial recognition afforded to artists snowballed from the letters pages carried in the earliest mainstream comics where fans attempted to guess which unaccredited artist had worked on a strip. This led to strips being credited with artists' names and the successful were given more strips to work on. That fan recognition now favors the star writer as well as the artist (as noted on online forums such as www.quartertothree.com) has further contributed to comics' recent redefinition as literary, rather than visual, entertainment.

Since the 1970s creators were given credit for their own work (in contrast to the anonymous assembly-line production of the early days of comics) and subsequently began to demand ownership of their material. This stands in contrast to the previous corporate mentality, and accredited authorship has brought about a new form of collaboration where both the writer and artist's input is more closely observed, if only for the purposes of ownership. In contrast to previous arrangements where comics were created anonymously in a publisher's house style, individuality of style and voice is now crucial to the narratology and production of contemporary mainstream comics.

Although the Vertigo core titles were all reworkings of established DC characters, the radical nature of most of these rewrites emphasized original and creator-owned material. Karen Berger explains: "We set the stage with the six titles that became Vertigo and a few creator-owned ones, like *Skreemer* and *World Without End*." She continues: "We [DC] did a few creator-owned books, the very first ones, before we even started Vertigo." Distinct creator-owned imprints are now part of both DC and Marvel and creators generally retain copyright of original material. The new diversity of the industry is reflected in this coexistence of multiple imprints within a main publishing company.

Copyright and intellectual property restrictions are well publicized in both the UK and the U.S. Within comics, although intellectual property law has restricted the freedom of writers to play with industry-owned characters, the same restrictions have also aided the coherent formation of a character (by limiting the body of work featuring them to that approved by the owner) and implicitly encouraged individuality of expression for those creators working on long-running titles. The law has also made space in the industry for creators' rights: DC now pays a "creator royalty" as well as writer and artist royalties— and the lion's share of most royalty money goes to creators in creator-owned projects. Partiality towards the creator (whether writer or artist) continues to emphasize the concept of literary authorship but, essentially, the coexistence of creators' rights and copyright restrictions has allowed the industry to sustain its dual status as both a business and a creative enterprise.

This diversity is also echoed in other areas of the industry's evolution. For example, changes in the distribution system and the introduction of the specialty comics store have led to an increased focus on associated merchandising and marketing. Licensing and merchandising have replaced sweatshop-style production to alleviate the financial strain, albeit to the point where Marvel and DC might even be described as divisions of a toy company. As a subsidiary of Warner Bros., DC runs advertisements for Warner projects prominently in its publications. Along similar lines, Marvel owns "over 4,700 proprietary characters" that it licenses "in a wide range of consumer products, services, and media such as feature films, television, the Internet, apparel, video games, collectibles, snack foods, and promotions" (Gotham Comics 2001). Crossovers to other consumer media are commonplace, such as movie tie-ins, fast-food promotions, and big-screen adaptations of comic books. With regard to the latter, like the move to the bookstores, this relocation of comics material again expands the market and audience (as smaller films such as *American Splendor* and *Persepolis* sit alongside the *The Dark Knight*).

A movie-inspired aesthetic has also redefined the medium in some respects—when speaking of the trade paperback repackaging process, Steve White notes that "The publishers are following the DVD market and are now doing 'extras'" (cover galleries, sketch books, reprinted scripts, interviews, and so on). *Preacher* artist Steve Dillon comments further: "Most of us think we have more in common with the TV format than the film format [. . .] superheroes, the best superheroes, tend to be more soap opera-ish—like the X-Men, and the old Spider-Man stuff. But that's for a continuing-forever sort of series" (Osborne 1998). The new focus on the trade paperback and creator-owned work has instead led to a preponderance of one-shot graphic novels or mini-/maxi-series with a finite end. Comparisons with the movies therefore seem more relevant to today's industry and likely to continue.

CRITICAL INTEREST

Before concluding, it is important to note the import of some of the changes discussed above. Critical interest in comics has increased exponentially in the latter half of the twentieth century, despite the intermittent press hostility towards comics running throughout the medium's history, particularly in the early 1950s.[4] Subsequent media and critical attention was similarly negative and focused on comics' advertising, discussing consumer culture, and specifically the role of the mass media in exploiting childhood. However, these treatments were soon offset by other critics' work, much of which offered a cultural and/or historical perspective in recording comics' evolution.

Comics today enjoy a new respect and have invaded the literary award scene, notable examples of which include Art Spiegelman's *Maus*, winner of the 1992 Pulitzer Prize; Chris Ware's *Jimmy Corrigan: The Smartest Kid on Earth*, which won the Guardian First Book Award in 2001; and Neil Gaiman and Charles Vess's "A Midsummer Night's Dream" (*The Sandman* #19), which won the 1991 World Fantasy Award for Best Short Fiction (after which the rules were changed to exclude comics from this category). Comics and associated publications are now reviewed in national newspapers, such as Douglas Wolk's reviews in *The New York Times*, and Roger Sabin and Paul Gravett's writing for (among others) *The Guardian*, *The Times*, *The Independent*, and *The Daily Telegraph* in the UK. Mainstream newspapers such as *The Independent* (UK) have also devoted entire issues of their *Sunday Review* to comics (1 October 2006), while in the U.S. literary journals such as *McSweeney's Quarterly Concern* have published special editions on comics (issue 13, July 2008).

Comics now have a solid presence in academia with an ever-increasing number of universities offering dedicated comics courses.[5] And it is drawing attention from academic subject areas as diverse as literature, art, cultural studies, history, philosophy, graphic design, pedagogy, visual language studies, and many others. Empirical surveys and evaluations of comics history now stand alongside studies of the medium itself, which have in turn contributed to the inclusion of comics in more traditional studies of visual language theory. More recently, comics criticism has focused on the superhero archetype in terms of its modern-day cultural functions.[6]

Critical attention has even extended to include metacriticism of the subject, such as Umberto Eco's 1999 article, "Four Ways of Speaking about Comics." The increasing acceptance of comics into academia is evidenced at both an international and grassroots level, examples of which include international academic journals such as the *International Journal of Comic Art*, *ImageTexT*, *SIGNs*, *European Comic Art*, and *Studies in Comics*. These are supported by resources such as the Grand Comic Book Database and the Comics Research Bibliography—and by both international discussion groups (e.g., the Comix-Scholars List) and localized initiatives (such as the Scottish Word and Image Group). Though space does not permit a full discussion of the much-valued efforts of both individuals and institutions here, it is clear that both critical and academic interest in comics is increasing exponentially.

THE NEXT STEP

It appears then that changes both within and outside the industry have brought the comic book closer to the notion of the literary text. Observable changes such as technological advances, in-house employment changes, the replacement of disposability with permanence, and a shift in distribution methods stand alongside the less quantifiable—a perceived shift in audience composition and attitude, the redefinition of the creator as singular author and the expansion of academic and critical attention. This has resulted in consequences regarding the notions of ownership within the wider cultural context of licensing and copyright law. The current shift towards graphic novels using original creator-owned characters and concepts are an outcome of the recognition afforded to the star creators through redefining comics as literature, as well as having their basis in the new distribution system and associated merchandising.

Using a reworked aesthetic, new technology, ideological departure, and innovative marketing, DC Vertigo has thrived by building on 1980s trends in a market that has redefined both the material product and cultural status of mainstream comics throughout the 1990s. The result is an industry where both the dominant and independent publishing companies now spend much of their energy on producing literary, creator-owned, book-length material. In addition to its alignment with literature, comics' technological and marketing developments have also produced parallels with other visual media such as film and television. Therefore, it may not be too much to say that, despite comics' expanding popularity, the traditional understanding of comics as a medium could be threatened in the current cultural context.

There can be no doubt that not only comics publishing but also perceptions of it have changed radically over the last seventy years. Although Karen Berger states that Vertigo has "no current plans for producing original content for the web," advances made in Internet publishing are bound to bring about a whole new set of changes. Despite differences of tactility and physicality, the possibilities of the web for creation and distribution are immense, and Berger believes that comics can exist successfully both in print and online. While Vertigo may not be producing comics directly for the web, in 2007 DC launched Zuda, an imprint dedicated to webcomics. Digital developments will continue, and it may be that the next evolutionary step for comics will have an even greater impact than the graphic novel.

NOTES

1. All quotations drawn from personal interviews. Full versions are available online at www.juliaround.com.

2. The title on the cover of *The Saga of the Swamp Thing* was changed to *Swamp Thing* with issue 31 (Dec. 1984), but for continuity this series is referred to by its original designation throughout.

3. Personal experience of author, reinforced by Steve White's observations and further evidenced by sites such as girl-wonder.org, which founded the Con Anti-Harassment Project in 2008 (cahp.girl-wonder.org/).

4. Jeet Heer and Kent Worcester's *Arguing Comics* (2005) offers primary evidence of the charges of immorality comic strips were subjected to in the 1906–1912 period (see also Gordon 38–43). Other prominent anti-comics writing includes Sterling North's article "A National Disgrace" in the *Chicago Daily News* (8 May 1940), the *National Education Association Journal*'s "An Antidote to the Comic Magazine Poison" (December 1940), and most famously, Dr. Fredric Wertham's *Seduction of the Innocent* (1953). See Amy Kiste Nyberg's *Seal of Approval* (1998) for a full discussion of this mid-twentieth-century history. *Arguing Comics* also collects together several early essays on comics from major writers and critics such as Umberto Eco, Marshall McLuhan, Dorothy Parker, e.e. cummings, and C.L.R. James.

5. A brief Internet search in January 2009 produced more than fifty universities offering dedicated comics courses. ComicsResearch.org lists over one hundred and seventy doctoral dissertations on the medium.

6. For a summary of early comics criticism, see above. Please refer to Ron Goulart, Ian Gordon, or George Pumphrey for critiques of comics, consumer culture, and childhood exploitation from various perspectives. The work of Roger Sabin, David Kunzle, and Paul Gravett offers historical surveys of comics. Will Eisner and Scott McCloud are at the forefront of those whose analyses have contributed to the inclusion of comics in other visual language studies, such as the work of Neil Cohn. Will Brooker, Roberta Pearson and William Uricchio, Richard Reynolds, and Stephen Rauch also provide various contemporary approaches to the superhero.

WORKS CITED

Brooker, W. 2001. *Batman Unmasked*. London: Continuum.

Cohn, N. 2007. Emaki Productions. *Visual Language*. http://www.emaki.net [accessed 14 Aug. 2008].

Comic Book Rebels. 2008. Neil Gaiman: A Man for all Seasons. *The Dreaming*. http://www.holycow.com/dreaming/lore/interview/neil-gaiman-a-man-for-all-seasons#more-1006 [accessed 14 Aug. 2008].

Cooke, R. 2006. The art of words and pictures. *New Statesman*. http://www.newstatesman.com/200609250051 [accessed 17 Dec. 2007].

Daniels, L. 2003. *DC Comics: A Celebration of the World's Favorite Comic Book Heroes*. New York: Watson-Guptill.

Eco, U. 1999. Four Ways of Speaking of Comics. *Fucine Mute*, 9. http://www.fucine.com/archivo/fm09/eco.htm [accessed 1 Feb. 2005].

Eisner, W. 1990. *Comics and Sequential Art*. Expanded ed. Tamarac, FL: Poorhouse Press.

———. 1996. *Graphic Storytelling and Visual Narrative*. Tamarac, FL: Poorhouse Press.

Gold, M. 1990. Introduction. In P. Moreno, *Batman: Digital Justice*, 2–3. London: Titan Books.

Gordon, I. 1998. *Comic Strips and Consumer Culture 1890–1945*. London: Smithsonian Institution Press.

Gotham Comics. 2001. Gotham Comics brings Marvel Universe to India. *Gotham Comics*. http://www.gothamcomics.com/html/Press.asp [accessed 13 May 2005].

Goulart, R. 1970. *The Assault on Childhood*. London: Victor Gollancz.

Gravett, P. 2006. The Second Golden Age of Comics: Selling the Graphic Novel into Bookshops. *On Comics and Graphic Novels*. http://www.paulgravett.com/articles/093_booksellers/093_booksellers.htm [accessed 7 Dec. 2007].

Hanley, J. 2000. Comics Distribution and Retailing forum. *Comicon.com*. http://www.comicon.com/ubb/ultimatebb.php/ubb/get_topic/f/3/t/000248.html [accessed 8 Sept. 2008].

Heer, J., and Kent Worcester. 2005. *Arguing Comics*. Jackson, MS: University Press of Mississippi.

Keene, R. 2003. *The Art of Comic Book Restoration*. http://www.g4tv.com/screensavers/features/45751/The_Art_of_Comic_Book_Restoration.html [accessed 15 Nov. 2007].

Kunzle, D. 1990. *The History of the Comic Strip: The Nineteenth Century*. Berkeley, CA: University of California Press.

Kwitney, A. 2000. *Vertigo Visions*. London: Titan Books.

Mayer, A. 2004. User Comment (Wednesday October 06, 2004): My Experiences as a Comic/Card Dealer. *Quarter to Three Online Forum*. http://www.quartertothree.com [accessed 27 Apr. 2005].

McCabe, J. 2004. *Hanging Out with the Dream King*. Seattle: Fantagraphics Books.

McCloud, S. 1993. *Understanding Comics*. New York: Paradox Press.

———. 2000. *Reinventing Comics*. New York: Paradox Press.

McCue, G. S., and Clive Bloom. 1993. *Dark Knights: The New Comics in Context*. London: Pluto Press.

Morrison, G., and Richard Case. 1992. *Doom Patrol: Crawling from the Wreckage*, #19–25. New York: DC Comics Inc.

Mulholland, T. 2007. More than words: Britain embraces the graphic novel. *International Herald Tribune*. http://www.iht.com/articles/2007/08/21/arts/gnovel.php [accessed 7 Dec. 2007].

Nyberg, A.K. 1998. *Seal of Approval: The History of the Comics Code*. Jackson, MS: University Press of Mississippi.

Osborne, S.L. 1998. Drinking with the Boys: An Evening with Garth Ennis and Steve Dillon. *Sequential Tart*, 1.1. http://www.sequentialtart.com/archive/sept98/ [accessed 22 Apr. 2005].

Pearson, R. E., and William Uricchio, eds. 1991. *The Many Lives of the Batman*. New York: Routledge.

Pumphrey, G. H. 1955. *Children's Comics: A Guide for Parents and Teachers*. London: Epworth Press.

Rauch, S. 2003. *Neil Gaiman's The Sandman and Joseph Campbell: In Search of the Modern Myth*. Holicong, PA: Wildside Press.

Reynolds, R. 1992. *Superheroes: A Modern Mythology*. Jackson, MS: University of Mississippi Press.

Rogers, M. C. 1999. Licensing Farming and the American Comic Book Industry. *International Journal of Comic Art* 1(2): 132–142.

Sabin, R. 2001. *Comics, Comix and Graphic Novels*. London: Phaidon Press.

Saenz, M., and Peter Gillis. 1988. *Shatter*. New York: Ballantine Books.

Salisbury, M., ed. 1999. *Writers on Comics Scriptwriting*. London: Titan Books.

Savlov, M. 1999. A Sort of Legend. *Austin Chronicle*. http://www.austinchronicle.com/issues/dispatch/1999-09-10/books_feature.html [accessed 1 May 2000].

Shainblum, M. 1993. The Information Barons. *Hour Magazine*. http://www.northguard.com/mbs/writing.html [accessed 8 September 2008].

Wertham, F. 1953. *Seduction of the Innocent*. New York: Rinehart & Company.

GROUPS AND ONLINE RESOURCES

Comicsresearch.org (Comics Scholarship Annotated Bibliographies): http://www.comicsresearch.org/

European Comic Art: http://www.liverpool-unipress.co.uk/html/publication.asp?idProduct=3793

Grand Comic Book Database: http://www.comics.org

ImageTexT: http://www.english.ufl.edu/imagetext

International Journal of Comic Art (IJOCA): http://www.ijoca.com

Scottish Word and Image Group (SWIG): http://www.dundee.ac.uk/english/swig/

Studies in Comics: http://www.intellectbooks.co.uk/journals.php

Studies in Graphic Narratives (SIGNs): http://www.graphic-narratives.org

The Comics Journal: http://www.tcj.com/

The Comix Scholars List: http://web.english.ufl.edu/comics/scholars/

CHAPTER THREE

Signals from Airstrip One: The British Invasion of Mainstream American Comics

—CHRIS MURRAY

When The Beatles made their first appearance on *The Ed Sullivan Show* on February 9, 1964, the American press proclaimed the "British Invasion" of rock and roll. Exactly twenty years later DC Comics published issue 21 of their then flagging *The Saga of the Swamp Thing* title, written by Alan Moore, a comics writer from Northampton, England. The British Invasion of American comics had begun.

The association between these two waves of cultural crossover is not made frivolously—in both instances British artists appropriated then revolutionized genres that seemed typically American, challenging audience expectations and creating waves of media interest. Also, in both cases the difference between British and American culture and politics created a space where something new and surprising could thrive. As the American success of The Beatles paved the way for The Rolling Stones and countless other British bands, Moore established the career trajectory so many of his contemporaries would follow—success in the small British comics marketplace, which then opened the door to a much larger audience in America.

The fact that this new cultural invasion began exactly twenty years after The Beatles were beamed into American homes would no doubt amuse Alan Moore, whose seminal works *V for Vendetta*, *Watchmen*, and *From Hell* are structured around his primary thematic conceit—that events reverberate through history, establishing patterns and resonances that unfold with mathematical precision. Moore's innovations inspired Neil Gaiman and Grant Morrison, who joined Moore as the first wave of the British Invasion.

The pattern was completed with a brash, opinionated, and excoriating second wave of British talent in the form of writers Garth Ennis, Warren Ellis, and Mark Millar.

This chapter will explore the early work of Moore, Morrison, and Gaiman. It will consider their entry into American comics, and will demonstrate that their perspective on superheroes was in large part a response to the complex political and cultural relationship between Britain and America. It will then outline the influence of the second wave—Garth Ennis, Warren Ellis, and Mark Millar. However, before exploring the work of these writers it is important to appreciate the interaction between British comics and American popular culture in order to understand the attitude of these writers toward American comics.

THE AMERICAN INFLUENCE ON COMICS IN BRITAIN

American comic books have always loomed large in the British comics buyer's consciousness. Since the late 1930s American superhero adventures had been reprinted in Britain, notably by Amalgamated Press (AP), which featured Superman stories in *Triumph* magazine, while Odhams Press published Disney reprints (Clark and Clark 1991, 34). These colorful American strips were quite different from traditional British comics such as *Comic Cuts* and *Illustrated Chips* (both 1890–1953), also published by Amalgamated. Firstly, British comics were published weekly, as opposed to monthly like American comics. This meant that stories were episodic and deadlines were much tighter.

In addition, the comics had formal differences. The usual AP style was to have a standard nine-panel image grid accompanied by text underneath, without captions or word balloons. Consequently, American comics seemed much more visually appealing and dynamic. AP's competitor, DC Thomson, based in the Scottish city of Dundee, seized on this new American style and produced *The Dandy* (1937–present) and *The Beano* (1938–present), anthology comics that met with immediate success, largely due to the talents of artists like Dudley D. Watkins and James Crichton (Gravett and Stanbury 2006, 70). These comics featured humor strips alongside action and adventure—and even a few short-lived homemade superheroes, such as The Amazing Mr X.

The outbreak of World War II brought American troops to British shores in the early 1940s and with them came American popular culture, including comic books. For a time reprints of Captain Marvel stories were incredibly popular, until DC's court case with Fawcett Publications brought an end to the supply of new material. However, British readers were soon kept happy with a character very closely based on Captain Marvel—Marvelman by Mick Anglo (Khoury 2001, 6).

In the 1950s the popularity of American horror comics provoked a similar moral crisis as it did in the U.S., with parents' groups and sections of the media calling for a ban (Barker 1984). This led to a resurgence of morally upright comics, such as *Eagle* and *Swift* by Hulton Press, the former featuring the square-jawed upholder of imperial values, Dan Dare, written and drawn by Frank Hampson. At this time *The Dandy* and *The Beano* concentrated on humor strips featuring characters like Dennis the Menace, Desperate Dan, and The Bash Street Kids, who were drawn by artists such as David Law, Leo Baxendale, and Ken Reid. Incidentally, the British Dennis the Menace appeared within days of the American strip of the same name by Hank Ketcham (both appeared in March 1951), although there is no established connection between them.

War comics also became incredibly popular in the post-war years, becoming a stable of British comics for decades, with the long-running *Commando* (DCT) appearing in 1961, later joined by *Warlord* (also DCT) in 1974. During the 1960s American comics were reprinted in Britain by Odhams Press under the Power Comics imprint, which tried to emulate the fan-friendly feeling of Stan Lee's Marvel Comics. In 1969 Odhams merged with George Newnes, Ltd. and Amalgamated Press to form IPC (International Publishing Company). At this point American superhero reprints disappeared from British newsstands for a few years until Marvel noticed the gap in the market and opened its own British arm, Marvel UK, in 1972.

In the mid-1970s the British comics market started to diversify, offering more violent stories to an older audience. IPC led the way, introducing *Battle* (1975) and the highly controversial *Action* (1976) (see Barker 1990). With the success of *Star Wars* (1977) science fiction became highly marketable, so IPC launched *2000 AD*, and DCT followed with *Starblazer* in 1979 (which in time would feature some of Grant Morrison's earliest comics work).

2000 AD (1977–present) was a punk science-fiction anthology showcasing Judge Dredd, a fascistic future lawman, and was created by writers Pat Mills and John Wagner. They had worked for DC Thomson and other well-established comics publishers but wanted to pursue more controversial themes outside the strictures of these publishers (Bishop 2007, 8–18). *Battle, Action,* and *2000 AD* were inspired by American popular culture, notably Hollywood films: *Battle* had the Rat Pack, modeled on *The Dirty Dozen* (1967), *Action* featured Hookjaw, a murderous great white shark inspired by *Jaws* (1975), and Judge Dredd was a science-fiction version of *Dirty Harry* (1971). This made IPC a strong competitor to DCT, and *2000 AD* one of the great success stories of contemporary British comics. In its long history (far outliving *Action* and *Battle*), *2000 AD* has nurtured the talents of Alan Moore, Neil Gaiman, Grant Morrison, and Garth Ennis, among countless others.

In 1982 Moore took over writing Captain Britain for Marvel UK in *Daredevils* and *Mighty World of Marvel*. Marvel UK was at this point publishing original material that rivaled the quality of the American reprints. Chris Claremont created Captain Britain in 1976 before he found success in America with his hugely popular run on *X-Men*, but Moore's Captain Britain was very different—and became a testing ground for many of the ideas he would develop later. When Moore left Captain Britain, Jamie Delano took over, leaving Moore to develop *Marvelman* and *V for Vendetta* for the short-lived but hugely influential *Warrior* (1982–1985), created by Dez Skinn, a former editor at Marvel UK, and published by Quality Communications. In *Marvelman* and *V for Vendetta* Moore produced some of the most significant British comics narratives to date, using them to highlight his political concerns, showing a society on the verge of collapse and divided by the inequalities associated with the government of Conservative Prime Minister Margaret Thatcher.

Despite the economic and social crises of early 1980s Britain, the mood of impending danger and unrest was accompanied by a burst of creativity in art and literature, which seemed full of oppositional energy. It seemed as if the art films of director Derek Jarman and television series like *The South Bank Show*, an arts magazine show, could really challenge the assumptions of the Conservative government, that the Left was truly in the right (so to speak), and that Thatcher's days as Prime Minister were numbered. This was optimistic thinking, but British comics shared some of the politics and complexity seen in contemporaneous cultural forms.

The tensions of the times created a generation of outspoken writers who used comics as a forum for political debate. A number of innovative anthology titles emerged, alongside a slowly growing underground, supported by the opening of specialty comics shops such as Forbidden Planet in the UK. By the mid-1980s the British comics scene was strong enough to support a range of intelligent, stylish, and influential magazines, including *Deadline* (home of Tank Girl by Jamie Hewlett and Alan Martin, and featuring work by the likes of Peter Milligan) and *Escape*, created by Paul Gravett, which reprinted the best comics from Europe and America.

There was also *Speakeasy*, a magazine of interviews and criticism similar to *The Comics Journal* from America. Fleetway (publisher of *2000 AD*) released *Crisis*, a darker, more socially engaged sister comic, and then *Revolver*, both aimed at the emerging adult market. *Toxic!* arrived in 1991, a rival to *2000 AD*, published by Apocalypse Ltd. and featured creator-owned work by former

2000 *AD* contributors (such as Pat Mills and John Wagner), but the title disappeared before the year ended, as did *Blast!* soon after (Sabin 1996, 140–45). This coincided with the great comics crash of the early 1990s, when the American speculator market collapsed and the adult comics boom lost the attention of the media—which had played a crucial role in driving it (Sabin 1993, 96–97; Wright 2001, 283).

As ever, the British market was closely tied to the American one, and problems in the American comics industry shot across the Atlantic faster than a speeding bullet, although by now the first wave of the British Invasion had secured a foothold in America where there was a notable demand for its talents. The formation of the direct market in the 1970s had aided in the formation of a stable fan-base, which established a much more visible and vocal adult readership (see chapters one and two in this collection). Publishers were keen to exploit this, and there was a generation of recognizable and marketable comics creators crucial in this regard, such as Frank Miller, but increasingly American publishers had to look beyond the American comics industry. Partly because they had learned the language of comics narratives as fans themselves, writers and artists within this industry were apt to repeat the same genre clichés proven popular in the past. Frank Miller was innovative in some ways, yet in most respects he aspired to be the Jack Kirby for his generation. It was time for something new, and the emerging British writers appeared at exactly the right time.

Needless to say, the writers who formed the British Invasion had more than a passing familiarity with American comics and the superhero genre, but they also possessed a degree of critical distance and ironic detachment from them that allowed these creators to deconstruct the superhero as a projection of American mythology. They also came from a different comics culture, where superheroes were only one small part of the equation. While British creators had made the transition to American comics before Moore—including Chris Claremont who had been born in England, and Peter Milligan, an Irish writer who worked for Eclipse in the early 1980s—they had not challenged the conventions of the American mainstream in significant ways. Indeed, Claremont's run on *X-Men* set the standard for mainstream genre writing in comics.

The impetus to do so arose due to the relationship between Britain and America in the early 1980s. For many liberal-minded Britons the right-wing policies of Thatcher were deplorable, as was her attachment to President Ronald Reagan's aggressive stance on communism. At a time when British and American politics converged in worrying ways for the political left, the superhero was a problematic figure for British writers and their works employed various strategies to deflate the myth. This was not anti-Americanism for the most part but an attack on the conservative values that seemed entrenched in British and American politics. The renaissance of British comics in the late 1970s and early 1980s seemed tailor-made to support a generation of comics creators eager to confront these issues, and the need for American publishers to source new talent combined to create the conditions for the British Invasion.

In Britain, Morrison gravitated towards 2000 AD, creating its first superhero, Zenith, in 1987. By this time Moore had successfully made his move into American comics, first through *The Saga of the Swamp Thing*, then writing memorable stories featuring DC's flagship characters—Superman and Batman—but his masterpiece was *Watchmen*, serialized in 1986, a dense and complicated story full of millennial anxiety and metafictional flair. *Watchmen*'s huge success was due in part to the upheavals in the comics industry in the mid-to-late 1980s. The nature of distribution was changing, new formats such as prestige editions and graphic novels heralded a wave of comics that garnered critical respect and new readership (as discussed elsewhere in this collection), and the idea of the comics writer/artist as an *auteur* moved out of the underground and independent market and into the mainstream.

With a new vision of the medium emerging, American comics diversified in ways not seen since the post-war/pre-Code comics of the early 1950s, resulting in the rise of so-called "adult comics" in a more respectable book format. In 1987 the collected edition of *Watchmen* joined *Batman: The Dark Knight Returns* by Frank Miller and *Maus* by Art Spiegelman as arguably the three most important American comics of the 1980s, leading the way in a revolution that led to mainstream distribution to bookstores and even best-seller lists (Sabin 1993, 87–95). The second wave would both pay homage to its predecessors and establish an altogether different legacy. In order to understand the context of the emergence of these important writers, the remainder of this chapter will examine the influence they had on the comics industry.

"THESE ARE NOT OUR PROMISED RESURRECTIONS" (MOORE AND CAMPBELL 2001): ALAN MOORE'S WORLDS OF DEATHLY DISAPPOINTMENT

Like all great writers, Alan Moore has an unmistakable voice, the power of which comes from an understanding of humanity in all its weakness and its failings, combined with a sense of empathy, tinged with an air of disappointment, a hint of unspoken frustration. This very English mood permeates

Moore's best work, from *V for Vendetta* through to the hugely influential *Watchmen*, the intricate *From Hell*, and the lavish *Lost Girls*. When Moore came to the attention of DC he soon found himself heading a project to produce more sophisticated superhero comics and led the way by subverting the genre through what was seen as "grim and gritty" cynicism. This was at a time when comics creators were starting to enjoy unprecedented acclaim due to the growth of fandom and independent comics retailers, both simultaneously encouraged by and nourishing the direct sales market.

Moore was the darling of a comics industry desperate to present itself as a legitimate adult art form, but he was too cynical or perhaps realistic to see this as anything other than what it was—a marketing strategy. Moore's work resisted the simple tags the media found for it—"realistic superheroes" and "grim and gritty," and with the work he had started in Britain (*V for Vendetta* and *Marvelman*, now called *Miracleman*) being published in America his anarchist leanings came more to the fore, as did the realization that he did not see himself as the savior of superhero comics. The roots of such rebellion against the status quo were visible as far back as Moore's first contribution to American comics, and as much in his working method as in his themes.

The story featured in *The Saga of the Swamp Thing* #21, "The Anatomy Lesson," was unlike anything seen in mainstream American comics to that point. It seemed to have an authorial voice, and was crafted with care and attention, unlike most of the products of the factory production line that had dominated the American comics industry (Wolk 2007, 231–236). Of course, underground comix had long celebrated the genius of the comics auteur, such as Robert Crumb, and several mainstream creators had individual styles, from Will Eisner in the 1930s, through Jack Kirby, to Frank Miller in the early 1980s, but these had often been writer-artists. Moore was no artist, although he had drawn some early strips—by the time he was starting to gain recognition he had turned exclusively to writing.

His scripts were dense, laden with description, suggestions for panel layout, transitions, expressions, mood—and often entire paragraphs were devoted to the description of a single panel (Smokey Man and Millidge 2003, 16; Baker, 2001, 43–53). This was far from the editor-led approach often practiced at Marvel and DC, where writers would suggest plots and the artist would work from quite threadbare scripts in order to turn around the issue, all the time consulting powerful editors who oversaw the interests of the property. In contrast, Moore's comics were clearly the product of a committed writer working in close collaboration with an artist operating as a creative partner. This was a defining characteristic of the British Invasion—the most important exports of British talents would be writers, not artists. While several important artists such as Dave Gibbons formed part of the British Invasion, the spearhead would be the writers.

No analysis of the British Invasion would be complete without some consideration of *Watchmen*, Moore's twelve-part mini-series, produced in collaboration with artist Dave Gibbons. Having impressed DC with *The Saga of the Swamp Thing*, Moore was asked to revive a set of characters previously part of Charlton Comics, but now owned by DC. Opening as a murder mystery, the story allowed Moore an opportunity to examine the superhero genre in a sophisticated and precise deconstruction of its workings. Underlying this was a sense of frustration that this genre, with all its absurdity and foibles, has retarded the development of the medium, but the text, like Moore, never hated superhero comics as much as it protested to.

The motif Moore deploys throughout is of a watch being assembled, mirroring the intricate story. He meditates on chaos theory and hidden patterns of order, and the form and style of the artwork reflects this, with its very traditional, reserved use of a nine-panel grid layout to reveal a much deeper structure of symmetry and synchronicity. This configuration recalls the newspaper strip format and the AP style common in Britain before reprints of Superman inspired DC Thomson's artists.

The story imagines what would happen if superheroes existed in the "real" world and not just on the comics page. One of its answers is that superhero comics would not dominate the industry (although they would dominate the world and could usurp human progress). The metafictional detail Moore weaves in is so layered that the very format of the comic itself is shaped in response to its themes. This is a serious story, despite its superhero trappings, and as with Miller's *The Dark Knight Returns* it is not surprising *Watchmen* captured the imaginations of adult readers.

It was visually stunning, beautifully poised, with disciplined artwork by Gibbons and a complex and challenging script by Moore, undercut with a sense of frustration at a world gone wrong. It drew upon art, philosophy, literature, science, and of course, nearly fifty years of superhero comics, offering a highly intertextual work which still serves as the watermark for writing in superhero comics. A young journalist named Neil Gaiman was so impressed by Moore that he set out to become a comics writer himself, taking Moore's literate comics to the next level, creating a hugely successful story about the nature of storytelling and imagination—*The Sandman*.

THE THEATRE OF DREAMS: ENTER NEIL GAIMAN

Gaiman's friendship with Alan Moore propelled him into comics, following in Moore's footsteps by contributing "Future Shocks" to *2000 AD* in 1986. His collaboration with artist Dave McKean led to three successful graphic novels, *Violent Cases*, *Signal to Noise*, and *The Comical Tragedy or Tragical Comedy of Mr. Punch*, then to *Black Orchid* for DC, which grew out of Moore's run on *The Saga of the Swamp Thing*. Karen Berger was the groundbreaking editor who headed Vertigo and established its brand of quality writing by headhunting British talent (Kwitney 2000, 9; Jones and Jacobs 1997, 332–36). When Berger recruited Gaiman his comic *The Sandman* became the cornerstone of Vertigo's success, along with Jamie Delano's *Hellblazer* (which also budded out from Moore's *Swamp Thing*).

Like *Watchmen*, *The Sandman* attracted people to comics who would not otherwise read them. Unlike *Watchmen*, the reader was not expected to have so much familiarity with the superhero genre. Wearing its origins as an update of a 1940s superhero very lightly, Gaiman moved the narrative away from the DC universe, creating his own world of "The Dreaming," the realm of Morpheus, lord of dreams. The story was engaging, sometimes warm (unlike the detached protagonist), and always well crafted. And the resolution of the series achieved something little seen in comics—real emotional power (Bender 1999, xi–xiv). Moore's influence was evident, and indeed, when Moore left *Miracleman* he picked Gaiman as his successor (in much the same way he picked Delano to follow him on *Hellblazer*), but by the time *The Sandman* reached the high point of its run, Gaiman had developed his own voice. Perhaps less cynical than Moore, Gaiman's stories were less about patterns, cycles, and frustration and more about evolution, growth, and hope.

Gaiman also brought an interest in the theatrical to comics, equating the comic page with a stage. This led him to focus much more on characterization, gesture, and nuance rather than action. Gaiman has suggested this on several occasions, with recurring references to Shakespeare in *The Sandman* (Round 2008, 18–33). Without Moore it is unlikely there would have been much of a demand for a writer like Gaiman in American mainstream comics, but with Moore establishing a market for intelligent, literate comics writers, Gaiman flourished, as did Scottish writer Grant Morrison, the first *enfant terrible* of the British Invasion.

POP GOES THE GLASWEGIAN: GRANT MORRISON
GETS TO PLAY WITH ALL THE TOYS

Scottish author Grant Morrison started with DC Thomson in the early 1980s while also pursuing a career in underground comics. In 1987 he started work on *Zenith* for *2000 AD*, intermingling the postmodern sensibility of *Watchmen* with his own interest in Romantic poetry, especially William Blake, and a fascination with Aleister Crowley and "pop magick" (Murray 2008, 34–53; Wolk 2007, 259). This sense that comics were magical, part of an incantation merging words and images, perhaps came from Moore, but Morrison moved it away from the psychogeography that fascinated Moore into anarchistic poststructuralist play where semantics and ritual were bound up with rebellion.

In the late 1980s Morrison was headhunted by DC Comics, which was eager to capitalize on the adult comics boom. Like Gaiman and Delano, Morrison would eventually contribute to DC's new Vertigo line after rejuvenating lesser-known superhero comics such as *Animal Man* and *Doom Patrol*. And as with Moore and Gaiman he offered radically different interpretations of these characters. In *Animal Man* the story became a platform for his animal rights views, and ultimately twisted in on itself to become a postmodern reconstruction of the comics form itself. Likewise, *Doom Patrol* became a surreal rumination on madness, disability, and art.

Morrison's subversion of these characters was striking, and he continued to make a name for himself as a serious writer with his disturbing vision of Batman's world in the graphic novel *Arkham Asylum* (1989), with artwork by Dave McKean. However, Morrison's most mature and personal work emerged in the mid-1990s and included *Flex Mentallo* (1996), *The Invisibles* (1994–2000), and later *The Filth* (2002). These works cemented his reputation as one of the most innovative and provocative writers in contemporary comics, fusing the myths of the superhero, apocalyptic anxieties, and a critique of notions of self and identity that moved far beyond the usual concerns of the genre.

Morrison followed this critical success with an unexpected move. Rather than continue with original characters or doggedly pursue personal works, Morrison's interest in archetypes and icons led him to helm high-profile revamps of Marvel's *X-Men* and to produce some of the most interesting work on Superman since the 1960s (perhaps excepting Moore's Superman stories in the mid-1980s). *New X-Men* reimagined the team as slick media stars and the epitome of twenty-first-century cool, while *All Star Superman* took Superman back to the wondrous years of the Silver Age (1950s and 1960s), reveling in the arcane history of the character, and offering Morrison's typically off-beat take on a popular culture icon. Both *New X-Men* and *All Star Superman* featured artwork by Morrison's frequent collaborator, Frank Quitely, which added considerably to the contemporary and stylish edge Morrison brought to these comics. Morrison occupied a niche as one of the most important and thought-provoking writers in the comics industry while "playing with the big toys"—the icons of popular culture that dominated the consciousness of an entire generation.

While some may feel Morrison has rejected the esotericism of his early writing to work with more obviously commercial properties in recent years, the reverse is actually true. He never claimed to hate superheroes as Moore did—or moved away from them into the realms of pure fantasy like Gaiman. His love of the genre permeates his work and his subversion of these icons is audacious, a kind of semantic hijacking of popular culture. What he aims to achieve by this is only made clear by a detailed appreciation of his themes and recurring concerns—an attack on the simple assumptions and conservative values that underpin the mythology of mass culture. He wants to make superhero comics better, and to show that as a metaphor they can be a positive expression of human potential, not the psychopaths and fascists Moore and Frank Miller portray. As Victor Hugo notes in *Histoire d'un Crime* (1852), "One can resist the invasion of an army; one cannot resist the invasion of ideas." This quotation sums up the ethos of Morrison's mature work.

The first wave of the British Invasion offered texts that drew upon literary and esoteric sources, notably Romantic poetry and the occult, as well as wider popular culture texts. Many of these comics offered postmodern deconstructions of the nature of comics storytelling and sequential art, and as such represent the emergence of a sophisticated and self-referential comics culture. One of the consequences of this was that the door was now open for a second wave of British talent to reach American comics.

THE SECOND WAVE: 1991–PRESENT

The huge success of Moore, Gaiman, and Morrison, as well as Delano, Milligan, and a host of British comics artists paved the way for more British comics creators to enter the previously impenetrable American comics industry. The perception was that British writers were edgier than American ones, who seemed permanently enthralled by the mythology of the superhero. The ironic distance achieved by the first wave came to be seen as the prerequisite for success in America, but a new generation of upcoming writers, particularly Garth Ennis, Warren Ellis, and Mark Millar, found a new strategy to differentiate their writing styles—irreverence, extreme violence, and profanity.

Garth Ennis came from Northern Ireland and drew much of his inspiration from the British comics of his childhood, notably *Battle* and *Action*. Ennis started in American comics with *Hellblazer* for DC in 1991, following Jamie Delano. Ennis was a much louder, brasher voice than Moore or Delano had been, replacing their dark subtle tones with a more violent and stark rendition of John Constantine's world. Ending his run in 1994, Ennis began writing the landmark series *Preacher* in 1995. This was the most American of comics, drawing from the western, the road movie, and American notions of Manifest Destiny, woven together with an attack on religious conservatism and pious values.

Working with British artist Steve Dillon, Ennis crafted a story that redefined mainstream comics, but there was no gimmicks, no clever plot twists, or metafictional gymnastics—instead there was plot, characterization, humor, action, and solid, consistent artwork. Since completing *Preacher* Ennis has brought those lessons to a popular run on *The Punisher*, also with Dillon, and has continued to demonstrate his distaste for superheroes in *The Boys*. This comic features characters that seem drawn from the British comics of Ennis's childhood, such as Dennis the Menace and Oor Wullie from DC Thomson, who are dedicated to destroying the superheroes who threaten to dominate the world with their arrogance and vanity. It is not difficult to read this in terms of a critique of the dominance of American superhero comics over the British comics industry, and a break with Morrison's love affair with the superhero genre. If Moore half-seriously proclaimed his hatred of superheroes, then Ennis really did—with a passion.

Warren Ellis, an English writer, followed quickly behind Ennis, first working for *Deadline* in 1990, then for *2000 AD*. His first notable work was "Lazarus Churchyard," which appeared in the short-lived *Blast!*; by 1994 he was working for Marvel, but failed to make much of an impact there. Ellis found success in America when he moved to Wildstorm, an independent company, and began work on *DV8*, a spin-off from the then very successful *Gen-13*. He took over on *Stormwatch*, turning a formulaic superhero comic into one of the best-paced, best-written action comics of the mid-1990s. With *Transmetropolitan* (1997), a creator-owned comic that was part of DC's ill-fated Helix imprint, Ellis garnered a huge fan following and critical acclaim; when Helix collapsed, *Transmetropolitan* survived and was transplanted to Vertigo.

In 1999 Ellis teamed up with British artist Bryan Hitch to launch *The Authority*, a spin-off from *Stormwatch*, turning up the intensity of action and violence. Hitch's artwork was perfectly suited to this high-octane blockbuster style nicknamed "widescreen comics." If Moore, Morrison, and Gaiman aspired to emulate literary influences, from Shakespeare and Blake through to Ballard and Moorcock—then the second wave wanted to be film directors, and Ellis the new Michael Bay. Ellis shared Morrison's excitement about superheroes but was more concerned with the various ways superheroes can inflict gruesome and shocking violence on others than with the potential of the superhero to revolutionize human potential.

Scottish writer Mark Millar, who claims to have been inspired to become a comics writer after meeting Alan Moore in his youth, began his career at 2000 AD in 1990 and collaborated with Grant Morrison. Millar started working for DC in 1994, taking on the now-ailing *The Saga of the Swamp Thing* series, but it was only in 2000 when he replaced Ellis on *The Authority* that he reached a substantial mainstream audience. Millar's hugely successful *The Ultimates* (2002), with Bryan Hitch, delivered the same kind of high-intensity "widescreen" action Hitch had popularized with Ellis in *The Authority*. Millar continued in this vein with *Wanted* (2003), a violent story about a world ruled by supervillains. Millar is one of the most successful writers of both waves of the British Invasion, at least in terms of his prolific output and sales—and is at the forefront of the current Invasion. And like Ennis and Ellis, he has succeeded in producing thrilling genre work that dominates the industry.

CONCLUSION

The implications of the British Invasion were huge and continue to shape the evolution of mainstream American comics. Whereas the writers and artists of American comics could be described as still under the shadow of Will Eisner and Jack Kirby, the British writers, at least in the first wave, seemed more indebted to a literary and theatrical culture. The appropriation of superheroes as a form of American mythology did not come from an ideological connection to those values, but instead stemmed from a deeply cynical attitude to power, having been raised in a country partially colonized by American popular culture and used as an outpost of American military might.

The political alliance between Britain and America in the 1970s and 1980s was one of mutual convenience, but it was not one of equals—and many felt that British novelist George Orwell's prediction that Britain would become "Airstrip One" had become a reality, with American airbases on British soil being part of the American nuclear defense strategy. The superhero was therefore a problematic figure for the British writers, and their works employed various means to deflate the myth. This remains a powerful imperative in the post-9/11 world where American interests once again determine world affairs.

Of course, discussing six writers as the leaders of the two waves of the "British Invasion" does no justice to the numerous other writers who have made the transition from British to American comics. Nor does it purport to give an account of the role of artists who formed the British Invasion. However, the tight focus on writers is not accidental—it underscores the point that the Brit Invasion was also a Lit Invasion.

Where American underground artists primarily focused on autobiography as a way of avoiding the clichés of genre, and the revolutionary American writer/artists of the 1970s and 1980s—such as Miller and Neal Adams—took film as their inspiration, the writers of the British Invasion saw themselves as *writers* in a long tradition of subversive imaginative production in a lineage that included Shakespeare, Blake, Wilde, Brecht, William Burroughs, J. G. Ballard, and Iain Sinclair. This perspective made them seem like a new presence in American comics, and being British (or to be more precise, English, Scottish, and Irish), gave them an altogether more cynical attitude towards America and what American power (cultural, political, and military) represented.

For a generation of British comics readers it was refreshing and empowering to see British comics creators finally influencing comics on an international stage. The dominant publishers now found themselves steered towards these voices of opposition and complaint, rethinking the politics of the superhero. The extent to which the second wave continued this trend or reacted against it is debatable, but what seems clear is that the relationship between British creators and American comics continues to flourish in innovative and productive ways.

WORKS CITED

Baker, William. 2005. *Alan Moore Spells it Out*. Milford, CT: Airwave Publishing LLC.
Barker, Martin. 1984. *A Haunt of Fears: The Strange History of the British Horror Comics Campaign*. London: Pluto Press.
———. 1990. *Action: The Story of a Violent Comic*. London: Titan Books.
Bender, Hy. 1999. *The Sandman Companion*. London: Titan Books.
Bishop, David. 2007. *Thrill-Power Overload: Thirty Years of 2000 AD*. Oxford: Rebellion.
Callahan, Timothy. 2007. *Grant Morrison: The Early Years*. Edwardsville, IL: Sequart Research and Literacy Organization.
Clark, Alan, and Laurel Clark. 1991. *Comics: An Illustrated History*. London: Greenwood.

Gravett, Paul. 2005. *Graphic Novels: Stories to Change your Life*. London: Aurum Press Limited.

Gravett, Paul, and Peter Stanbury. 2006. *Great British Comics*. London: Aurum Press Limited.

Groth, Gary, and Robert Fiore, eds. 1988. *The New Comics*. New York: Berkley.

Jones, Gerard, and Will Jacobs. 1997. *The Comic Book Heroes*. Rocklin, CA: Prima Publishing.

Kaveney, Roz. 2008. *Superheroes! Capes and Crusaders in Comics and Films*. London and New York: I. B. Tauris.

Khoury, George. 2001. *Kimota! The Miracleman Companion*. Raleigh, CA: TwoMorrows Publishing.

Kwitney, Alisa. 2000. *Vertigo Visions: Artwork from the Cutting Edge of Comics*. London: Titan Books.

McLue, Greg S., with Clive Bloom. 1993. *Dark Knights: The New Comics in Context*. London: Pluto Press.

Moore, Alan, and Eddie Campbell. 2001. *Snakes and Ladders*. Paddington, Queensland: Eddie Campbell Comics.

Murray, Christopher. 2008. Subverting the Sublime: Romantic Ideology in the Comics of Grant Morrison. In *Sub/versions: Genre, Cultural Status and Critique*, ed. Pauline MacPherson, Christopher Murray, Gordon Spark, and Kevin Corstorphine, 34–53. Newcastle: Cambridge Scholars Publishing.

Reynolds, Richard. 1993. *Superheroes: A Modern Mythology*. Jackson, MS: University Press of Mississippi.

Round, Julia. 2008. Subverting Shakespeare? *The Sandman* #19: A Midsummer Night's Dream. In *Sub/versions: Genre, Cultural Status and Critique*, ed. Pauline MacPherson, Christopher Murray, Gordon Spark, and Kevin Corstorphine, 18–33. Newcastle: Cambridge Scholars Publishing.

Sabin, Roger. 1993. *Adult Comics: An Introduction*. London and New York: Routledge.

———. 1996. *Comics, Comix & Graphic Novels*. London: Phaidon.

Smokey Man and Gary Spencer Millidge. 2003. *Alan Moore: Portrait of an Extraordinary Gentleman*. Leigh-on-Sea: Abiogenesis Press.

Spurgeon, Tom, ed. 2006. *The Comics Journal Library Vol. 6: The Writers*. Seattle: Fantagraphics Books.

Versaci, Rocco. 2007. *This Book Contains Graphic Language: Comics as Literature*. New York and London: Continuum.

Wolk, Douglas. 2007. *Reading Comics*. New York and Cambridge, MA: Da Capo Press.

Wright, Bradford W. 2001. *Comic Book Nation: The Transformation of Youth Culture in America*. Baltimore and London: John Hopkins University Press.

Interview

—JEFF SMITH

To date, Jeff Smith's commercial success and critical attention has concentrated on his black-and-white bimonthly series *Bone*, published by Cartoon Books. *Bone* narrates the adventures of the three Bone cousins, who are slowly drawn into the political machinations and history of a valley filled with humans, dragons, rat creatures, talking bugs, and other fantastical beings. Based in Columbus, Ohio, Cartoon Books is an example of the creator-owned comics companies the self-publishing movement of the early 1990s was based on (Smith established Cartoon Books in July 1991, and his wife Vijaya Iyer is credited as publisher of Smith's comics).

It would not be an exaggeration to say that *Bone*'s success as a self-published comic was unprecedented and unmatched in the 1990s. Further, that success took place in an industry experiencing profound economic uncertainty. In 1993, American comics sales peaked at $1 billion, but from 1995 onwards sales fell dramatically; inflation, the evaporation of comic book speculation purchases by investors, and Marvel's ill-judged acquisition of various comic- and non-comic-related assets were some of the reasons later cited (Wright 2003, 283).

In 1995 Smith decided to publish *Bone* through Image Comics to safeguard and extend his book's ability to be distributed to comics shops. Image had been established in 1993 as a partnership between various creators who left Marvel in order to publish their own comics featuring characters they created and owned. Smith's tenure at Image was a short one, however, and according to former Image Executive Director Larry Marder, Smith returned to publishing *Bone* solely through Cartoon Books when it was clear that his production costs as a self-publisher were less than the fixed production costs incurred by publishing through Image (Dean 2000).

From 1993 onwards, the *Bone* comics have been reprinted in various formats: as a graphic narrative in its entirety, as a series of graphic novels collecting each of the nine chapters constituting the *Bone* narrative, and in smaller-sized, full-color books published by Scholastic, to name but three of its versions (it was first published in collected editions under the rubric *The Complete Bone Adventures*). Since *Bone*'s conclusion Smith's projects have included a miniseries featuring the original Captain Marvel, co-editing Fantagraphics's new series of *Pogo* collections (Walt Kelly's seminal mid-twentieth-century comic strip), and in March 2008 the release of Smith's *RASL*, an ongoing bimonthly self-published black-and-white comic from Cartoon Books, featuring a dimension-jumping fine art thief.

The following is a summary of an interview conducted by telephone on December 4, 2007. Initially the interviewer asserted how *The Rise of the American Comics Artist* was exploring a transformation in the perception of comics in the press, in universities, and in the wider reading public since the late 1980s, before mentioning some of the writers discussed in this collection, such as Chris Ware and Jim Woodring.

Jeff Smith: What happened in the last twenty years was down to a lot of the people you named, who were outside the mainstream at the time, but doing what basically became graphic novels. Will Eisner and a few others were trying to get people to call them graphic novels, but even in the early 1990s we were more likely to call them collections or trade paperbacks.

Paul Williams: You raise the issue of graphic novels: *Bone*'s been available in a few different formats: the *Complete Bone Adventures*, and then you had the nine books [publishing each chapter of the story together].

JS: OK, well, from the beginning I saw *Bone* as a 1,300-page novel: *Huckleberry Finn* meets *Moby Dick*. I knew the story would have to be tight, and have a beginning, a middle, and an end, but in a marketplace driven by pamphlets—monthly or bimonthly chapter books—the story also had to be exciting and accessible for the reader. The question I asked myself was "How do I keep this story available for the reader?" If this is a single, giant story, how do you keep the first chapter available for new readers? At that time there was not really a trade paperback or graphic novel market. There was a back issue market, which was a big part of the economy of that time for comic stores. But with back issues, once they are sold, they're gone. You can't buy that comic any more.

So after a series of false starts, I was still experimenting to see how people would take to complete collections. Some comic companies, such as Kitchen Sink and Fantagraphics (with their complete *Krazy Kat*), were entering this market. So I took a block of six issues for a year of *Bone* and collected them into a book. After three of those, I could see that the natural rhythm of the story didn't go in 6-issue chunks. Some arcs, or chapters, were only five issues long, or eight or nine issues by the end. After the third *Complete Bone Adventures* collections, I scrapped that version and repackaged the story in books that felt like chapters. Having scrapped the *Complete Bone Adventures*, I gave the collections new titles. So the first chapter when the Bone cousins are run out of Boneville was titled "Out of Boneville." But the idea was always a one-volume edition. Fortunately the technology appeared to make this possible when the story was finished; otherwise I don't know how I would have had the whole thing bound!

The collections were obviously going to affect the store owners' ability to resell back issues. Me and other indy creators would sit around at conventions, and this could be Glasgow or Oakland, we would have long discussions about whether there was a market for these books. The comic business didn't seem to operate like other businesses. I didn't understand why a comic store didn't work like a hardware store, where if you sell out of a hammer you restock the hammer. But with comics, if you sell out of something you can't order any more. I can't think of any other industry like that. If I go into a music store, I can't imagine not being able to buy *The White Album*; if you go into a bookstore, you can always buy *Moby Dick*. But in the early 1990s, you couldn't buy *Superman* #1! Neil Gaiman was just starting to collect *The Sandman* into books. We were browbeaten by retailers thinking we were undercutting their profit, but we pointed out that the profit margin on an $11 book was better than a comic that cost $2, $3. And with a book, if it sells you can restock it, and it's even more profitable. We would talk about this all the time, Scott McCloud and I.

PW: I was hoping you would say a little more about that really, because it *was* controversial. It seems so commonplace now but 15 years ago it wasn't that well heard of. Was there much browbeating?
JS: Oh yes. In the mid-to-late 1990s, I did an interview with *Comics Retailer* magazine, and I referred to a revolution in format. This put the interviewer on edge; they were upset by the word "revolution." Discussing the idea that the marketplace would turn upside down was frightening.

PW: What do you think the status of back issues is now, given that things really have gone 180 degrees? Walking past the local comic shop, the things they have in the window are graphic novels or trade paperbacks. You really have to dig for the comics now.

JS: I was trying to get out of the back issue market but I succeeded too well in getting *Bone* into other markets and being a "book." My next project is going to be released in issues: this thing is for comic stores.

PW: It sounds like you already have firm ideas about how your next project, *RASL*, will be serialized and collected together at the end.

JS: Of course. I wrote out a business plan in 1989, before I started self-publishing *Bone*. You kind of have to, it goes alongside the creative process. If you were making a movie you would have to plan it out completely before it started. Way ahead of the ending I knew how the story was going to conclude.

PW: How far do you see the success of *Bone* as your success in finding viable distribution deals at pivotal times in the history of the industry? It is not as if comics have been an unmitigated success story in the last few years—the industry is so convulsive it is often hard to track. It seems to me one of the reasons for Cartoon Books's success is in the negotiation of those distribution pitfalls that have put many companies and comic shops out of business.

JS: The reason why *Bone* was a perfect thing for me is because I wasn't a publisher trying to find commercial properties. With *Bone*, I had lived with it for so long it was more like having a child and finding places for it to go. But I didn't want it to starve: it wasn't that we said, "There's a door here, let's go through it," but "Let's make a door go there."

With the libraries, *Bone* switched to hardcover editions when we moved from the *Complete Bone Adventures*. The durability of hardcover editions made it more friendly to librarians, and they played a large role in *Bone*'s success, getting the book into the hands of children. That would have been impossible to do in the comic book-directed marketplace. So in terms of distribution being part of *Bone*'s success, that was a big part of it! The *Superman* and *Spider-Man* comics, they sold to a certain collector type, a certain type of reader obsessed with certain details about the character, and their vulnerabilities or whatever. And then there are underground comix, whatever you want to call them, that are a broader genre, including serious autobiography, and the kind of fantasy that Jim Woodring and I do.

PW: Do you want to say a little about the difficulties involved in trying to promote comics as a credible artistic medium, while at the same time young readers through the libraries have been a big part of *Bone*'s success story? Are you very conscious of the balancing act there, between promoting comics for their literariness, as a viable artistic medium, while aware of the fact that popularity comes from a universal audience?

JS: First, I don't think something that's universal should be shallow or without artistic merit. In terms of negotiating, there wasn't much to do. Through the libraries the book was being read by children and their parents, by parents to their children, and then by parents on their own. This was happening without my knowledge; librarians were putting it on their must-read lists. By about 2002, the graphic novel seemed to be making money in Barnes and Noble and Fnac [two entertainment store chains]. By 2004 to 2005—and I think manga was a big part of this, because they made graphic novels a profit center for book stores—at this time there was a big enough body of work to start stocking shelves, so you could have a whole section of graphic novels. I don't have to tell you which, you know the ones I mean, the twelve books everyone can name!

As for publishing comics as an art form, any piece of literary symbolism I'm aware of I can put into *Bone*. It doesn't matter whether kids get it or not, but it's there.

PW: How do you feel about comics, and your work in particular, becoming the subject of academic study? Being put on reading lists, say, or lectures being given on it on twenty-first-century literature courses?

JS: I'm ambivalent about it. I mean, I won't lie, I am rejoicing in the serious acceptance. But part of me, the part that got into comics when I was nine, is thinking "Did we actually manage to make comics *boring*?" But I do love the dignity comics have now. Back in the early 1990s Scott McCloud and I would talk a lot about how it was unbelievable these great comics were things that weren't taught. That was a good time to sit in the bar at conventions getting drunk and discussing comics at midnight.

PW: In that short space of time since the early 1990s it seems the whole field and the status of creators has changed. Do you feel that the battle for respectability is over?

JS: Almost. It's partly over. Back then we treated it as a lost cause. Gary [Groth] and Kim [Thompson] at Fantagraphics had a lot to do with the fact that it wasn't. Most people's attitude at the time was you just do it—you do it for the people that get it. You didn't do it for kids, you did it for cartoonists. I did it for me and other people that got it. But as for the current levels of respectability—I didn't think it was possible! With *Bone*, I knew the medium could handle it, a full-length story, that it could be read by more people than *were* reading it. I often get requests from professors for information, so somebody is getting it—I like that.

PW: In terms of the medium, it seems alongside the consolidation of graphic novels there has been a raiding of the archive and bringing to light a hundred years of comic creators. Can you say a little about your involvement with Fantagraphics and the republication of Walt Kelly's *Pogo*? I am tempted to say now is the best time to be reading comics, because you can get hold of comics you simply couldn't have got hold of five years ago, let alone twenty, thirty years ago.

JS: I've been saying this for years, Paul—it just keeps getting better. I stated this in *Bone*. When I got hold of the complete *Popeye*, I had never seen all of them. To see all of them, to get a feel of it together . . . it was like when Fantagraphics republished *Krazy Kat*. I knew who these artists were, I had seen their work in different places, but now you had a resource you can draw on. The complete *Peanuts* was long overdue, because by the end of the run you forgot how good the early stuff is.

My involvement with *Pogo* began with Fantagraphics republishing Walt Kelly's *Our Gang*, which was based on *The Little Rascals* films. They are not that fantastic. But it's still Walt Kelly, right? With the republication of *Pogo*, it has been slow going because Kelly's syndicate did not survive [unlike *Peanuts*'s syndicate]. That means it has been a longer story to get good, acceptable prints. Each book will contain about two years of material. It is all being published from the start for the same thing happened to *Pogo* that happened to *Peanuts*—you don't remember how good the early ones are! They hold up really well. That first year is so funny. And as we get into the early McCarthy era, that material is so relevant today. So working on this project is Gary Groth, me, and Carolyn Kelly, Walt's daughter.

PW: As a sense of twentieth-century comics solidifies into a real history of comics with its big figures being put back into place, is there anyone you think is due a revival? Do you think the world of comics has forgotten some people that should be remembered?

JS: For me, Walt was the last one. The greats for me are Barks, Schulz, and Kelly. I do think that Joe Kubert needs a monster book. He is a different kind of figure altogether, but a great comic artist whose work should be collected. Of course, he drew comic books.

PW: That's interesting because the people who are being republished are primarily known for their comic strip work.

JS: Yeah, I think cartoon strips are where the most interesting work was being done in comics in its first one hundred years. The big work being done today is in comics and graphic novels. This is partly because the space the newspapers dedicate to strips is shrinking and the strips are getting smaller.

PW: Are there strip artists you read today? Do you still turn to the funny pages?

JS: Actually, I think *Dilbert* is a funny comic strip. My brother works in a partitioned office so he doesn't think so! Apart from that, the only recent comic strip I have been impressed with is *Calvin & Hobbes*.

Y'know, this wasn't what I was expecting to be talking about!

PW: Well we are interested in an industrial point-of-view. One of the ways we are approaching the field of comics is from a cultural studies background, so we are particularly interested in the material text, production and distribution, and similar issues. Do you often talk to academics, and do you have an idea about what academics do with comics?

JS: The kind of people I talk with are, say, librarians writing about graphic novels. Also, high school-level teachers, who are finding they can get people who won't read anything to read *Bone*.

I started out on two tracks: to create the art and to get people interested in the story, but to finish it I had to make sure it made money. I did not try to get rich but I did want to make enough money to get to the end of the story! By putting a spine on the story you look at it as something more real. It structures that work by fitting it into the spine of the graphic novel. It needs a beginning, a middle, and an end spoken in a single voice. I rarely read collections of superhero comics produced by a team of creators—actually, except for that 1960s *Fantastic Four* stuff.

When I go to talk in schools, or to any group in fact (and I get invited to talk to all kinds of groups: national librarians' conferences, managers of Borders, universities, high schools), I give a very similar talk to all of them. I say that comics are a literary art form: the smallest unit of a comic is any two given panels. You need that to make time elapse and for actions to occur. You read it left-to-right and top-to-bottom, like a prose page. The other thing I talk about is the graphic novel itself, the form. When I talk about the art itself I refer to my symbolism.

For instance, I use water as a symbol. This because I'm a *Moby Dick*, *King Arthur* fan. When Arthur comes across any fountain surrounded by women in the middle of the woods you know something good is going to happen! In *Bone*, water signals that an important point has been reached in the story: when Fone Bone enters the valley in "Out from Boneville" [the first chapter of the *Bone* narrative], he leaps from the waterfall; when he is being chased, he says "Stupid, stupid rat creatures!" while he is suspended on a branch by the waterfall; when he first meets Thorn, she is bathing in a stream. The Dragon comes out of a well when Fone Bone goes to fetch water from it, and at the end of the story, when the water is rushing by, all the dragons come out in the flood, that kind of thing. Like *Huckleberry Finn*, water is an integral part of the story's symbolism.

PW: I am enthused to hear you talk about the two together, these two tracks, because I find that even very good students who have no problems tucking into *Huckleberry Finn* do find reading comics unusual. I don't mean from the position of "Why are you giving us a comic instead of a book?" but literally the act of reading—you do need to practice it. If you are brought up reading comics it is easy to forget that if you are *not* brought up reading comics they are actually quite alien ways of telling a story, and you can't just throw students a comic and say "Look at the symbolism." The eye has to be trained to read the comic *and* the symbolism in a symbiotic relationship.

JS: I remember sitting around at a convention, and some of the older cartoonists, like Sergio [Aragonés], or Mark Evanier, were telling the story of how they had gone, as a group, to Africa on an official visit. They were showing comics to people who had never seen them ever before. And they were asked the question "Why does this character have no legs here?" when the cartoonist had gone in for a medium shot. This was probably in the 1960s, so perhaps these first-time readers were not really familiar with the vocabulary of television or film images more generally, like the long-shot or the close-up. No, now I think I might have read this story in Mark Evanier's book! Wherever I came across this story, I think it shows that comics do operate as a language you have to learn to become fluent in.

PW: It does sound like you see a great deal of continuity between *Bone* and other Great American Novels, say *Huckleberry Finn* and *Moby Dick*. Did you have that in mind as you were executing it?

JS: Without trying to be pretentious, I was trying to do something like Melville does in *Moby Dick*, which is a book I enjoy reading for the sheer act of reading. The book spends so much time when nothing is happening with the story, but for the reader it is a pleasure just being in the presence of the author. I think that is why it has never been a really good movie. There are also its layers and layers of symbolism. I did try to get a *Moby Dick* style of narration where you just stay with the story because of the pleasure of being in its company.

If we are dignifying issues as chapters, *Huckleberry Finn* was perfect for the overall structure. It starts like a boy's adventure story (which I enjoy anyway) like *Tom Sawyer*—it has the start of a swashbuckling boy's adventure, but goes on to get darker and more sophisticated as the story progresses. When I was reading Uncle Scrooge written and drawn by Carl Barks, I wished there was an Uncle Scrooge story that was as long as *Huckleberry Finn* and *The Odyssey*, which is where *Bone* came from. I hope it worked.

WORKS CITED

Dean, Michael. 2000. The Image Story. *The Comics Journal*. http://archives.tcj.com/3_online/n_image4.html [accessed 12 Mar. 2010].

Wright, Bradford W. 2003. *Comic Book Nation*. Rev. ed. Baltimore: The John Hopkins University Press.

II: Demo-Graphics: Comics and Politics

CHAPTER FOUR

State of the Nation and the *Freedom Fighters* Arc

—GRAHAM J. MURPHY

I am born from the collective consciousness of a nation.
—Uncle Sam, *Uncle Sam and the Freedom Fighters*

Comic books have generated increased critical, scholarly, and popular attention; in 2007, Daniel McCabe wrote that they are "much more sophisticated since the advent of *Archie* or *Superman* and are now a legitimate area of scholarship." Recent scholarly studies of the superhero narrative alone include Richard Reynolds's *Super Heroes: A Modern Mythology* (1994), Will Brooker's *Batman Unmasked: Analyzing a Cultural Icon* (2001), Geoff Klock's *How to Read Superhero Comics and Why* (2002), Danny Fingeroth's *Superman on the Couch: What Superheroes Really Tell Us About Ourselves* (2004), Tom Morris and Matt Morris's *Superheroes and Philosophy* (2005), Jeffrey Kahan and Stanley Stewart's *Caped Crusaders 101: Composition Through Comic Books* (2006), Peter Coogan's *Superhero: The Secret Origin of a Genre* (2006), and Angela Ndalianis's *The Contemporary Comic Book Superhero* (2008).

While "comic books no longer automatically mean superheroes" (Coogan 2006, 4), monthly sales data show superhero narratives are still the top-sellers in a fiercely competitive North American marketplace. These narratives, often featuring long-underweared (or too-often scantily-clad) clashes between good and evil, continue to be popular and, for better or worse, typify the genre and have unfairly (and incorrectly) characterized the medium as youthful escapism, at least in popular consciousness. Over the decades, however, superhero narratives have shown a mature sophistication by repeatedly engaging with political issues and tackling corruption, government scandals, bigotry, racism, alcoholism, domestic violence, gender discrimination, drug abuse, warfare, the War on Terror, and

> questions regarding ethics, personal and social responsibility, justice, crime and punishment, the mind and human emotions, personal iden- tity, the soul, the notion of destiny, the meaning of our lives, how we think about science and nature, the role of faith in the rough and tumble of this world, the importance of friendship, what love really means, the nature of a family, the classic virtues like courage, and many other impor- tant issues (Morris and Morris 2005, x–xi).

DC's Uncle Sam and the Freedom Fighters is a lesser-known but well- established superhero team with a 70-year pedigree. Quality Comics intro- duced Uncle Sam in *National Comics* #1 (July 1940) and then premiered most of the remaining Freedom Fighters between 1939 and 1941. Led by Uncle Sam, the Freedom Fighters typically includes the Ray (absorbs and projects light, electricity, and electrical blasts; super-speed flight), the Human Bomb (gener- ates biochemical explosions), Black Condor (flight, enhanced strength, wind control), Phantom Lady (invisibility, blackout ray devices), and Doll Man (six inches in height, retains normal-size strength, military weapons).

Other members included Miss America (mental powers, enhanced strength), Firebrand (athlete, generates explosive bolts of energy), Red Bee (possesses specially trained bees, stinger gun, advanced armor), Invisible Hood (invisibility cloak), Magno (magnetic abilities), Hourman (miraclo pill provides enhanced abilities for one hour), Red Torpedo (captains a flying sub- marine), Neon the Unknown (projects energy bolts, flight), and Damage (a living fusion reactor; increased strength, durability, and speed). DC Comics eventually acquired copyright and "premiered" Uncle Sam and the Freedom Fighters in *Justice League of America* #107 (1973). Other notable appearances in the DC universe include *Freedom Fighters* (1976–1978), *All-Star Squadron* (1981–1987), *Crisis on Infinite Earths* (1985–1986), and *Kingdom Come* (1996) (*The DC Comics Encyclopedia*).[1]

Justin Gray and Jimmy Palmiotti have recently relaunched the Freedom Fighters in a multi-title narrative arc that culminates (in my analysis) in the eight-issue limited series *Uncle Sam and the Freedom Fighters* (2006–2007). This *Freedom Fighters* arc[2] is particularly topical in its fusion of adventurous escap- ism with pointed political commentary that showcases what the medium and its creators can accomplish: it is explicitly indebted to, and draws upon, the negative utopia (i.e., dystopia)[3] to critique post-millennial America under the Bush administration by positing a trade of freedom for potential fascism, self-determination for security, and heroic individualism for horrific institutionalism, an allegory of Bush-era post-9/11 America operating under the aegis of a War on Terror, intense self-monitoring, and national security.

"THOSE WHO ARE FIT TO RULE KNOW THERE IS NO MORALITY AND THAT THERE IS ONLY ONE NATURAL RIGHT, THE RIGHT OF THE SUPERIOR TO RULE OVER THE INFERIOR."

The *Freedom Fighters* arc begins ignominiously in *Infinite Crisis* #1: a secret society of supervillains decimates the team. While the Ray and Damage survive the villainous attack, Uncle Sam is left floating in a river while the rest of his heroes are killed. This event, coupled with the destruction of the fictional Blüdhaven in *Infinite Crisis* #4, prompts the renaissance of an all-new Ray, Phantom Lady, Doll Man, and Human Bomb in *Infinite Crisis Aftermath: The Battle for Blüdhaven*. These super-powered successors are initially agents of the Super Human Advanced Defense Executive (S.H.A.D.E.), a government agency led by the enigmatic Father Time.

S.H.A.D.E. is transforming Blüdhaven survivors into superpowered government operatives while also defending government control of Blüdhaven from protestors and displaced citizens located on both sides of a wall that cordons the shattered city. One such agitator, Andre Twist—the new Firebrand—has a vision from Uncle Sam (who does not appear in the *Blüdhaven* series) of a dark and oppressive near-future America. He leaves Blüdhaven (and the series) to find Uncle Sam, all the while guided by a voice that "says there are forces at work that will destroy the world. It says the time is coming where we will have to stand up against tyranny and speak for freedom" (7). The eight-issue *Uncle Sam and the Freedom Fighters* (2006–2007) continues the narrative trajectory by reintroducing Uncle Sam, reforming the Freedom Fighters, and staging the resistance to this tyrannical and dystopian near-future (but strangely contemporary) America.

The story line is replete with superhero tropes: superpowered battles, origin stories, witty banter, exaggerated body types (the males have abdominal six-packs; Phantom Lady is saddled with an embarrassingly large bust), and an alien antagonist in Gonzo the Mechanical Bastard.[4] It is a mistake to dismiss the *Freedom Fighters* arc for its all-too-familiar superhero clichés, namely because even spandex-clad characters can "remind us of the importance of self-discipline, self-sacrifice, and expending ourselves for something good, noble, and important" (Loeb and Morris 2005, 16). As Justin Gray explains in an online interview with AICN Comics, *Uncle Sam and the Freedom Fighters* is a "political superhero book" that hits "hot button issues and kitchen table discussions. We just stuck our big toe in an interesting and sometimes frightening new century ... Uncle Sam looks at these changes in the context of a superhero universe, which means everything is larger than life." Thus, under its skin-tight spandex surface, *Uncle Sam and the Freedom Fighters* is all-too-familiar: a cataclysmic attack on urban America—Blüdhaven, now called "Ground Zero"—scars the physical, emotional, political, and cultural landscape, which then prompts the rise of a government agency sworn to increase domestic security by bending Constitutional liberties. S.H.A.D.E. operates under the aegis of the Department of Homeland Security and is dedicated to the threat posed by "the groups threatening America, the metahumans [read: terrorists] responsible for endangering our future" (132).

S.H.A.D.E. must be judicious and ruthless in combating the perceived metahuman threat. Conversing with Senator Knight, a presidential candidate and Phantom Lady's parent, Father Time defends S.H.A.D.E.'s experiments on Blüdhaven's survivors: "These people . . . are under S.H.A.D.E. jurisdiction and protected by Homeland Security . . . The only way to shut down the program would be to file an appeal with Congress to have a significant portion of the Patriot Act overturned" (33). Father Time also revels in trimming "some of the societal fat" and advocates an American unilateralism that leads "the world by example, with the force to back it up" (133).

He laments America's deplorable domestic condition, targeting "[g]ay marriage, abortion, rampant gluttony, stem cells, Romanesque obesity, chemical pollution, global warming and the worship of false idols . . . I'm going to restore this nation to greatness by any means necessary" (132). He tells Firebrand that "people need to be led. Those who are fit to rule know there is no morality and that there is only one natural right, the right of the superior to rule over the inferior" (36). Thus, he is willing to "defend" democracy by deploying (non-human) suicide bombers in densely populated American cities and assassinating Senator Knight to substitute the Gonzo doppelgänger. With his new President (Gonzo) Knight in office, Father Time implements the National Identification Law requiring all Americans to submit to R.F.I.D. (radio-frequency identification) implants: in the interests of a country conducting a War on Terror, citizens need to be tracked and monitored by the government.

Bush-era post-9/11 parallels in the *Freedom Fighters* arc—homeland security and the Patriot Act, divisive social issues (e.g., gay marriage, stem cell research), American unilateralism, domestic surveillance—are inescapable. They are also entirely not surprising for these two writers. Gray and Palmiotti's Wildstorm series, *The Resistance* (2002), is a particularly useful thematic precursor to the issues they explore in the *Freedom Fighters*. Gray explains to Jennifer Contino that *The Resistance* is set in an oppressive near-future "where people are born illegally, basically the poor and unfortunate are hunted down by government agents and androids. We have a complex network of underground [freedom] fighters living among a population that is constantly told, by the media and their leaders, that children are criminals" (Contino 2008). As Jonathan Ellis learns, a fair amount of *The Resistance* explores "the role that the politics play in controlling the public. Public perception and all about the way the system manipulates its citizens into thinking a certain way and making them believe what they want so there is an order to the chaos that is the world . . . With people still emotionally raw from the tragedy of 9/11, they embraced nearly any action designed to make them feel safer and more secure" (Ellis 2008). Although *The Resistance* only lasted eight issues, the *Freedom Fighters* arc is Gray/Palmiotti's thematic continuation in a "political superhero book" whose superhero tropes allegorize a post-9/11 cultural climate. Gray and Palmiotti tell *Newsarama.com* that "the timing of the series came together perfectly as it mirrored real world changes [that] were taking place. We were trying to uncover a sense of optimism and renewed faith in what it means to be a superhero or on a larger scale, an American" (Brady 2007).

Uncle Sam and the Freedom Fighters is then less about (super) heroic battles between good and evil so much as staging an allegorical struggle between *state* and *nation* and the consequences when the two are at odds. Father Time embodies a dystopian (police) state: he bends the American constitution, spies on the populace, and assembles First Strike, a metahuman government task force. First Strike throws into sharp relief the violence of unrestricted state power and authority. For example, the super-speedster Spin Doctor pronounces: "Never let the Spin Doctor get a hold of you. Now you can't tell up from down or left from right!" (84). There is also Embargo, a woman who can project isolating force fields around her opponents. Finally, Propaganda is a telepath who can "spread cerebral misinformation. I can undermine your free will, subjugate your ideology and crush your opinion of your self-worth" (84). The S.H.A.D.E. laboratories in *The Battle for Blüdhaven* #2 also show other state powers being decanted, including Electorate, Civil Defense, Republic, Judiciary, and Veto (26–27).

The superpowered battles between the Freedom Fighters and First Strike showcase an oppressive state of the nation. Chief Justice, for example, tells Uncle Sam: "We have been sent to dispose of you. While I personally disagree and feel you should be court-martialed, I still have to execute Father Time's orders" (81). It is an unsettling admission: (chief) justice is beholden to Father Time and is used to usher in an America that is "an orderly society based on a single power structure" (*Blüdhaven* #3 21). This (mis)carriage of justice reaches its apotheosis when Chief Justice is demoted to second-in-command by Strike Force's new leader, the militaristic Americommando. Father Time replaces (chief) justice in this brave new America with martial law. In a rematch with the Freedom Fighters, First Strike bears no shred of justice when Americommando offers the Freedom Fighters two options: suicide or death (112).

"I SEEM TO REMEMBER WE HAD US A CONSTITUTION"

Terrorizing children, conducting illegal assassinations, and justifying civilian deaths as collateral damage in a War on (metahuman) Terror exemplify the incongruities of the brave new America Uncle Sam is challenging: "[I]s this heroic? Is this your patriotic duty, to murder men in front of their children, even if they are drug lords? Where are the courts, the laws we set in place? I seem to remember we had us a constitution" (52). Ironically, Uncle Sam and most superheroes typically ignore the judicial system and violate the U.S. Constitution in their pursuit of justice. Heroes and villains alike are quite literally more-than-human and often rise above the laws that govern mere mortals, but it is *motivation* that makes all the difference.

While both Father Time and Uncle Sam violate the U.S. Constitution, Father Time and his (first) strike force explicitly herald a dystopia with images of an America founded on Constitutional flexibility and the repeated allusions to Aldous Huxley's classic dystopia, *Brave New World* (1932).[5] For example, in the weeks between the conclusion of *Infinite Crisis Aftermath: The Battle for Blüdhaven* and the launch of *Uncle Sam and the Freedom Fighters*, DC Comics advertised a handful of new series in an eighty-page standalone comic book called *Brave New World* that included a hinge narrative connecting *Infinite Crisis Aftermath: The Battle for Blüdhaven* and *Uncle Sam and the Freedom Fighters*. In the *Freedom Fighters* limited series that followed *Brave New World*, characters repeatedly reference their Huxleyian inspiration. Father Time tells Uncle Sam: "This is the brave new world, Samuel. What scares me is a world without control, a planet where there's no morality and no homogenization . . . if I have to violate the civil liberties of a few thousand people, that doesn't bother me one bit" (132). President (Gonzo) Knight even betrays Father Time (prompting the S.H.A.D.E. chief to temporarily help Uncle Sam and claim he has actually been trying to help the Freedom Fighters, an erroneous and disingenuous statement and/or weak plot device) and says "[t]here's nothing you can do to stop it. You may as well embrace the brave new world" (178).

Uncle Sam's resistance to this brave new America is predicated on the strength of its people: Uncle Sam is *of* the people and *for* the people. Unlike the oppressive state embodied by Father Time, Uncle Sam is a synecdoche of the American *nation*. His powers are nation-based: "Superstrength, invulnerability; can change size; powers are proportionable to the country's faith in the ideals of freedom and liberty" (Anon. 2004, 319). He is thus described as "the spirit of a nation [who] is coming back after a long, restless sleep" (71), and the back cover of the trade collection unsubtly announces: "The Spirit of the People Rises!" Uncle Sam tells the Ray that "I'm one with this nation, son. The land, the rivers, mountains, cities . . . they all speak ta me" (98). Interestingly, Uncle Sam should embody *both* state and nation in one heroic package: the classic Uncle Sam recruitment poster ("I Want You for U.S. Army")—the same poster Father Time holds when he shouts at First Strike to "Bring me Uncle Sam!" (40)—depicts the unified state of the nation. Yet the conflict between Father Time and Uncle Sam highlights the schism between *state* and *nation*. This is clearly articulated when Father Time admits Uncle Sam remains incomprehensible to him: "We got your test results back, Samuel. The problem is we have no answers for them. You're not human, at least not in the traditional sense. You're not entirely meta or magical either. What are you?" Uncle Sam responds: "I am born from the collective consciousness of a nation" (131).

The state/nation dichotomy is also visually reinforced in key political speeches. Senator Knight (before his assassination) campaigns on the strength of American liberty and freedom while Doll Man, the Ray, and Phantom Lady, initially working for S.H.A.D.E., conduct an illegal assassination. Senator Knight's hopeful optimism—"This century will be freedom's century" (22)—is juxtaposed against S.H.A.D.E. agents training their guns on men, women, and children. Later, President (Gonzo) Knight's televised speech is full of American jingoism: "I see a great day coming for our country and our people. Government-sanctioned metahumans—rather than vigilantes—will protect ordinary citizens. I'm putting those who would wear a mask on notice! You're either for America or you're for eternal darkness" (93). During this speech the heroic Freedom Fighters are battling First Strike, the corrupt task force that ignores civil liberties and kills civilians. In essence, Gray/Palmiotti's *Freedom Fighters* arc suggests the *state* is divorced from the will of those people who encompass the *nation*.

Tellingly, Uncle Sam is adversely affected by a nation beaten down by state oppression. In his final battle with First Strike, he begins to lose his immense stature and the Washington Monument is smashed over his head. It then turns to the non-powered citizenry to stand against the state and defend U(ncle) S(am)—they proclaim, "Get away from him you inhuman bastards! He saved our lives. We have to do something." Uncle Sam responds with Bob Dylan's infamous "The times . . . they are a'changin'" (192) while the general popula-tion pelts First Strike with bricks and bottles. In spite of First Strike's violent reprisals (several citizens are vaporized in the melee), the American people stand up for their *nation* at great cost; it is at this point the remaining Free-dom Fighters arrive to defeat First Strike and Uncle Sam regains his stature. In the end, Uncle Sam and the Freedom Fighters defeat Gonzo and Father Time (although he does escape) and promise to reform S.H.A.D.E. for the better-ment of the American nation-state, thereby (re)creating an organization whose duties include protecting America from metahuman threats, both domestic and abroad, without the sacrifices Father Time was willing to exact.

The successful resistance to Father Time's brave new America and S.H.A.D.E.'s eventual change in leadership situate the *Freedom Fighters* arc in a difficult position. On the one hand, Uncle Sam and the Freedom Fighters *react* to Father Time, President (Gonzo) Knight, and the metahuman threats to America. Peter Coogan argues "proactivity seems to be a narrative dead end in the superhero genre . . . the superhero has to be reactive to operate effectively, at least in terms of open-ended serial narratives" (115). This (re) activity raises questions regarding political efficacy: superheroes may typi-cally envision a better world but rarely do they actually implement or achieve it. Instead, as Matthew Wolf-Meyer argues, "The vast majority of superheroes are intent on retaining the status quo subservient to the popular politics and will of the people they endeavor to protect . . . acting against humanity, rather than for it, retaining the hegemonic capitalism they defend, rather than pro-moting utopia" (501).

Ensconced in the superhero genre, the *Freedom Fighters* arc appears to retrench this status quo: the heroes defeat both Father Time and President (Gonzo) Knight only to take up posts in a newly re-christened S.H.A.D.E. On the other hand, Coogan admits that "proactivity as a central focus seems to cause a shift in narrative strategy away from the superhero formula and towards a use of the superhero as metaphor, along the lines of literary fiction" (2006, 115). Thus, as a "political superhero book," the *Freedom Fighters* arc goes beyond a simple reactivity of the superhero narrative to enact a "shift in narrative strategy," using a dystopia chassis to deploy explicitly the social dreaming that is utopianism and edge the series closer to the metaphor and allegory common to "literary fiction." The *Freedom Fighters* arc draws on standard superhero tropes while simultaneously incorporating Utopia's literary tropes and allegory in its political commentary. The *Freedom Fighters* arc is perhaps a closer brother to the critical dystopia in its political allegory than the typical superhero slugfest. Raffaella Baccolini explains the critical dystopia rejects "the traditional subjugation of the individual" that often concludes the classic dystopia (such as *Brave New World*) to "open a space of contestation and opposition" that maintains the "utopian impulse *within* the work" (Baccolini 2000, 18). In this sense, Uncle Sam and the Freedom Fighters, agents of the *nation* contra Father Time's oppressive *state*, embody that space of contestation typical in the critical dystopia and resist the dystopia foreshadowed by an America under the aegis of Father Time and President (Gonzo) Knight.[6]

While the *Freedom Fighters* arc contains the familiar ingredients of the superhero narrative, the series is more important as an allegorical commentary on utopian resilience to a darkened post-millennial America that, as Manuel Castells writes in *Power of Identity* (2004), exhibits an "Orwellian prediction" because "under the new information agency set up by the Homeland Security Act . . . it is clear the United States has entered a period of recession of civil liberties" (353).[7] The *Freedom Fighters* arc can be read as an allegory for a Bush era, post-9/11, pseudo-Huxleyian (or -Orwellian) America, a country governed under the aegis of a war on terror where surveillance programs have been conducted on its own citizens and national security can conflict (and trump) civil liberties. Yet, this arc has more to do with hope than it does despair and is unwilling to allow dystopian darkness and a tempestuous political climate to take root; rather, its allegorical critique of post-9/11 America calls forth a country whose citizens, (super) powered or otherwise, carry the torch of utopianism to envision a brighter state of the nation.

NOTES

Section titles are quotations taken from *Uncle Sam and the Freedom Fighters*.

    1. Of ancillary interest is *Uncle Sam* (1997), a two-issue prestige graphic novel by Steve Darnall and Alex Ross for the DC imprint, Vertigo Comics. That series does not exist in DC's mainstream continuity nor does it feature the Quality/DC Comics Uncle Sam

character, but the narrative parallels are notable, including an Uncle Sam wandering the streets of a darkened America in desperate need of finding its roots in utopianism. Greil Marcus writes (in a manner applicable to the *Freedom Fighters* arc) that *Uncle Sam* announces, "the country may have betrayed every promise on which it was founded—and that means that the promises remain to be kept" (3).

2. The *Freedom Fighters* arc under discussion encapsulates a narrative trajectory across *Infinite Crisis* (2005–2006), *Infinite Crisis Aftermath: The Battle for Blüdhaven* (2006), *Brave New World* (2006), and *Uncle Sam and the Freedom Fighters* (2006–2007). The eight-issue *Uncle Sam and the Freedom Fighters* was released as a trade paperback (2007) that also collects *Brave New World*; therefore, relevant page references are to this anthologized collection. I do not include a second eight-issue *Uncle Sam and the Freedom Fighters* (2007–2008) series in this arc due to its non-Utopia thematic and narrative focus.

3. Lyman Tower Sargent defines utopia as a "non-existent society described in considerable detail and normally located in time and space" (1994, 9). The positive utopia (eutopia) is a utopia "that the author intended a contemporaneous reader to view as considerably better than the society in which that reader lived" (9) while the negative utopia (dystopia) is a utopia "that the author intended a contemporaneous reader to view as considerably worse than the society in which that reader lived" (9).

4. Gonzo the Mechanical Bastard's inspiration lies in George Brenner's Bozo the Iron Man, a crime-fighting robot introduced in Quality Comics' *Smash Comics* #1 (1939) and whose popularity lasted more than 40 issues. Justin Gray explains to *Newsarama.com* that Gonzo the Mechanical Bastard is not "an updated version of Bozo the Iron Man" so much as a character evolved "from Grant [Morrison's] original proposal into something very different" (Anon. n.d.). The contemporary Gonzo has effectively become the antithesis of the Thirties-era Bozo: yesterday's crime-fighting iron man has been replaced by today's criminal mechanical bastard.

5. A near-future dystopia that critiques consumer capitalism, Fordism, and Taylorism, Huxley's novel depicts the World State (circa 2540 or After Ford 632) as an oppressive metropolis that maintains social stratification through eugenics, the abolition of private property, state-sponsored addictions to the drug *soma*, and carefully regimented sexual interactions. The narrative follows the political and internal struggles borne by Bernard Marx and Helmholtz Watson; in addition, John the Savage, a young boy raised on a primitive Reservation and introduced back into the World State, struggles with the seductions and bawdy pleasures the World State offers. In the end, resistance is futile: both Marx and Watson are exiled while John, in a mix of both defiance and despair, hangs himself.

6. This site of contestation is literalized in Uncle Sam's base of operations: it is an idealized piece of the American heartland that exists in its own space-time continuum, thereby folded up in the fabric of America without being tainted by the brave new America heralded by Father Time.

7. Castells is clearly referencing George Orwell's *Nineteen Eighty-Four* (1949). Orwell's novel follows the trials and tribulations of Winston Smith in a nightmarish dystopia ruled by the totalitarian Big Brother and founded on perpetual surveillance, tight censorship, and the control of the historical archive, social engineering and brainwashing programs, and a seemingly never-ending war between Oceania and either Eurasia or Eastasia.

WORKS CITED

Anon. N.d. Gonzo the Mechanical Bastard. Uncle Sam & The Freedom Fighters
    Sketchbook. *Newsarama.com*. http://www.newsarama.com/dcnew/FreedomFighters/
    sketchbook/preview.html [accessed 22 Apr. 2008].

Anon. 2004. Uncle Sam. In *The DC Comics Encyclopedia*, 319. New York: DK Publishing.

Baccolini, Raffaella. 2000. Gender and Genre in the Feminist Critical Dystopias of
    Katharine Burdekin, Margaret Atwood, and Octavia Butler. In *Future Females, The Next
    Generation*, ed. Marleen S. Barr, 13–34. New York: Rowman & Littlefield.

Brady, Matt. 2007. Headed Toward a Star-Spangled Finale: Gray & Palmiotti on Freedom
    Fighters. *Newsarama.com*. http://forum.newsarama.com/showthread.php?t=101588
    [accessed 29 July 2007].

Castells, Manuel. 2004. *The Power of Identity*. 2nd ed. Malden, MA: Blackwell.

Contino, Jennifer. N.d. Resistance is Encouraged: Jimmy Palmiotti and Justin Gray.
    Strange-Haven.com. http://www.strange-haven.com/news/110102/news4.html
    [accessed 22 Apr. 2008].

Coogan, Peter. 2006. *Superhero: The Secret Origin of a Genre*. Austin: MonkeyBrain Books.

Ellis, Jonathan. N.d. Interview: Justin Gray and Jimmy Palmiotti: Live Free or Die.
    PopImage. http://www.popimage.com/content/viewnews.cgi?newsid1026452328,40256,
    [accessed 22 Apr. 2008].

Gray, Justin, Jimmy Palmiotti, and Daniel Acuña. 2007. *Uncle Sam and the Freedom
    Fighters*. New York: DC Comics.

Gray, Justin, Jimmy Palmiotti, and Dan Jurgens. 2006. *Infinite Crisis Aftermath: The Battle
    for Blüdhaven*. #1–6. New York: DC Comics.

Klock, Geoff. 2002. *How to Read Superhero Comics and Why*. New York: Continuum.

Loeb, Jeph and Tom Morris. 2005. Heroes and Superheroes. In *Superheroes and Philosophy:
    Truth, Justice, and the Socratic Way*, ed. Tom Morris and Matt Morris, 11–20. Chicago:
    Open Court.

Marcus, Greil. 1998. Introduction. In *Uncle Sam*, Steve Darnall and Alex Ross, 3–4. New
    York: DC Comics.

McCabe, Daniel. 2007. Just don't call it Mickey Mouse. *University Affairs*. http://www
    .universityaffairs.ca/issues/2007/march/mickey_mouse_01.html [accessed 1 May 2007].

Morris, Matt and Tom Morris. 2005. Men in Bright Tights and Wild Fights, Often at Great
    Heights, and, of Course, Some Amazing Women, Too! In *Superheroes and Philosophy*, ed.
    Tom Morris and Matt Morris, ix–xii. Chicago: Open Court.

Ndalianis, Angela. 2008. *The Contemporary Comic Book Superhero*. New York: Routledge.

Sargent, Lyman Tower. 1994. The Three Faces of Utopianism Revisited. *Utopian Studies*
    5(1): 1–37.

Taylor, Robert. 2007. Reflections: Talking with Jimmy Palmiotti. *Comic Book Resources*.
    http://www.comicbookresources.com/?page=article&id=10767 [accessed 17 Mar. 2010].

Wolf-Meyer, Matthew. 2003. The World Ozymandias Made: Utopias in the Superhero
    Comic, Subculture, and the Conservation of Difference. *Journal of Popular Culture* 36 (3):
    497–51.

CHAPTER FIVE

Critique, Caricature, and Compulsion in Joe Sacco's Comics Journalism

—ADAM ROSENBLATT AND ANDREA A. LUNSFORD

I want to get away from the pretense of the reporter as artificial construct. Reporters have feelings about a situation and that impacts the way they write. My work is a way to demystify a process that may otherwise seem strange to people.
—Joe Sacco (Qtd. in Yusuf 2007)

Since the early 1990s, when Art Spiegelman's Holocaust memoir in comic book form, *Maus*, won a Pulitzer Prize, comics creators have gained increasing attention for producing comics about contemporary events. Joe Sacco's comics about Palestine and the former Yugoslavia, Ted Rall's "graphic travelogue" *To Afghanistan and Back*, a comic book adaptation of the 9/11 Commission Report, and Seth Tobocman's *Portraits of Israelis and Palestinians: For my Parents* and *War in the Neighborhood* all represent the growing interest in using properties of word and image specific to comics to capture "the news." As a result, comics journalism has begun to pop up in newspapers, from *The New York Times* to *The Oregonian*, though as Kristian Williams notes in the *Columbia Journalism Review*, these publications still tend to "relegate comics journalism to cultural coverage and human interest stories. When it comes to the front page, newspapers favor plain language" (Williams 2005). The "plain"-ness of newspaper prose, for most people, promises unadorned journalistic objectivity. Meanwhile, comics call to mind caricature, slapstick, and superheroes;

and the unapologetic "personal touch" of drawings done by hand seem to lend themselves to exaggeration, subjectivity, and sometimes irony.

For the most part, comics journalists like Sacco, Spiegelman, Rall, and Tobocman have taken this set of associations in stride, acknowledging—even championing—the deeply subjective viewpoint of their comics, using word and image to create something very different from the standard news article. But no one captures the potential—as well as the challenges—of comics journalism more fully than Joe Sacco, whose books on Palestine and the former Yugoslavia have led the way in establishing this new genre. More than any other creator of comics reportage, Sacco's work is closer to traditional journalistic practices, and more than any other creator, Sacco self-consciously redefines journalism for the comic book medium. He uses comics not just to create a new kind of journalism, but also to question the orthodoxies of more traditional reporting. Sacco holds a degree in journalism, and at various points has traveled on UN convoys with a press pass, hired local "fixers" to find him interviews and translate for him, and stayed at hotels swarming with foreign correspondents. At the same time, more than any of his peers, Sacco levels harsh criticism at himself and other journalists for the effects of these practices on their reporting and on the war-torn communities they visit.

Central to Sacco's critique of journalism is self-awareness about both the strengths and the perils of his own work. In stressing his subjective position, Sacco distinguishes himself from the traditional journalistic aims of distance and objectivity. Obsessed with narrowing the distance between reporters and their subjects, Sacco sticks around in war zones and occupied territories which have received either only the "proverbial fifteen minutes" (2001, 6) of fame, or no coverage whatsoever.

In a small town in Eastern Bosnia, Goražde, which gives the title and setting to his masterpiece, *Safe Area Goražde*, several locals ask him why he has come. In search of an answer, he realizes that he wants to find out more than simply "what happened" during the war that tore Bosnia apart. His reply, probably never delivered to his actual audience in Goražde (aside from those who have read the book): "Why? Because you are all still here . . . not raped and scattered, not entangled in the limbs of thousands of others at the bottom of a pit. Because Goražde had lived, and—how?" (2001, 14–15). That search for "how" leads Sacco, in *Safe Area Goražde* and other books, to depict late-night conversations over tea, people chopping wood for winter, and fleeting romances in the same careful detail other reporters reserve only for battles and politics.

This hunger to capture every dimension of experience in these troubled places, however, is also where Sacco fears he might lose himself, and his graphic novel *The Fixer* is devoted precisely to exploring the ethical and emotional boundaries of war reporting. Sacco recounts his friendship and symbiotic relationship with Neven, a "fixer" whose job is to find him interviews and tell him stories from the war. Sacco knows Neven may be lying to him and is, at a bare minimum, ripping him off. But as is typical of Sacco, he shows us that the truth about Neven, which in any case can never be fully captured, is immensely complicated. At the end of the book, after having said goodbye to Neven, Sacco talks to an old acquaintance of Neven's, who tells him several things that surprise him, that "make me feel like I didn't know half of what Neven was about . . . that I'd barely traced the edges of his secrets" (2004a, 108). In this way and many others, Sacco's mature work traces the limitations of journalism and of historical knowledge even as it attempts to create new forms of journalism and history.

"I'm not an objective journalist," Sacco says, though "I am showing something that is essentially journalistic; I'm telling someone's story that is factual, that I got from an interview and also trying to add something to it, which is something you can do with the medium of comics" (2004b). For Sacco, then, comics journalism is a hybrid form that uses images and words in sequenced panels to take his readers directly into the situations on which he reports. "Prose writers can be very evocative," he says, "and I appreciate what they do, but I find there is nothing like thrusting someone right there. And that's what I think a cartoonist can do" (2004b). Sacco seems to be saying that comics are unmatched in their ability to combine words, images, and sounds to create immediacy—to take the reader directly into the scene and action through mixing image and text—while also being obviously enough an artificial language (of panels, figures, speech balloons, and more) that we are encouraged to stop and reflect on our experience in ways that film, for instance, may not always demand.

Sacco's comics journalism may stand above that of similar creators in terms of popularity, critical recognition, and self-reflection on comics' formal qualities, but it is not without major influences. He began his career making autobiographical comics influenced by the underground giants Robert Crumb and Harvey Pekar. When he began publishing his own series, *Yahoo* (1988–92), he initially focused on his own personal crises and time spent touring with a rock band. But his interest in politics and in the conflicts in the Middle East and in Eastern Europe soon led him to drawing/telling other people's stories as well. In retrospect, Sacco talks of his work as evolving as much through serendipity as clearly planned progression: "I wanted to be a journalist and then fell back on an intense hobby to make a living. I don't think too much about where I place myself and I never really had a theory about what I was doing" (Qtd. in Yusef 2007).

Sacco does, however, see himself as connected loosely to a tradition of reporting best illustrated by *Dispatches*, Michael Herr's brilliantly evocative literary treatment of the Vietnam War, which started out as a free-wheeling assignment to report on the war for *Esquire* but ended up a painstakingly rendered product of Herr's subjective imaginative process. In the end, *Dispatches* is less about constructing a grand narrative for the Vietnam War than it is about Herr's own experiences as a reporter who spent a year in the trenches of Vietnam. Rather than focusing on presidential policies or on generals and commanders, Herr takes readers into the horrific minutiae of everyday battle as experienced by the "grunts." As Herr says toward the end of the volume, "My life and death got mixed up with their lives and deaths, doing the Survivor Shuffle between the two, feeling the pull of each and not wanting either very much" (Herr 1991, 261). Sacco's reporting in Bosnia and Palestine reflects the same kind of deep psychic engagement that allows readers an intimate contact with the experience of the people with whom Sacco interviews and interacts.

Sacco's work can also be seen as related to the long tradition of illustrated coverage of war, from *Harper's* and the *London Illustrated*'s Civil War reporting to the extensive and increasingly caustic editorial cartooning that responded to George W. Bush's war in Iraq. Sacco's comics, however, are both more sustained in their narrative and more focused on *character*: though his mission is journalistic, his portraits of himself and his subjects have a literary richness that single editorial cartoons can seldom achieve.

Sacco's war reporting also recalls a long history of engagement between fine art and war, including Francisco Goya's series of etchings *Disasters of War* and Pablo Picasso's *Guernica*. These works of art have a strong subjective point of view, expressing horror and outrage, and they thrust the viewer into the scene in the same way Sacco believes comics journalism can do. In addition, Picasso and Goya aim to present truths about war by moving beyond realism into the hallucinatory, fragmented, and speechless horrors that war always entails—in much the same way that Sacco says his work moves beyond the official "realism" of the news genre in order to get at more particular, microscopic human truths. Sacco uses exaggeration and caricature to make his drawings feel "loud," the way he says some paintings do: "Like Brueghel's *The Triumph of Death*. I see that painting as . . . just so loud. I mean, its skeletons drumming, you know, herding people into these huge coffins, and . . . it's

Fig. 5.1 In Sarajevo, Sacco heads into "an awful silence." Joe Sacco, *The Fixer*, 2004. Reproduced by permission from Sacco 2004a, 12.

shattering to my ears almost. And that's part of what I wanted somehow to get at in my own way" (2004b).

But Sacco is not interested only in loudness, or in shocking the conscience. He also takes the time to depict, more than most photojournalists do, the silences of war: a giant, nearly-empty Holiday Inn at the beginning of *The Fixer*, bombed-out buildings and shell-marked streets, the feeling of cities and settlements that live in fear or that the United Nations, the press corps, and the world have abandoned. There is an almost musical quality to the variation between loud and quiet in Sacco's stories, and the moment that hits you like a kick in the chest can happen just as easily over tea in someone's living room as on a battlefield.

Sacco's work might also be productively compared to photojournalism of the kind practiced by Matthew Brady in reporting on the Civil War, Margaret Bourke-White on World War II, or Robert Galbraith on the Iraq War. But Sacco looks for opportunities available to the cartoonist alone: "The good thing about being a cartoonist is that . . . you can be in your own mental crane, your own mental helicopter, and take yourself above a situation. I defy a photographer to do that" (2004b). Sacco also uses sharp angles in his panels to give a sense of the world gone topsy-turvy in wartime, exaggerated or flattened perspectives that make space seem more confined and overcrowded (as in the occupied territories) or large and lonely (as in the bombed-out streets of Sarajevo).

Setting Sacco's work in the larger arena of journalism and photojournalism allows readers to appreciate the degree to which Sacco challenges the conventions of these fields as well as the contributions he makes to both. His comics journalism is complex and multifaceted, rewarding close reading and interrogation. In examining his comics, particularly *Palestine*, *Safe Area Goražde*, and *The Fixer: A Story from Sarajevo*, we have identified three major features that create productive, and sometimes troubling, tensions that highlight the contrast between his technique and traditional journalism, as well as give a sense of what really makes his comics tick. The first of these, already noted, is his critique of journalism, which we will discuss further below. In addition to critique, we will explore his use of caricature, as well as his compulsion, controlled or uncontrolled, for detail.

CRITIQUE—AND SELF-CRITIQUE

In his meditation on the war in Bosnia, *Safe Area Goražde*, Sacco thrusts his readers into the no-man's-land of a U.N.-protected "safe area" (a designation

Fig. 5.2 Sacco reports on the attempts by foreign reporters to "set a good example." Joe Sacco, *Safe Area Goražde*, 2001. Reproduced by permission from Sacco 2001, 131.

that turns out, in this case, to provide very little "safety" to the area's occupants) with a convoy of trucks nearing the city, now an enclave "surrounded by separatist Serb forces." Sacco's point of view from the convoy depicts crowds of citizens lining both sides of the road to roll out the "red carpet" for their international visitors. In the middle of the road, Sacco uses a block of text, placed as if to interrupt or rebuke the spectacle spreading out all around it, to report: "'I wish Goražde would go away,' I heard one American correspondent say."

This kind of dehumanization, in which an entire town of people becomes a "problem" or bargaining chip for a peace process taking place thousands of miles away, is replicated in all kinds of daily practices among the foreign press. Sacco observes foreign photographers "throwing candy at kids to capture the predictable mad scramble" (2001, 131) that will confirm their audience's notion of Goražde, and Bosnia, as a place of desperation, a place where the rules and conventions of human life have disappeared. Almost as offensive to Sacco's sensibilities, other journalists develop complicated "policies" of candy distribution for the children, which seem to replicate the superiority and distance that muddles the political relationship between the United Nations and the people under its sometime protections. In response, Sacco explains, "<u>My</u>

Fig. 5.3 Sacco "interrogates" two former prisoners from Iraq. Joe Sacco, "Trauma on Loan," 2006. Reproduced by permission from Sacco 2006, 8.

bon-bon policy was to give them out to every kid asking so long as they all got one. As to how they ought to eat their bon-bons, I couldn't care less. I figured the children in Goražde could make their own bon-bon decisions" (2001, 132). This last sentence appears in a panel depicting a child against a backdrop of bombed-out buildings, reminding us of the gap in lived experience between the inhabitants of Goražde and the foreign journalists, so eager to reeducate Goražde's children in decent, human behavior.

But Sacco's criticisms of journalistic practice become most interesting, both conceptually and visually, when he turns them on himself. Starting before his turn towards comics journalism, in a piece he did about his "addiction" to Gulf War coverage called "War Junkie," and continuing through *The Fixer*, Sacco has dissected his own sometimes predatory journalistic instincts, and the uncomfortable places they can take him. On January 21, 2006, the British newspaper *The Guardian* ran "Trauma on Loan," an eight-page report of Sacco's interviews with two Iraqi men detained and, according to their account, tortured by the U.S. military.

The panels on the final page offer a fine example of Sacco's often scathing self-critiques (fig. 5.3). Note that though Sacco depicts himself in earlier pages of this story, as in his other works, with blank glasses and an inflated nose and lips, here the focus is almost exclusively on the men being interviewed and the story they have to tell. The drawing is composed as if a light were shining from behind Sacco onto the two men, exposing their faces but leaving him mostly in shadow. He is, in other words, depicted not unlike an interrogator, and his notebook and pen, the only objects in the panel, occupy the place of implements of torture.

Sacco's remark that he can "smell" the men's exhaustion is made in sympathy, but also evokes the careful attention interrogators pay to those being questioned, the way they alternate kindness and cruelty, watching for signs the prisoner might "break." Sacco is offering us both an interview of the Iraqi men and a set of associations that link the hungry press with the other tormenters these men have faced. As his interview concludes, Sacco writes, "Once again they are released," echoing the story the Iraqi men have just told about their own "release" from detention.

As these examples suggest, throughout his work Sacco offers stinging critiques, often focusing on his failures as well as his triumphs in getting beyond the dominant paradigm of traditional war reporting, a paradigm in which people's stories of suffering too often become commodities, sorted into genres and presented in tidbits by the journalists who collect them. Sacco turns the spotlight of his comics journalism on such commodification, perhaps most strongly when he sees himself as in some ways complicit with it.

Fig. 5.4 Sacco's "rubbery" depiction of Palestinian women protesting the Israeli occupation. Joe Sacco, *Palestine*, 2002. Reproduced by permission from Sacco 2002, 56.

CARICATURE AND CRITIQUE

Caricature, another hallmark of Sacco's work, may be the most uncomfortable one for many readers, especially those unfamiliar with the underground comix tradition that has influenced Sacco's style. In *Palestine*, the chapter "A Thousand Words" (2002, 53–58) opens with a series of full-page panels, the first of which depicts marching Palestinian women and children, their mouths all open and turned down at the corners, teeth exposed as they protest expulsion orders before being intercepted, clubbed, and thrown into jeeps by the border police. The caricature here walks a fine line: are the protesters being portrayed as crazed beasts, undermining the legitimacy of their political acts? Is Sacco, even unintentionally, evoking a history of caricatures in Western newspapers that portray the "enemy" (whether Japanese, African-American, or Muslim) as looking all the same, and all ugly? Or does caricature allow him to evoke a sense of seething rage, adding more emotional depth to this event

Fig. 5.5 Sacco's caricatured version of himself, drunk and dancing. Joe Sacco, *Safe Area Goražde*, 2001. Reproduced by permission from Sacco 2001, 10.

than traditional journalism could capture? And what does our potential discomfort, as we consider these different interpretations, mean for our reading experience?

When Sacco began work on *Palestine*, he says, his drawing "was a bit rubbery and cartoony because that's the only way I knew how to draw. It became clear to me that I had to push it toward a more representational way of drawing" (Qtd. in Gilson 2005). Readers can see the evolution of Sacco's style in later work, as his angles and perspectives grow more restrained, his lines less energetic and more photorealistic. Nor does Sacco, in the tradition of racist and xenophobic newspaper cartooning, only caricature "the other." His representation of himself is an instantly recognizable and devastating caricature: the round face accentuated by large round glasses that are always blank, the broad nose and thick lips, stooped shoulders, and downtrodden

Fig. 5.6 Watching Goražde's "Most Horrifying Home Videos." Joe Sacco, *Safe Area Goražde*, 2001. Reproduced by permission from Sacco 2001, 120.

look that often comments indirectly and ironically on his fantasies of capturing the perfect story or winning a Pulitzer for his photographs. Sacco depicts his own needs, especially in frequent scenes of eating, drunkenness and lust, as equally human, pressing, and flawed as those of his subjects. His body is also just as, if not more, frail, leveling the power dynamic usually established between the journalist—who is not hungry, is not wounded—and the people whose vulnerable lives he or she records.

Because Sacco has gained the technical skill and self-control to use caricature only when he chooses to, it is worth taking a look at how he draws faces at different moments. In Goražde, Sacco and a Turkish reporter find themselves more or less trapped in the apartment of a local who insists on showing them amateur footage of what Sacco calls "Goražde's own Most Horrifying Home Videos," a compendium of acts of violence from the war. Their host appears as a gruesome caricature, his face contorting more and more as he repeats, "Look! You must look!" (2001, 120–21). War and need distort this man into a caricature, and the whole scene becomes more uncomfortable as it was unclear whether his need is for someone to bear witness to his suffering or merely for the money that would come from selling his tape.

Sacco and his friend leave disgusted by both the footage and the sales ploy, but of course the man's desire for witnesses and his financial desperation stem from the same source, the war. Left unanswered is the question of whether Sacco and his friend's disgust is fair, whether the boundary it draws between testimony and salesmanship has any moral weight, or simply reflects the perspective of the privileged journalist who has the luxury to be disgusted by another man's desperation. Even making room for this ambivalence, however, Sacco's disgust rubs off on his drawing style, and he renders the man with crazed, zombie-like eyes.

Some of Sacco's most realistic and most subtle figure drawing, on the other hand, comes at moments of domestic comfort or joy—for example, in recurring scenes with a group of Goražde teenagers, whom he calls the "silly girls." Despite the dismissive name and the major topics of conversation, which include blue jeans and boyfriends, Sacco takes great pains to draw each of these young women as distinct individuals with realistic faces and expressions. Once again, it is only the war and its offspring—hatred, fear, desperation—that distorts this realism. At the end of "Silly Girls, Part II," Sacco asks one of the "silly girls," Dalila, about the Serb friends and neighbors who used to live in Goražde (Dalila, the other "silly girls," and most of the people now in Goražde are Muslim).

Dalila offers a stark, angry reinterpretation of the past: "I never had any Serb friends. How could they have been your friends if then they tried to kill you?" (2001, 154). At this moment, her face hardens into a glassy, indistinct mask, as if all the markers of emotion or individuality had been taken from it. But toward the end of *Safe Area Goražde*, a TV set brings news of the Dayton Accords, establishing an official end to the war in the Balkans, and we return to this same Dalila.

In a set of lovingly rendered panels, Sacco portrays Dalila as she cycles rapidly through a series of emotions, including shock, joy, disbelief, and grief (2001, 210–11). At no moment in Sacco's work does anyone look less caricatured, or more recognizably human, than in these panels where Dalila slowly

Fig. 5.7 "It's peace and I don't know how to behave." Joe Sacco, *Safe Area Goražde*, 2001. Reproduced by permission from Sacco 2001, 210.

realizes "It's peace and I don't know how to behave" (2001, 211). Sacco's use of caricature, then, presents a series of roles that can dehumanize himself and his subjects (hungry journalist, needy or resentful victim) as well as a set of conditions and places (peace, home) that dignify and differentiate them. Perhaps this tendency points to wishful thinking on his part, as if war were always an external force that comes along and transforms us from our best selves into something different. But it certainly establishes a role for caricature in his work as part of his moral perspective rather than as purveyor of racial stereotypes or political lampooning.

CRAFT AND COMPULSION

The complex ways critique and caricature work together is complicated by the role compulsion plays in Sacco's comics, from his insistence on reporting the most minute and quotidian details of life in war zones—precisely how wood is chopped, what brand of cigarettes people smoke and how they smoke them—to his intense graphic attention to landscapes, architecture, and weapons. As Christopher Hitchens writes in his introduction to *Safe Area*

Fig. 5.8 Sacco gets a different perspective on his fixer, Neven. Joe Sacco, *The Fixer*, 2004. Reproduced by permission from Sacco 2004a, 61.

Goražde: "Sacco's combined word-illustration makes me remember that distinctive Bosnian domestic architecture—the gable ends and windows—with a few deft strokes. You know where you are, in other words, and it's not in some generic hotspot. Then the additional details, such as the unforgettable 'bear's paw' scar that a mortar-shell makes on pavement" (2001, n.p.). If his use of caricature paints people in broad, vivid strokes, his compulsion for detail deepens his portrayals, revealing, through the places and things with which people interact, a more nuanced picture of how they live.

Sacco's meticulous drawing process is bound up in complex ways with his interviews, like the ones he conducted with three men who had been at Ansar 3 Prison. Sacco listens intently as they describe the prison and then strives to render the scene in a way that is minutely faithful to their recollections. Nevertheless, as Sacco himself points out—especially throughout *The Fixer*—interviewees have agency and purposes of their own that may escape the reporter's ability to see and to listen. In fact, if "Trauma on Loan"—Sacco's interview with the detained Iraqi men—is a story of how reporters can "prey"

On April 22, NATO gave the Serbs an ultimatum demanding an immediate cease-fire and the withdrawal of their forces from Goražde.

NATO DEMANDS OF SERB WITHDRAWALS

ROGATICA

PULL-BACK TROOPS 3 KM BY APRIL 23

MEDEDA

KOPACI

PULL-BACK HEAVY WEAPONS 20 KM BY APRIL 26

GORAZDE

CAJNICE

Drina

FOCA

The Serb artillery barrage intensified.

The Russians, ostensibly sympathetic to the Serb cause, dropped their previous objections to air-strikes. Said Foreign Minister Andrei Kozyrev, "The Bosnian Serbs' military command has criminally defied the elementary norms of humanity."

Fig. 5.9 Sacco goes photorealistic. Joe Sacco, *Safe Area Goražde*, 2001. Reproduced by permission from Sacco 2001, 184.

on their subjects, *The Fixer* is a study in the opposite (or complementary) process.

Sacco's "fixer," Neven, whom he hires to help him find stories in Sarajevo, is adept at providing Sacco with just the sort of climactic narratives Sacco hungers for, but it becomes increasingly unclear whether Neven is lying to keep the money flowing, telling the truth, or something in between. Perhaps he revises his memories in Sacco's presence in order to ascribe meaning to his own story and to a war whose importance seems increasingly pointless. In other words, the further Sacco's compulsion to get as close to the Truth of the grittiest details of the war extends, the greater the risk from people and narratives with their own agendas that may be counterproductive.

Sacco's near-obsessive hunger for visual detail has its own dangers too. As he leaves behind the highly caricatured, always askew style he used in *Palestine* and earlier works, he seems less aggressive in his focus on his own subjectivity and more in tune with the traditional journalistic search for realism and objectivity. Having expressed his doubts about journalism in general, and about himself in particular, Sacco seems to have decided to live with those limitations and move on, allowing other characters and other issues to move to the center of his books. But as his drawing style has developed, his relationship with photography has become more troubled.

Sacco's most detailed drawings, particularly landscapes, often approach photography in their intense realism. Because they are *not* photographs, however, but rather drawings done painstakingly with pen and inkwell, they become as much a record of Sacco's own obsession for getting as close to the truths of war as possible as they are of the wars and conflicts he has followed. Ultimately, in this way, Sacco winds up back where he started with his early comics: his journalism becomes a form of autobiography, the diary of an unsatisfied journalist compulsively trying to answer the unanswerable "how" of a place like Goražde.

Readers following Sacco's journey, both his drive to capture and report the truths of those who experience the hell of war and his realization that these efforts can never be fully successful, may wind up examining their own assumptions about how close to true understanding any other person or event they can get. But Sacco's compulsive and meticulous attention to detail suggest that something other than hopelessness or nihilism is the answer: it reminds us just how much we do stand to gain from attention to the quotidian, seemingly mundane details of life, even in a war zone.

CONCLUSION

Our exploration of Sacco's comics journalism—and particularly of his use of critique, caricature, and compulsion—leads us to recognize and appreciate the complexity of his work, the tensions and contradictions that animate it. As this essay was being written, the Serb leader Radovan Karadzic, accused of planning and ordering genocide, torture, and systematic rape, was captured in Belgrade, where he had lived for over a decade with a radically changed appearance and identity. Seeing a picture taken before he went into hiding took us back immediately to Sacco's *War's End: Profiles from Bosnia 1995–96* (2005) and particularly to his face-to-face encounter with Karadzic, whom Sacco calls "a man I have despised with all my heart for years" (2005, 59).

Sacco's story, "Christmas with Karadzic," prominently features all of the elements we have explored: critique, caricature, and compulsion. In terms of critique, Sacco portrays himself and his fellow journalists, in typical fashion, as crazed vultures, speeding through checkpoints, calculating the cost of

Fig. 5.10 Radovan Karadzic through Sacco's eyes.
Joe Sacco, *War's End*, 2005. Reproduced by
permission from Sacco 2005, 61.

their trips versus the cash value of a good story, haranguing government ministers, and ogling women—all with a strange, perhaps adaptive, detachment from the horror and suffering that has brought them to the Balkans in the first place. One frustrated newspaper correspondent, hoping for a recording of gunshots to make his radio broadcast more vivid, yells "Come on! Shoot! Fuckers! Will someone open up with a machine gun out the window!! This is bullshit!" (Sacco 2005, 55).

The gap between these moments of crassness and absurdity, on the one hand, and Sacco's reflective captions, on the other, illustrate Sacco's struggle with competing imperatives: his search for meaning versus his search for a juicy story, or what he glibly calls "the fight between being a journalist and being someone who actually cares about what they write about" (Qtd. in Gilson 2005). We also see Sacco's characteristic compulsion in his depiction of the bureaucratic twists and turns it takes to find Karadzic, as well as of the lingo and inside jokes tossed around among his cadre of foreign correspondents. Sacco renders these experiences at a level of detail that ultimately overwhelms the reader, to the point of almost breaking his narrative apart.

What particularly made us think back to this particular comic, however, was Karadzic's face and the question of caricature. Sacco's portrayal of Karadzic, one of the few people in his books who could unequivocally be called a monster, is not exactly photorealistic—but we would also be hard-pressed to call it caricature. The rich gray ink washes that replace Sacco's usual cross-hatching in this story, as if chosen especially for the task of representing Karadzic, give his face depth and texture unusual in Sacco's comics. Karadzic's full head of hair and aquiline features are instantly recognizable, but unlike most newspaper images of him, he looks surprisingly old and tired, with an expression of resignation.

The problem with Karadzic, according to Sacco, is that he's "not enough" (2005, 60). Seeing him in person does not add anything to Sacco's understanding of him, and the encounter seems to question the cartoonist's faith that images and faces contain some special truth that words cannot offer. Like Hannah Arendt watching the Adolf Eichmann trial, Sacco finds himself in front of someone too commonly human, too banal, for the deeds he has committed. Sacco looks to him for answers, or for a new surge of outrage, and instead just feels vaguely embarrassed.

While he may feel embarrassed, Sacco is the journalist and cartoonist doing what he does best: even as he deflates the journalist-confronts-monster drama we might have expected, he creates a new drama about what it means to be a human witness to inhuman events carried out by other human beings. Having concluded that "bigwigs" like Karadzic are worthy of horror and rage, but rarely a source of any new or meaningful information, he heads back to the apartments and cafés where ordinary people, survivors of war and everything that comes after, spend their time—and where Sacco's comics get their life force. "That's where things are really happening," says Sacco (Qtd. in Gilson 2005). As admirers of the courage with which he tackles the toughest assignments and of the critical spotlight he often turns on himself and his craft, we are happy to keep following along with him.

WORKS CITED

Gilson, Dave. 2005. The Art of War. *Mother Jones Online*. http://www.motherjones.com/arts/qa/2005/07/joe_sacco.html [accessed 14 July 2009].

Herr, Michael. 1991. *Dispatches*. New York: Vintage.

Hitchens, Christopher. 2001. Introduction. In *Safe Area Goražde*, n.p. Seattle: Fantagraphics.

Jacobson, Sid, and Ernie Colón. 2006. *The 9/11 Report: A Graphic Adaptation*. New York: Hill and Wang.

Rall, Ted. 2002. *To Afghanistan and Back*. New York: ComicsLit.

Sacco, Joe. 2001. *Safe Area Goražde*. Seattle: Fantagraphics.

———. 2002. *Palestine*. Seattle: Fantagraphics.

———. 2004a. *The Fixer: A Story from Sarajevo*. London: Jonathan Cape.

———. 2004b. Presentation at the 2002 University of Florida Comics Conference. *Image/Text: Interdisciplinary Comics Studies* 1(1). http://www.english.ufl.edu/imagetext/archives/v1_1/sacco/ [accessed 29 Oct. 2009].

———. 2005. *War's End: Profiles from Bosnia 1995–96*. Montreal: Drawn and Quarterly.

———. 2006. Trauma on Loan. *The Guardian*, Jan. 21 [Weekend Magazine].

Spiegelman, Art. 1993. *Maus*. New York: Pantheon.

Tobocman, Seth. 2000. *War in the Neighborhood*. New York: Autonomedia.

———. 2003. *Portraits of Israelis and Palestinians: For My Parents*. New York: Soft Skull Press.

Williams, Kristian. 2005. The Case for Comics Journalism. *Columbia Journalism Review*. http://cjrarchives.org/issues/2005/2/ideas-essay-williams.asp [archive available with subscription only].

Yusuf, Huma. 2007. Interview with Joe Sacco. *Confessions of an Aca-Fan: The Official Weblog of Henry Jenkins*. http://www.henryjenkins.org/2007/03/an_interview_with_comics_journ.html [accessed 14 July 2009].

III: Artists or Employees?

CHAPTER SIX

Too Much Commerce Man? Shannon Wheeler and the Ironies of the "Rebel Cell"

—JAMES LYONS

You made a lot of money from your commercial. You lucked out with your gimmicky character.
—(Wheeler 1999, 113)

"Coffee," Rossini told me, "is an affair of fifteen or twenty days; just the right amount of time to write an opera."
—(Balzac 1996, 273)

In the end pages of *Wake Up and Smell the Cartoons of Shannon Wheeler* (1996), a collection of the comics artist's early work, Wheeler provides a short professional biography that is worth quoting in full:

Shannon Wheeler's cartoons first appeared in college newspapers and obscure publications throughout the country. Shannon graduated from UC Berkeley's architecture department in 1989. After a couple of years of angst ridden meaningless retail work, Wheeler re-located to Austin, Texas, where he continued to work retail jobs. It was during this time that he hooked up with Blackbird Comics, who published his first collection of cartoons: *Children With Glue*. It was while trying to find a promotion for that book that Wheeler created Too Much Coffee Man.

Starting as photocopied mini-comics Too Much Coffee Man eventually evolved into full color comics, a weekly strip, t-shirts, mugs, and even an animated television commercial.

Too Much Coffee Man has become an industry unto itself. Along the way Wheeler collected an Eisner award for best new comic, a Hatch award for best animated commercial, and a Harvey nomination for most promising new talent, as well as several other nominations and awards. Shannon Wheeler's cartoons now appear in college newspapers and obscure publications throughout the country (1996, n.p.).

While the descriptive trajectory of Wheeler's career is clearly tongue-in-cheek, it nevertheless offers something revealing about the nature of success as a professional comics artist. In its evocation of circularity—all that output and acclaim serves merely to position Wheeler pretty much where he was when he started—the artist necessarily underplays the amount of talent and dedication required simply to stay the course and earn a decent living from his work. Fittingly, the Too Much Coffee Man (hereafter TMCM) character that has proved so successful for Wheeler was by his own admission born of expediency, and has achieved a level of popularity that has made subsequent non-TMCM work a somewhat difficult commercial undertaking.

As Wheeler commented in a 2007 interview, "I tried to do other comic books, and the numbers were 50-percent. I don't know if it's the fan base—I tend to think it's the store owners that see it as something new and cut orders" (2007a). Wheeler's magazine, launched in 2001 and suspended in 2006, persisted with the title *TMCM*, despite the fact that most of its content was a diverse range of material from Wheeler and other contributors such as Craig Thompson, Jeffrey Brown, and Jhonen Vasquez, a decision which allowed him to use the distribution deal set up with Diamond for the TMCM character, as well as draw on its continuing popularity.

The circumstances Wheeler found himself in were by no means unique; other comics creators, as well as numerous authors, musicians, and film directors have struggled with the consequences of an unexpectedly successful creation that sets up commercial and artistic expectations about subsequent work, and which can be hard to shake. Two things, however, make the case of Wheeler and TMCM particularly interesting. The first is that Wheeler's TMCM character, during the course of his comic lifespan, began to reflect increasingly, and in intriguing ways, on the complexities and ironies of his popularity and the impact of this on the life and career of Wheeler. The second is the trajectory the TMCM character made outside comics, which saw Wheeler disenchanted by his experience of attempting to use TMCM as the basis for a Comedy Central network cartoon series, but then subsequently adapt him for the world's first-ever opera based on a comic strip, which debuted at the Portland Center for the Performing Arts in 2006. Taken together, these events make TMCM a revealing study of the complex symbiosis of commercial and creative impulses involved in alternative comic production.

GETTING HIGH ON CAFFEINE: THE RISE OF TMCM

We rejected the "Sexy Woman" cover, even though it had greater
"Market Appeal." Please support our integrity by buying several
copies of this book . . .
—(Wheeler 2001, 4)

Few art forms better illustrate the complexities of what media sociologist Dick Hebdige terms "artisan capitalism" than alternative comics (1989, 93). Drawing inspiration in part from the punk movement to which Hebdige's term refers, alternative comics have been seen similarly to distance themselves from the "profit-driven escapism" (Sabin 1996, 178) that often characterizes "mainstream" superhero fare. Yet as Hebdige points out, "It is difficult to maintain any absolute distinction between commercial exploitation on the one hand, and creativity/originality on the other" (92).

Perhaps no recent creation expresses this as acutely as Shannon Wheeler's Too Much Coffee Man, a brooding, existential, caffeine junkie with a parodic superhero outfit and a large coffee mug attached to his head. Wheeler conceived of the character in the early 1990s initially as a "joke . . . an iconographic character that would allow me some recognition with an audience" (Wheeler 1998, 142), to be published in 25-cent mini-mags he hoped would attract readers to his other more expressly autobiographical work. As Ted Rall writes in his foreword to Wheeler's How To Be Happy (2005): "'Too Much Coffee Man,' Shannon has told me, began as a somewhat cynical exercise in 1990s Gen X consumerism: an edgy strip meant to appear in the sort of publications that are often read in coffeehouses by disaffected thirtysomethings" (9–10). Indeed, Wheeler's own residential journey took him through U.S. cities that had precisely the kind of critical mass of highly educated but often underemployed young people that helped sustain alternative comics' production and their coffeehouse consumption in the 1980s and 1990s. From Berkeley,

California, to Austin, Texas, and on through Seattle, Washington, and then to Portland, Oregon, Wheeler moved through a range of locations noted for their alternative/underground arts and music scenes, and the coffeehouses and bars around which such activity took place. Wheeler's first *TMCM* strip was self-published out of Austin in 1991, the same year that saw the release of *Slacker*, Richard Linklater's milestone low-budget independent movie. Located in the neighborhoods around the Austin campus, the movie followed the physical and verbal rambles of its assorted collection of characters, some of whom engaged in angst or paranoia-ridden, coffeehouse-located flights of fancy not dissimilar to those of Wheeler's creation.

The title of Linklater's film soon entered media parlance as a synonym for disaffected, seemingly directionless young people, and was often used interchangeably with "Generation X" in mass media discussions from 1991 onwards. As was clear to anyone who picked up a copy of *Advertising Age* at that time, part of the beguiling nature of this supposedly enigmatic demographic was its elusive quality as a target market for commodities (Frank 1997, 233). Characterized as a cynical, media-savvy, corporate-skeptical cohort who seemingly failed to respond to traditional marketing techniques, advertisers responded with a range of strategies and campaigns seeking to appeal to "hip consumerism," many of which were embarrassingly wide of the mark. Others, however, were not, and as Thomas Frank's *The Conquest of Cool*, Naomi Klein's *No Logo*, and Joseph Heath and Andrew Potter's *The Rebel Sell* make abundantly clear, many products have been sold successfully through their appeal to non-conformist, "alternative," or rebellious sensibilities, marketed for their capacity to signify rejection of "mainstream" values. *Too Much Coffee Man*, a comics creation that lampooned the righteousness and simple-minded hubris of "mainstream" superheroes (never more vividly than when TMCM fought the sculpted superhero Cliché, and faced down his barrage of trite expressions) was, as Wheeler freely admits, designed to appeal in such a way, and could be quickly grasped through its "high concept" design.

What Wheeler could not have foreseen when designing his comics creation at the beginning of the decade was the remarkable explosion in the number of coffeehouses across the U.S. as the decade progressed. By the time of the publication of *Too Much Coffee Man's Amusing Musings* in 2001 there were over 12,000 specialty coffee retail outlets in the U.S., up from 250 in 1980. At the same time, U.S. retail sales had rocketed from $60 million to $3.3 billion in 2001 (Sturdivant 1990, 60; Crabtree 2001, E4). Drinking coffee in public had become a serious national pastime, with the number of people who could identify with coffee-fixation and the experience of public caffeine overdosing multiplying exponentially. As Wheeler commented in 1998, "My biggest burden now with Too Much Coffee Man is having people tell me they love my comic because they love coffee" (142). Moreover, while Wheeler's initially imagined coffeehouse was the sticky-floored independently-owned bohemian hangout long part of the urban furniture in locations such as Berkeley and Austin, the expansion of "coffee culture" in the 1990s was in contrast the work of deep-pocketed NASDAQ-listed companies such as Starbucks, which had over 3,500 stores worldwide by the end of the 1990s (Anon. 1999). The coffeehouse had gone corporate in a big way, which served only to amplify the conditions for TMCM's existential anguish. In a 1999 cartoon titled "What has happened to Too Much Coffee Man? Since he's dead!" Wheeler depicted TMCM in hell, which comprised a cell showing him standing outside the entrance to a Starbucks (99).

Yet the cartoons have largely refrained from commenting on the "coffee culture" phenomenon as typified by Starbucks. Instead, Wheeler devoted an issue of his *Adhesive Comics* to addressing what he saw as the widespread misrepresentation of the McDonald's coffee lawsuit (Liebeck v. McDonald's restaurants, 1994). The lawsuit, filed as a result of seventy-nine-year-old Stella Liebeck spilling McDonald's coffee in her lap and suffering third-degree burns, had, in Wheeler's opinion, been used unfairly as an indictment of a hysterical "litigious culture" based upon fallacious reporting. Wheeler also criticized McDonald's callous defense tactics and implied that their financial and political clout also played a part in the misreporting of the case. Following on the heels of the widespread reporting of the so-called McLibel Trial (McDonald's Restaurants v. Morris & Steel) in the British High Court, prompted by the corporation's issuing of libel proceedings against Greenpeace activists in 1991, and anticipating Morgan Spurlock's indie documentary *Super Size Me* (2004), Erich Schlosser's *Fast Food Nation* (2005), and Richard Linklater's film adaptation of Schlosser's book in 2006, Wheeler employed TMCM's caffeine hook to draw readers in to a much more substantive critique of corporate malfeasance.

By and large, however, the machinations of coffee-pushing corporations have featured rather less frequently in the comics than the derision and scorn heaped on coffeehouse poseurs. Wheeler's observations, gleaned from "sitting in a coffee shop, looking at the people around me, making fun of the people around me" (2007b), have formed the basis for exposing the pretensions and hypocrisies of those who use the signifiers of "alternative" status as a mark of superiority. In a one-page comic included in *How to Be Happy* Wheeler draws TMCM entering the "Urban Hipster" coffeehouse and announcing: "I may not dress cool, and I don't have tattoos or piercings, but I'm just as alienated, depressed, and apathetic as the rest of you!" (2005, 115). Another comic collected in *Amusing Musings* depicts TMCM quitting the city for the countryside, seeking isolation but instead finding another urban émigré, who has holed up with "a lot of counter-culture stuff" such as "*The Anarchist's Cookbook*, Zinn, Burroughs, Chomsky, and Bukowski" and "a nice stereo" to listen to "Dylan, Ice-T, Rage Against the Machine, MC5, and The Dead Kennedys" among other creature comforts. The penultimate cell depicts TMCM objecting: "Hold on. Just because you consume rebel culture, you're not automatically a rebel. In fact, all you are is a consumer" (2001, 117).

Wheeler's spearing of the "Rebel Sell" at the heart of alternative cultural consumption has added poignancy, because, as a producer of "alternative" comics, he is, like it or not, operating in a sphere of cultural production where the symbols of "cool" and "hip" are, at least for some, valued currency. Indeed, TMCM's iconic appeal has been exploited commercially by Wheeler, used to adorn T-shirts, coffee mugs (of course), and lunch boxes—the joke being that anyone who has actually *read* the *TMCM* comic may well have encountered a strip mocking characters wearing TMCM T-shirts as a sign of hip individuality. In somewhat cynically exploiting those individuals apparently more concerned with subcultural style over substance, Wheeler has realized the profitability of what Tom Tomorrow calls "a satire on consumerism masquerading as a consumer icon" (2001, 8).

Things get somewhat more complex when Wheeler has segued from (to quote Tomorrow) his calling as "an unparalleled master at coming up with weird shit to sell you" (2001, 8), to dealing with major corporations who have also cottoned on to the adaptability of TMCM for merchandising ends. In the mid-1990s Wheeler worked with Converse to create an animated commercial based on the TMCM character. The commercial depicts a Converse sneaker-wearing TMCM realizing he has run out of coffee filters, and, in a fit of cold-turkey anxiety, jams one of his sneakers in his coffee percolator to fashion a makeshift filter. The resulting brew is so potent that TMCM's heart bursts out of his chest.

The commercial is a superb piece of work, masterfully capturing the concentrated caffeinated mania of the TMCM character with rapid cuts and tight close-ups, and with a typically abrupt and absurd ending. Yet the character's Converse sneakers are, it must be said, a contrivance, since TMCM is not otherwise drawn with footwear of any kind, not even apparently non-descript sneakers that can be "revealed" as Converse in the commercial. But this is perhaps less problematic than the fact that the character's connection with

Converse inevitably involves him in a reciprocal relationship of "cool" association; both the brand and the man come off as more hip as a result, which
arguably cancels out any residual satire on consumerism left over from the
Comic-Con stand of embossed lunchboxes. Moreover, the commercial pulls
the character much closer to the caffeine-junkie "hook" aspect of the comic,
and offers no space for the existential musings and verbal diatribes that prolif-
erate on paper. Perhaps somewhat predictably, reflecting their differing forms
and functions, the commercial ends where the comic books really take off.

A number of Wheeler's cartoons in the aftermath of the success of the
Converse ad ponder the consequences of the fact that a *great* commercial for
a major corporation is still a *commercial for a major corporation*, which sets up
some unwelcome assumptions. In a strip included in *Parade of Tirade* Wheeler
depicts himself as cartoonist drawing TMCM, and answering the door to two
young fans who have heard "This is where the girl who draws Too Much Coffee
Man lives," punning on the gender assumption created by his first name. One
of the boys asks "why did you do a comic book from a commercial?" and the
other follows up with "is it because it's such a *cool* character?" After explain-
ing patiently that the comics preceded the commercial, the boys respond,
"You made a lot of *money* from your commercial," "You were *smart* to do a
coffee character," and "Coffee is *trendy*" (1999, 113). As Wheeler has stated in
an interview, "Some kids really did think that I got the idea for my comic book
from the commercial" (2008), with the frustration that opportunities and circumstances that occurred either consequently or coincidentally are taken to
be formative in TMCM's genesis. Wheeler closes the strip with his cartoon
alter-ego reflecting on the encounter, stating that "They want to believe that
success is based on something cheap like 'Selling Out,' exploiting others, a
deal with Satan, or rich parents," and ending with the reflection that "the only
deal with the devil is that you have to sacrifice so much of your own life to do
well in your work" (114).

In another strip Wheeler *does* show the perils of making a deal with the
devil, in the guise of a representative for a "large coffee company who wants
[TMCM] as a spokesman." After initially announcing, "You're perfect for this
job. We don't want you to change a thing!" the spokesman states that "They
love everything about this project except the name," finally whittling TMCM's
name down to just "man," and then switching to "person" as "'man' is too gen-
der-specific" (1998, 116). They tell TMCM that "we're looking at other actors
to play your part. Someone younger—a name—to hit the youth market!"
TMCM, who has remained dumbfounded as the spokesman has sucked him
into a vortex of agent-speak, is eventually dropped out of a limo and handed

a check, which he looks at with puzzlement (117). The next installment of the comic begins with his compadre (and occasional rival) Too Much Espresso Guy proclaiming "You sold out!" (118).

Arguably the high-water mark for this anxiety over corporate proprietorship occurs in the strip that opens *Parade of Tirade*, where TMCM is pitched into battle with Trademark Copyright Man (TM©M). After receiving a puzzling letter in the mail, TMCM travels to the sender, arriving at a skyscraper emblazoned with the TMCM lettering. Inside he is directed to cease and desist from "using the TMCM logo" (1999, 8). After TMCM hires a lawyer to help him fight back, TM©M retaliates: "I've filed a trademark on the 'cup-on-the-head' and copyrights on manic behavior, paranoia, coffee addiction, and exaggerated expressions" (9). Once TMCM's lawyer counters with evidence of his client's personality appearing in work "prior to [the] filing of the bogus copyright" (9), TM©M eats him. In this typically outlandish finale, the failure of legal bullying to work results in a consuming rage, which literalizes the devouring appetite of an aggressive corporation. Here, the consequence of success is not the prospect of "selling out" but being *frozen out*, outmaneuvered as others seek to capitalize on legal naiveté to exploit TMCM's commercial potential.

Many of these issues were played out for real in Wheeler's subsequent experience of attempting to use the TMCM character as the basis for an animated series. In 1999 the Canadian entertainment company Nelvana optioned *TMCM* as a TV show and began the process of finding potential network investors. Nelvana, which had a long history of transforming children's books and comics into animated shows (e.g., *Babar, Pippi Longstocking, Tintin*), had struck gold in the 1980s with its acquisition of the character rights to *Care Bears* (Anon. 2002). Although the company's origins were in the late-1960s counterculture (co-founder Clive A. Smith had worked on *Yellow Submarine*), its subsequent activities were firmly in the family entertainment market. Its optioning of *TMCM* should be seen as an attempt to diversify its activities, using its clout and connections with TV networks to establish itself in the potentially lucrative teen/college cartoon sector occupied by shows such as *Ren and Stimpy, Beavis and Butt-head*, and *South Park*. Nelvana succeeded in interesting Comedy Central, home of *South Park*, and Wheeler went to Los Angeles to work on a pilot script. The script was completed and submitted, but the network declined to take up the option (Wheeler 2007b).

While Wheeler's experience of a near miss with a network puts him in good (not to mention extensive) artistic company, his ensuing thoughts on the process are nevertheless revealing. Above all, Wheeler has expressed what appears to be a genuine sense of relief about Comedy Central's decision. This is based principally on his avowed dissatisfaction with the way the writers involved in the pilot sought to reshape the TMCM character, and his unease at the fact that he no longer had the final word on his creation's identity and activities. As Wheeler stated:

> I was supposed to be an intimate part of creating the show. The writer and I worked together on a script and I didn't like it, but I was a minority. They made TMCM a mean person, and they explained to me that television and comic books are very different things. I was very unhappy with the script and thankfully Comedy Central agreed with me that it sucked . . . (Wheeler 2002).

While we have no way of knowing if Comedy Central thought that the pilot "sucked" for precisely the same reasons that Wheeler did, issues of translatability and creative control are at the heart of most, if not all, negotiations to take comics characters from page to screen, and Wheeler is not the first (and will by no means be the last) creator to become disenchanted with the realities of the enterprise. Arguably, it is what may have attracted Nelvana to the TMCM character, specifically a "high concept" look and name which invites the possibility of wide-ranging usage, which is key in this instance. While a fifteen-second Converse commercial is brief enough to be propelled satisfyingly by the character's caffeinated mania, a longer sequence requires more extensive decision-making over characterization, plotting, and story arcs.

In other words, it is more straightforward to translate the kinetic exuberance of a one-page coffee-oriented strip into a commercial than the introspective, existential musings of some of the longer comics into a TV show. Wheeler's comments regarding the introduction of a "sexy" secretary character into the animated version, against his reasonable protestation that "this is sexist," indicate an attempt to situate TMCM into a rather more hackneyed set of scenarios, presumably for wider appeal. Wheeler consulted his lawyer to see if it was possible to stop the pilot process, to which s/he apparently replied "Well, they've really invested a lot of money in this, and what you need to do now is divorce yourself emotionally from the project." Wheeler states, "So I did, but thankfully it died" (2007b).

The nature of Wheeler's experience with Nelvana might have been predicted to end his willingness to sanction the translating of TMCM into other guises, particularly if it meant ceding to third-party input. However, in September 2006 the Portland Center for the Performing Arts (PCPA) programmed the world premiere of *Too Much Coffee Man*, a one-hour chamber opera based on Wheeler's comics creation. As the PCPA box office website made clear, this was the first opera ever to be based on a comic book. Wheeler had collaborated on the production with the composer Daniel Steven Crofts, and with "Dorkboy" comic creator Damian Wilcox, who helped write the opera's libretto. Crucially, both were friends of Wheeler.

In an interview Wheeler stated that Crofts had approached him several years previously with the idea of an opera based on TMCM, but he had resisted, finally relenting and working on it sporadically for a few years as "just sort of a lark" (2007b). A serendipitous meeting with the executive director for the PCPA had made the possibility of its performance "a once in a lifetime opportunity" (2007b). The opera ran at the PCPA for a month, and then was reprised for a short run in San Diego for the attendees of the 2007 Comic-Con, with some additional public performances. As a result of the original opera's popularity, a sequel debuted at the Stumptown Comics Fest in Portland in September 2007.

At first glance, part of the attraction of TMCM: The Opera is perhaps the absurdity of the premise. Like Jerry Springer: The Opera, first performed in 2001, the translation of popular culture subject matter into opera, which, as John Storey notes, represents for many people "the very embodiment of 'high culture'" (2002, 32), is intriguing and unlikely. Yet as Storey has usefully pointed out, the 1990s actually saw opera undergo a significant transformation in cultural status to become again "art that can be entertaining," as it had been prior to its isolation as high culture by social elites at the end of the nineteenth century (37). Like Jerry Springer, TMCM: The Opera is in a sense a manifestation of this transformation, and one similarly constructed with a very skilful sense of what can constitute the compelling subject matter of a musically scored dramatic work.

In TMCM: The Opera, this revolves around TMCM's love for a local barista, whom he is too shy to approach. His pain is compounded when Too Much Espresso Guy also makes advances on the object of his affections. However, the barista has other ideas, and selects to become a superhero in her own right, rather than merely become the love interest of another. The basic storyline was adapted by Wheeler from some of the comics, and stays exceedingly faithful to its source material, a consequence of the dynamics of the creative process and the lack of commercial imperatives impinging upon it. As one review noted, "There's no whiff of a Hollywood ending in the way the barista sings about hating her service industry job, its measly tips, and the geeks who lust after her" (Gallivan 2006). More interesting, perhaps, are Wheeler and the cast's observations on the surprising adaptability of his comic book material to operatic form. As Wheeler notes:

> I've tried to translate TMCM to animation several times and never felt like it was working. In part because the strip is so heavy on internal dialogue. It's all about emotions and animated cartoons are very plot driven and have a lot of physical humor. TMCM translated really well to opera. Opera is all about internal dialogue of a character and the emotions. They're singing how they feel. TMCM is very much about how he feels . . . (2007c).

While Wheeler perhaps underplays the importance of plotting to the operatic tradition, not to mention the vaudeville-derived bodily humor of the opéra-comique, the tendency of opera to provide opportunities to over-dramatize the externalizing of interior states certainly suits TMCM's caffeine-fueled anguish. From a rather different perspective, Matt Dolphin, the tenor who played the part of Espresso Guy in the Portland premiere, pointed out that "the scoring resembles a cartoon, with its quick cuts" (Gallivan 2006). Yet unlike a cartoon, the propulsion in *TMCM* is more often than not provided by dialogue, rather than action.

While this caused difficulties for a satisfactory translation to animation for Comedy Central, it has proved more assimilable to opera, where the score provides the pacing and drive for the libretto. Thus while animation may be able to more accurately render the graphical qualities of *TMCM*'s character world, Wheeler and his co-creators discovered that opera, an art form seemingly much further from the "grammar of Sequential Art" (Eisner 1985, 8), is more able to convey the sentiment of the original. What is "lost in translation" from comic to animated cartoon is clearly not *reinstated* in opera, but is instead *replaced* with the particular expressive qualities of the form. Thus while *TMCM: The Opera* may have been begun as "a lark," Wheeler and his co-creators stumbled upon a form, and, just as important, a stratum of cultural production which, if not autonomous from the dictates of commerce (opera houses have to sell seats too), then one in which the primacy of artistic expression has a highly prized and privileged place. The result has been the opportunity to develop the character in ways that, for both commercial and aesthetic reasons, proved much more difficult with television animation.

CONCLUSION

Thomas Frank refers in *The Conquest of Cool* to what he characterizes as the "genesis of the counterculture as an enduring commercial myth, the titanic symbolic clash of hip and square that recurs throughout post-sixties culture"

(1998, 32). If alternative comics are, as Roger Sabin argues, "in many ways an extension of the old underground comix" of the counterculture, a number have also been assimilable to the codes of "hip consumerism" that work dramatically to animate symbolic rebellion. As Frank suggests, "Rebel youth culture remains the cultural mode of the corporate moment" (31). In a strip collected in *Too Much Coffee Man's Guide for the Perplexed*, TMCM responds to anxiety regarding his own popularity, and the inevitable consequence that "hip" people will now be compelled to regard him as "unhip" with the statement: "You're not any sort of rebel if you're reacting to popular culture" (1998, 120).

Of course, the irony is that the TMCM character began life as a calculated reaction to mainstream superhero fare, parodying its traits and tropes through Wheeler's absurdly "high concept" hooks. More ironically, the remarkable popularity of the character offered him the chance to participate in the commercial packaging of "rebel youth culture" in the guise of the TMCM Converse commercial and the Nelvana animated TV series. While the success of the commercial would seem to suggest that there's nothing hip consumers like more than a "satire on consumerism," the aborted TV series shows how an ostensibly less brazen commercial undertaking can be hamstrung by generic expectations that in fact require much greater compromise.

More ironically still, the anxieties that accompanied the vicissitudes of TMCM's commercial trajectory made for increasingly compelling comic material, as the character, and Wheeler's cartoonist proxy fretted over "selling out," being successful, popular, or cool. Most ironically of all, Wheeler found an opportunity for enhanced creative expressivity in opera, the "square" art form for social elites, and thus in many ways the antithesis of countercultural rebelliousness. If this epoch has seen the "Rebel Sell" become the modus operandi of the commercial mainstream, when it comes to the Rebel "Cell," it is perhaps on occasion more hip to be square.

WORK CITED

Anon. 1999. *Business Wire*. http://www.businesswire.com/webbox/bw.111899/193221527 [accessed 5 Dec. 2002].

———. 2002. Nelvana gets the inside story - on Nelvana. *Toronto Star*, Mar. 16, AR10 [Arts Section].

Balzac, Honore de. 1996. The Pleasures and Pains of Coffee. Trans. Robert Onopa. *Michigan Quarterly Review* XXXV(2): 273.

Crabtree, S. 2001. Straight coffee serves up goodwill with a hot cup of java. *San Jose Business Journal*, Mar. 9.

Eisner, Will. 1985. *Comics and Sequential Art*. Paramus, NJ: Poorhouse Press.

Frank, Thomas. 1997. *The Conquest of Cool*. Chicago: University of Chicago Press.

Gallivan, Joseph. 2006. Coffee fan tutti: Caffeinated comic character goes to the opera. *The Portland Tribune*, Sept. 18.

Heath, Joseph & Andrew Potter. 2005. *The Rebel Sell*. Chichester, West Sussex: Capstone.

Hebdige, Dick. 1989. *Subculture: The Meaning of Style*. London: Routledge.

Klein, Naomi. 2000. *No Logo*. London: Flamingo.

Sabin, Roger. 1996. *Comics, Comix, & Graphic Novels: A History of Comic Art*. London: Phaidon Press.

Storey, John. 2002. "Expecting Rain": Opera as Popular Culture. In *High-Pop*, ed. Jim Collins, 32–55. Oxford: Blackwell Publishing.

Sturdivant, S. 1990. Coffee in the next decade: upcoming trends. *Tea & Coffee Trade Journal* 162(1): 60/65.

Wheeler, Shannon. 1997. *Wake up and Smell the Cartoons of Shannon Wheeler*. Austin TX: Mojo Press.

———. 1998. *Too Much Coffee Man's Guide for the Perplexed*. Milwaukie, OR: Dark Horse Comics.

———. 1999. *Too Much Coffee Man's Parade of Tirade*. Milwaukie, OR: Dark Horse Comics.

———. 2001. *Too Much Coffee Man's Amusing Musings*. Milwaukie, OR: Dark Horse Comics.

———. 2002. Interviewed by Tom Waters. *Acid Logic*, Aug. 16. http://www.acidlogic.com/shannon_wheeler.htm [accessed 15 July 2009].

———. 2005. *How to Be Happy*. Milwaukie, OR: Dark Horse Comics.

———. 2007a. Interviewed by Brian Heater. *The Daily Cross Hatch*, May 15. http://thedailycrosshatch.com/2007/05/15/interview-shannon-wheeler-pt-3-of-3/ [accessed 14 July 2009].

———. 2007b. Interviewed by Brian Heater. *The Daily Cross Hatch*, Apr. 11. http://thedailycrosshatch.com/2007/04/11/interview-shannon-wheeler-pt-2-of-3/ [accessed 14 July 2009].

———. 2007c. Interviewed by PinkRaygun. *PinkRaygun.com*, Apr. 16. http://www.pinkraygun.com/2007/04/16/pink-raygun-interviews-shannon-wheeler/ [accessed 14 July 2009].

———. 2008. Interviewed by Steve Johnson. *Associated Content*, June 12. http://www.associatedcontent.com/article/813339/the_man_behind_too_much_coffee_man.html?cat=38 [accessed 14 July 2009].

CHAPTER SEVEN

Comics Against Themselves: Chris Ware's Graphic Narratives as Literature

—DAVID M. BALL

The recent rise in scholarly interest regarding graphic narratives has been precipitous and remarkable. This intellectual ferment is evidenced both by the strength, volume, and range of the comics produced, as well as an attendant enthusiasm and productivity in comics criticism and theory.[1] Graphic narratives' ability to reinvigorate literary theoretical questions of temporality, narrative, and periodization, among others, points toward the catalytic effect that studies of comics are beginning to provide for conventional literary scholarship (for examples, see Chute and DeKoven 2006; Chute 2008; Baetens and Blatt 2008).

In this essay I will concentrate in particular on periodization and explore the ways comics complicate most conventional notions of modernism and postmodernism in twentieth- and twenty-first-century literature.[2] Namely, the development of comics can be seen as an inverted history of an admittedly caricatural, but nonetheless widely held trajectory of twentieth-century literary history, one that moves from the formal experimentation and putative disdain for mass culture in modernist texts to the playful self-referentiality and celebration of consumption in postmodern fiction.[3] Using the recent work of Chris Ware as a paradigm, I argue that contemporary graphic narratives' characteristic ambivalence about their status as popular cultural productions repeats modernist anxieties about literary value that reemerge precisely at the moment graphic narratives are bidding for literary respectability.

Considered at face value, however, no American medium appears better suited to the expectations of literary postmodernity—ludic irony, the willful disruption of high and low, "the consumption of sheer commodification as a process"—than that of the comics (Jameson 1991, x). Given their historic genealogy within technologies of mass production, comics remain symbolic of a near total homology of popular culture and creative expression. Their appropriation by quintessentially postmodern visual artists such as Roy Lichtenstein and Andy Warhol as mass media emblems seems only to ratify the unassailable postmodernity of the comics medium. As evidence of this literary critical concept, take the inclusion of graphic narratives throughout the Norton anthology *Postmodern American Fiction*. The book, which includes work by Lynda Barry and Art Spiegelman, the graphic adaptation of Paul Auster's *City of Glass* by Paul Karasik and David Mazzucchelli, and references to George Herriman's seminal comic strip *Krazy Kat* in Jay Cantor's novel of the same title (as well as the collage between visual and textual materials in selections by Theresa Hak Kyung Cha, Kurt Vonnegut, and others), insists that literary postmodernity be both seen and read (Geyh, Leebron, and Levy 1998, 85–93, 162–73, 196–225, 295–300, 450–57).[4] Yet, the inclusion of Herriman's figures, even in the context of Cantor's novel, is a curious one. Herriman's most productive years were the 1920s and 1930s, a time when he was feted by many arbiters of literary modernism such as Gilbert Seldes and E. E. Cummings—and working within one of American modernism's most recognizable visual registers: the iconography of the American southwest that drew modernist writers and artists in the wake of Mabel Dodge Luhan such as Willa Cather and Georgia O'Keefe (Seldes 2004; Cummings 2004).[5]

Newspaper comics achieved a period of formal inventiveness in the work of Winsor McCay, Herriman, and Rudolph Dirks, among many others, contemporaneous with the development of artistic *and* literary high modernism. Indeed Dirks, whose comic strip *The Katzenjammer Kids* was imported from America to Paris and passed lovingly between Gertrude Stein and Pablo Picasso during their foundational modernist collaborations, was himself exhibited at the influential 1913 Armory Show, the artistic epicenter for American modernism (Stein 1990, 23).[6] Despite such rich overlap between comics and modernism, however, comics have made only fleeting appearances in conventional anthologies or histories of modernist literature. If they seem only to be able to signify the postmodern, it is because American comics' popular cultural medium appears as their only possible message. In these terms, the rapid rise of the "graphic novel" in publishing and contemporary literary criticism could be viewed as the ultimate conflation of visuality and postmodernity, a

belief that characterizes the majority of contemporary work in visual studies and visual culture (for example, see the introductory gambits in Mirzoeff
1998; Cohen 1998; Manghani, Piper, and Simons 2006).

In this essay, I want to put forward a counterargument to such claims,
revealing instead the persistence of modernism in that most unlikely of
places: the contemporary American graphic narrative. To do so is to revisit
critical debates over modernism's uneasy relationship with mass media, and
the once-secure assumptions of literary *and* artistic modernism's austere
distance from popular culture. These stem from a long tradition of theorists
ranging from Theodor Adorno and Clement Greenberg to Andreas Huyssen,
arguments that have recently been challenged and complicated by contemporary interventions in American modernist theory and literary criticism.
Foremost among these is the work of Michael North, who in *Reading 1922*
states:

> The common dichotomies by which literary modernism . . . is distin-
> guished from the larger culture of the time cannot be maintained against
> the evidence that the very terms those dichotomies depend on were
> being redefined by literature and culture in concert. . . These dichotomies
> cannot be used to divide modernism, for their ironic interdependence
> defines the modern (North 1999, 29–30).

North's point here is well taken, as evidenced by his influence on many
recent studies in American modernism. However, these studies threaten to
undervalue the felt antipathy the high modernists often held for mass culture. Fitzgerald's and Faulkner's widely acclaimed disdain for the periodical
press or Ezra Pound's revulsion in "Hugh Selwyn Mauberley" for the "taw-
dry cheapness" of the modern age coexist with their very reliance on popular
cultural materials within their work. Modernism's characteristic bricolage of
high and low—*Ulysses'* Homeric cipher and its quotidian Dublin setting, the
high literary footnotes and "Shakespeherian Rag" of *The Waste Land, Let Us
Now Praise Famous Men*'s cacophony of intellectual luminaries and sharecrop-
pers in its opening listing of "People and Places"—all can be said to emerge
exactly within this failed divide, or the divide within this divide, between
high art and mass culture. It is the force of this ambivalence toward popular
culture, as much as the inevitability of popular cultural influence in modernist production, which remains an important engine of the formal ingenuity
and intellectual ferment of the era. The characteristically modernist text
thus achieves one of its most recognizable forms in the generative tension

between the ideal and the possible, between the desire for an art produced in pure isolation from the world and that world suffused throughout the art.

Which is to say that what makes recent graphic narratives so thoroughly, persistently modernist is their continued desire to disassociate themselves from the mass media forms in which they were first produced. Despite their aforementioned avant-garde strains, American comics began in the realm of mass media and yellow journalism (the etymology for the term itself coming from Richard Outcault's "The Yellow Kid," one of the earliest, archetypal American comics characters), where they served first as a boon to mass readership. Later, with the rise of the comic book in the 1930s, comics became a vehicle for an almost exclusively adolescent audience, one resisted by the later rise of "underground" and then "alternative" comics in the 1960s and continuing to the present, shifting the medium toward the confessional, craft-focused, often self-produced avant-garde of contemporary graphic narratives today.

In doing so, this current generation of comics artists instantiates the most recognizable characteristics of modernist literature in the contemporary graphic narrative: epistemological difficulty, moral ambiguity, formal experimentation, and a conspicuous rhetoric of literary failure. This sea change has come about precisely as graphic literature aspires to the status of literature as such, and in this transformation what the reader of contemporary graphic narratives can observe is a phenomenon of *comics against themselves*: an ambivalent, yet determined resistance to the generic conventions and mass media associations of conventional comics artistry within the emergent field of graphic literature. This resistance, I argue, repeats and extends the most recognizable symptoms of literary modernism, confirming the claims of T. J. Clark, among others, that the intellectual crux of postmodernity may well be nothing more than the persistence of the modernist dilemma (Clark 2000).

I have been painting with very broad strokes here, and I would like to model some of these assertions in a reading of the work of Chris Ware, who is quickly becoming one of the central voices in the emerging field of graphic narratives. Ware's work has been appearing in serial form since 1993 in his *The ACME Novelty Library*, significant portions of which were collected as the American-Book-Award-winning graphic novel *Jimmy Corrigan: The Smartest Kid on Earth* (2000). Described variously as the James Joyce, the Samuel Beckett, and the Emily Dickinson of comics, Ware's work is distinguished for its simultaneous narrative complexity and richly detailed vision of human experience. More recently, Ware has also emerged as an extremely prolific arbiter

Fig. 7.1 "Stuffing" pictures a solitary, elderly man feeding pigeons on Thanksgiving Day. Chris Ware, "Stuffing," 2006. Reproduced by permission from Ware 2007, n.p.

of contemporary comics, editing both the comics anthology *McSweeney's Quarterly Concern* #13 (2004) and the Houghton Mifflin *Best American Comics 2007*, in addition to having his own work appear in such highly prestigious publications as *The Virginia Quarterly Review*, *The New York Times Magazine*, and *The New Yorker*. Described by Art Spiegelman as having an "uncanny . . . recollection of the history of comics, and the talent to expand upon it" (Kidd 1997, 42), Ware's already prodigious body of work as author, critic, editor, and archivist places him second only to Spiegelman himself as a shaping and determinant force in the development of graphic narratives' prominence in twenty-first-century literature.

It is one of his contributions to *The New Yorker* I will focus on here: a series of four serial covers and an online supplement to the November 27, 2006, cartoon issue, all of which have been collected as *The ACME Novelty Library No. 18½* under the title "Thanksgiving."[7] The first four compositions of this sequence served as four alternate covers of the November 27 issue, one of which was delivered to subscribers with no indication of the existence of the other three beyond an inset "map" buried within the glossy advertisements in the magazine's opening pages. Indeed, it is safe to assume that a majority of subscribers read the magazine with no knowledge of the other three covers. In this format alone, I would argue, Ware is invoking familiar techniques of literary modernism: narrative fragmentation, conspicuous difficulty, and the cultivation of a trained, cerebral, coterie audience.

When read in sequence, these covers together—consecutively titled "Stuffing," "Conversation," "Family," and "Main Course"—trace a storyline accessible only to the most vigilant and patient of readers, revealing an almost Nabokovian sense of narrative games.[8] At the same time they articulate a narrative of increasing visual and representational complexity, the number of panels on the page expanding exponentially from a single, wordless image in "Stuffing" to two-, four-, and twenty-four-panel compositions, culminating in a vast canvas for an online supplement titled "Leftovers" that is based on a 256-panel grid. Taken together, "Thanksgiving" serves as a rigorous reading lesson in contemporary comics, one that both exemplifies the possibilities of graphic narratives and satirizes the very impulse for comics to become literature.

The first cover, "Stuffing" (fig. 7.1), pictures a solitary, elderly man feeding pigeons on Thanksgiving Day, his back turned toward the reader. Taken by itself, it appears to be nothing more than one of the typical, single-panel illustrations conventionally seen on the cover of the magazine. Read in sequence, however, "Stuffing" establishes the dominant theme of the series of covers—loneliness and disassociation amidst the Thanksgiving celebration of

Fig. 7.2 "Conversation" juxtaposes the warm tones and familial conversation of a 1942 Thanksgiving against the same dining room on a contemporary Thanksgiving, distracted by the flat screen television. Chris Ware, "Conversation," 2006. Reproduced by permission from Ware 2007, n.p.

community—and introduces readers to a central character who will reemerge throughout the narrative. By itself, "Stuffing" can be read as an antitype to that most iconic of *The New Yorker* cover images, Eustace Tilley, whom Ware took as the subject of a study of movement in the comics medium for his cover illustration in February 2005.[9] Rather than foppishly viewing the butterfly through his monocle, our character shies from a gas light in the figure of that same butterfly, at the same time disregarding the miniature illuminated scenes of Thanksgiving feasting that surround and isolate him in the facing buildings.

One of these miniature scenes is the subject of the second cover, "Conversation" (fig. 7.2), which zooms in on one of these lighted windows (the fourth floor of the leftmost building), depicting the same home during the old man's childhood in 1942 and its present-day tenants. Already expecting a severe degree of visual literacy—the careful reader can match the teenager on her cell phone in the bottom panel of this cover with one of the tiny figures in the windows of the previous cover—this second image demands a great deal more of the reader, expecting them to shift seamlessly between two separate time frames and to establish a rough equivalence between the isolation of the old man and this disaffected young woman. Both occupy the same corner of their respective panels, the old man in his childhood years (Ware signals this connection through his use of color as well as narrative contiguity) reading comics as his family is engaged in post-dinner conversation, while the teenager speaks with friends on her cell phone as her family watches a football game on television. The contrast overall is seemingly as stark, literally and figuratively a binary opposition between the warm tones and communion of the earlier scene of familial conversation against the cold, almost antiseptic dining room whose flat screen television disallows conversation in the present-day scene. The palpable nostalgia for the earlier time frame—a putative golden age of both communal values and the comics that the young boy reads—is tempered, however, by the boy's older brother being away at war. In many respects the "conversation" of the cover's title is between the two halves of its diptych, a camouflage-clad relative in the bottom center of the present-day panel serving suggestively as an Iraq war analogue of the brother-soldier's portrait on the side table above.

The third cover, "Family" (fig. 7.3), charts the intersection of these two narratives, the disaffected daughter of the second family singing the praises of the old man's "emo" quality ("No, seriously—you have to check that guy out! He is so EMO . . . DUDE YOU ARE SO EMO!") as she passes him in the park outside their home.[10] In doing so, she mistakes his very real melancholy as

"No, seriously—you have to check that guy out! He is so EMO …
DUDE! YOU ARE SO EMO!"

Fig. 7.3 The disaffected daughter of the second family in "Conversation" shouts at the old man in "Stuffing." Chris Ware, "Family," 2006. Reproduced by permission from Ware 2007, n.p.

Fig. 7.4 The imminent demise of Penrod the pigeon. Chris Ware, "Main Course," 2006. Reproduced by permission from Ware 2007, n.p.

an affectation of despondency cultivated by contemporary teens. It is also a misrecognition of their connections, the dramatic irony allowing the astute reader to acknowledge that they share a common experience in the same apartment that transcends their generational differences, a common experience neither character can begin to recognize.[11] A similar flattening takes place elsewhere on this cover in the comparison of her suffering, being subjected to her mother's non-vegan stuffing ("I mean, I TOLD her not to use butter in the stuffing . . . She has absolutely no respect for me or my political beliefs!"), with that of slavery ("Well, at least we can be thankful there's no slavery anymore, right? I mean, that, like, totally sucked."). Such professions of hyperbolic teen-age angst signal the development of her story as an occlusion of the nascent political critique of the series, shifting instead to the more trivial, everyday concerns of disaffected youth. Her voice is manifestly one that seeks to undo the contemplative mood established with respect to the old man, vying with him for the emotional and hermeneutic center of the entire sequence.

As such, the reader can begin to detect a pattern throughout "Thanksgiving": the establishing of a somber storyline—one of loss, loneliness, and human alienation that elevates comics to such serious subject matter—and its subsequent interruption and lessening in nearly the same stroke. These

Fig. 7.5 The brother's letter arrives after his death, illustrated with the comics he had forsaken as a child. Chris Ware, "Leftovers," 2006. Reproduced by permission from Ware 2007, n.p.

two forces are represented broadly by the two major characters: the old man and the teenager, respectively. This self-disruptive quality characterizes not only the content, but also the form of much of Ware's work, from his earliest comics for *The Daily Texan* during his college days, where characters have the ability to manipulate the panels into which they are drawn, to his 2000 novel *Jimmy Corrigan*, where its multigenerational storyline abruptly gives way to cut-out dioramas, instructions to the reader, and other extradiegetic interruptions. These disruptions bring into question or disallow the long-form, richly developed storylines aspired toward in contemporary graphic narratives, undercut as they are with the more insensate, adolescent energies conventionally associated with comics.

This pattern is magnified to an almost sublime (or sublimely ridiculous) level in the fourth cover in the sequence, "Main Course," which penetrates the consciousness of the pigeons pictured in the previous three covers. Ware slyly signals this thematic, tonal, and metatextual shift in the previous comic by leaving a copy of *The New Yorker* on the apartment's side table that turns out to be the very issue of the magazine represented in this final cover. Indeed, if the movement of the narrative up until this point has been one of increasing interiorization, unfolding narratives, and interconnections between characters by way of an increasingly magnified and sensitive vision, this final gesture holds that vision up to a kind of ridicule. It is a narrative of Penrod the hen-pecked, nebbish pigeon, forced to forage for food on Thanksgiving Day despite his misgivings that the historical violence done to turkeys on the holiday might spill over to all birdkind. Played for laughs, Penrod's fears are nonetheless confirmed in the final panel, when it seems imminent that he will be run down by what is presumably the old man's car (fig. 7.4), his narrative serving as a mise-en-abyme for the sequence's larger leitmotifs.

By acceding more readily to the expectations of comics as they are conventionally understood, "Main Course" ironizes and confronts the barriers that have been traditionally erected to dissociate comics from high cultural prestige. Noted comics theorist Thierry Groensteen has outlined these obstacles, describing what he terms a "four-fold symbolic handicap":

> 1° [Comic art] is a hybrid, the result of crossbreeding between text and image; 2° Its story-telling ambitions seem to remain on the level of a sub-literature; 3° It has connections to a common and inferior branch of visual art, that of caricature; 4° Even though they are now frequently intended for adults, comics propose nothing other than a return to childhood (Groensteen 2000, 35).

All are characteristic of this fourth cover, in opposition to the previous three. "Main Course" most fully integrates image and text, appearing most recognizably as a comic strip. It emphasizes a more caricatural style, both in its iconographic, starkly rendered forms and in its antic humor that draws on para-literary genres such as sitcoms and vaudeville for its social commentaries (particularly its two-dimensional representation of gender). Indeed, some of Ware's most direct commentaries on the high art tradition—his condensation of art history from cave drawings to postmodernism, "Our History of Art" (originally composed for his inclusion in the 2002 Whitney Biennial), as well as his brief history of literary influence from Homer to Joyce (a cover illustration for *Virginia Quarterly Review*'s "Writers on Writers" special issue)—are rendered in similarly caricatural stick figures, the purported seriousness of the subject deflated by the droll jocularity of the style (Ware 2005, 6–9; Ware 2006b). Penrod's name also derives from a popular cultural source, Booth Tarkington's eponymous collection of boys' stories (as evidenced by the reproduction of the cover of Tarkington's *Penrod* in the vast grid of "Leftovers"), one that, like comics themselves, anticipates a youth audience. As such, these allusions purposefully cut across the otherwise high literary references in "Thanksgiving," including everything from Tolstoy to Chaucer's story of Chanticleer in the *Nun's Priest's Tale*.

Taken together, the premium placed here on authorly innovation and readerly expectations in these four comics, combined with the ambivalence to contemporary culture, all signal classically modernist concerns. Ware's very title, *The ACME Novelty Library*, represents two high modernist anxieties simultaneously: the gesture toward radical originality that is itself a conspicuous archaism (in this case of the palette and line of earlier twentieth-century and Golden-Age-era comics) and the false promises of commercialism in those same comics. Ware ruthlessly parodies capitalist consumption in a series of fake advertisements in *The ACME Novelty Library*, selling such lugubriously titled merchandise as "Success Brand Snort" and "Genuine Smile." An ongoing feature of Ware's is "Tales of Tomorrow," which imagines a future world defined entirely by advertising culture, its citizens' daily routine comprised of navigating a shimmering, unredeemable consumer culture in a perpetual state of buyer's remorse (Ware 2005, 9, 76, 78, 84, 86, 91–93). Above all else, Ware directs his satirical ire toward this accelerated promise that meaningfulness can be purchased on the cheap in the modern age. More so than his relationship to literary or art historical forebears, it is this deep suspicion of commercially available, success-oriented commodity capitalism that aligns his work in a recognizably modernist trajectory (for other important critical considerations of Ware in terms of modernism, see Prager 2003; Worden 2006).

At the same time, I would argue that Ware, like many modernists before him, recognizes that such an austere distance from commodity culture is impossible. The very engine of Ware's characteristically fragmented and conspicuously difficult narrative in "Thanksgiving," the serial cover, is also a consummate marketing strategy. Long used by the comic book industry to boost sales—back issues of these original issues of *The New Yorker* sold out in days—Ware's serial covers generate consumerism in their very critique of its practice. Repackaging this narrative as #18½ of *The ACME Novelty Library*, Ware also reissued these covers in two differing editions, "Lower East Side," a widely available folio of the four covers, and "Upper East Side," a limited and signed edition that includes a reproduction of Ware's sketchbook notes during the composition of the "Thanksgiving" series. In a label on the inside cover of the "Lower East Side" edition, Ware writes:

> An outrageously expensive edition of this folio in a limited, unfolded impression of 175 with hardcover covers and a facsimile reproduction of the author's tepid notes and doodles subsequently signed and possibly further defaced by said author himself {i.e., the "Upper East Side" model} is available to interested exclusive parties and nominated individuals willing to pay for the privilege of handling sheets of paper upon which flakes of skin, essential epidermal oils, or perhaps even DNA from the corpus of its artist have briefly made abrasion or even permanent affiliation. Interested parties will please consult thenewyorkerstore.com for further details.[12]

In doing so, he acknowledges, however parodically, the voracious appetites of the comics collector, and the mass-market economic forces of the comics industry more generally, generating the very consumerist tendencies his comics criticize so relentlessly. Treating the author's body as a reliquary and deploying the language of real estate sales (one all too familiar to the stereotypically monied and leisured reader of *The New Yorker*), these paratextual claims codify literary value as a function of collectability. In almost Hegelian fashion, the felt presence of commerce is simultaneously preserved and annulled, the coterie audience so prized by the modernist impulse at the same time revealed to be a symptom of an all-embracing consumer culture.[13]

The same could be said for Ware's equally acute ambivalence for comics as a medium, which he has described as a "woefully underdeveloped and commercially handicapped narrative form" (Ware 2006a, 7). Indeed, for every exploration of a high-minded, literary theme, Ware's narratives ensure that those meditations are relentlessly undone. In the online supplement to the previous four covers, a vast composition entitled "Leftovers" offers the back story to the old man: the death of his brother in 1942, the news of which arrives immediately after the first Thanksgiving celebration pictured in "Conversation."

In the ironic reversal of the two titles—the most caricatural and seemingly unrelated composition titled "Main Course," and the most ambitious titled "Leftovers"—Ware signals his characteristic rhetoric of failure, one that persistently inflects his stated goal to write comics with the texture, depth, and sophistication of literary fiction (Ware n.d.). Comics figure centrally as a self-referential motif in this composition, which is an intricate and beautiful canvas that seeks to visualize and map the workings of the old man's memory. The reader learns that both brothers aspire to be comics artists, a dream cut short by the older brother "outgrowing" comics and enlisting in the military. Several panels of "Leftovers" are devoted to an abortive attempt they made together (in the vein of Shuster and Siegel and other comics creators) to script a comic book of their own, these incomplete pages serving as a testament to the brothers growing apart.

"Leftovers" concludes tragically with the older brother's death, a trauma the reader comes to understand as the cause of the old man's solitary meditation in "Stuffing." Struck by a jeep in a training accident, the brother's death seemingly confirms the tacit war commentary of the second cover, this final contemplation of the human costs of war an apparent ratification of the entire sequence's insistence on the perdurability of trauma and loss. Yet at almost the same stroke, Penrod's slapstick demise, his also being struck by a vehicle, anticipates and flattens the latter tragedy, the unwitting pigeon's death unwriting, to some degree, the tragic resonance of the sequence's end (fig. 7.5). All that remains of the brother at the conclusion of "Leftovers" is a letter that arrives after his death, one illustrated with the comics he had forsaken as a child. Both mute reminder of his loss and insignificant register of his life, these final caricatures are wholly incommensurate to the tragedy of his death. Comics are thus both the medium through which his life is so beautifully told and remembered, as well as the insufficient residue of that very life.

Resisting even this final word on the narrative of loss, however, Ware reanimates his world-weary teenager in the collected "Thanksgiving" folio in an epilogue titled "3mpir3stat3.jpg." In doing so, he continues to oscillate between his somber septuagenarian and his blithely uncaring teenager, between narratives of a literary texture and their subsequent unraveling. In the manner of "Leftovers," this final composition follows a day in her life, as recorded in her own voice as she updates her MySpace page. Again, her dialog undoes whatever pretension the comics sequence might have toward literariness. She writes, "**OMG** I am **so** xcited . . . today I discovered sugar-free pudding at only **35 cals** per cup && I am now like, feeling so good about myself," and several panels later, "I'm just so upset that my family has **no respect** for me or my personal space at **all!!** I mean is it really too much to ask?? && then they have to make everything so supremely **gross** by commenting on things that are **none of their fucking business, OK??!!** && if their [sic] reading this right now then they deserve it bcz this is **really** none of their business, understand??!! **NOYFB!!**" Clearly, the fickleness of her emotional state and

Fig. 7.6 The teenage girl takes a photograph of the Empire State Building on her cell phone for her MySpace page. Chris Ware, "3mpir3stat3.jpg," 2006. Reproduced by permission from Ware 2007, n.p.

her dialog punctuated with visible typographical errors and text-message contractions places into question whatever sympathy the reader might have for her presumed difficulties. The specific bone of contention in this passage is a cell phone picture she has taken of the Empire State Building, one complimented on by her father and reproduced on the recto of "3mpir3stat3.jpg." As the tone has shifted from the old man's heart-wrenching memories to the teenager's banal gripes, so too has the visual focus of this final composition shifted from his comics to her digital photos.

It is tempting to read this transition as an evacuation of meaning in the present day, a narrative of degeneration in everything from "family values" to the care, craft, and attention paid to contemporary visual media. Yet, allegories of authorship are present in both the old man's comics and the teenager's digital photos. Ware's finished comics incorporate both exquisitely hand-drawn compositions and digital coloring, a hybridity shrewdly alluded to in the image-within-an-image composition of the Empire State Building (fig. 7.6). In turn, this image was originally designed by Ware for the October 3, 2005, cover of *The New Yorker*, yet another intersection in Ware's history with the magazine and a powerful point of comparison between Ware's teenager and her creator.

As relentlessly as its narrator is held up to scorn, "3mpir3stat3.jpg" concludes with a quite genuine sense of loneliness and anomie, one shared with the old man in "Leftovers." "I am walking around in this house," writes the teenager, "feeling like a total ghost . . . like I died, or, (even better) like I'd never been born." The panels correspond with these sentiments, silently surveying the empty expanses of her apartment and the surrounding buildings, recalling the very first image of the sequence, "Stuffing." Indeed, despite the differences between them, these two characters are unexpectedly brought together in this final gesture. Ware's draft notes reveal his intention to bring these characters into a more proximate relationship with one another—"That is what I want to be, right there," she states in discarded dialog, "the lonely old pigeon guy . . . Where do I apply?"—her character going so far as to claim "I think I was a lonely old pigeon guy in another life."

Likewise, for all the self-flagellating doubts about the putative value of comics as the means of literary sophistication, these characters' proximity also calls into question those very doubts. The narrative of "3mpir3stat3.jpg" turns on the fate of an image: the teenager and Ware's rendition of the Empire State Building. Mortified though she is by her father's praise of her photograph, the comic suspends the reader's knowledge of whether or not the file is deleted at narrative's end, picturing a deletion prompt with the "save" function highlighted. The dialectic of preservation and annulment that is at the core of the entire "Thanksgiving" sequence comes to a head here, concluding with a final gesture toward the preservation of the image: the teenager continuing to snap photos in the comic's final panel. It is one of these pictures that presumably occupies the second half of the recto of "3mpir3stat3.jpg," a companion nightscape of the Empire State Building that stands alongside the imperiled original. For all of its missed connections and reversals, its ambivalence about the power of the comics medium as literature, "Thanksgiving" thus ends on a final note of possibility in the virtues of the visual.

This unwriting, this working at odds with itself, I argue, is the hallmark not only of Ware's work, but of an entire generation of graphic novelists who aspire to the status of literature. It is a rhetoric of failure, one of conspicuous difficulty and willed ambivalence learned from literary modernism and extending both its intellectual anxieties and intellectual rewards (see Ball for a more complete investigation of Ware's use of the rhetoric of failure). Early in his career, Ware stated in an interview: "If one wants to tell stories that have the richness of life, [comics'] vocabulary is extremely limited. It's like trying to use limericks to make literature" (Kidd 1997, 43). Acknowledging the tensions articulated here—between comics and literature, mass culture and high art—and the slipperiness of these very distinctions remains the linchpin for beginning to discuss the role of graphic narratives in the literary canon. Doing so will not only make important shifts to our understanding of comics as a vehicle for intellectual work, but will also place Chris Ware at the center of that renewed appreciation.

NOTES

I have benefited greatly from conversations and debates with students, colleagues, and friends about my interpretation of Ware's work, including audiences at Dickinson College, Princeton University, and the narrative fiction panel on the theme of "text and image" at the 2007 Modern Language Association conference. I am particularly indebted to my conversations with Martha Kuhlman, Elizabeth Lee, and Benjamin Widiss.

1. Nomenclature has proven a vexed question for comics/comix/graphic novel/graphic narrative scholars, as discussed in the introduction. Without going into exhaustive detail, "comics" is the preferred term by contemporary authors in the medium to distinguish their distinctive use of words and pictures presented in sequence to give the illusion of temporal and spatial progression. By the term "graphic narrative," I mean to indicate the recent trend of comics artists to produce comics with the weight and import of literary fiction, including much of the nonfictional and short-form work for which the term "graphic novel" proves overly narrow.

2. My focus here on Ware's import to literary history and periodization is not meant to discount the other disciplines with which his work makes important interventions: art history, architecture, American music, and so forth. For the full range of Ware's reach into these contiguous fields, see Ball and Kuhlman 2010.

3. The terms "modernism" and "postmodernism" have generated decades of critical debate and volumes of exegetical labors. My investment in these terms for the purposes of this essay is in tracing the American literary canon's shifting investment in popular cultural and mass media emanations. For a particularly lucid explanation of the modern/postmodern distinction, and its many complications, see Harvey 1990.

4. The most recent edition of *The Heath Anthology of American Literature* (Volume E Contemporary Period: 1945 to the Present) has followed suit, including graphic narratives by Spiegelman, Barry, Alison Bechdel, Joe Sacco, and Ware himself.

5. For the most part, the proximity between Herriman's work (and the early-twentieth-century corpus of American comics more generally) and the aesthetic and intellectual achievements of American modernism has gone largely unrecognized by both literary and comics scholars. An important exception to this critical neglect is Inge 1990, 41–57. Contemporary graphic novelists, however, have shown a keen and fanciful interest in revisiting these intersections. See Jason 2006; Bertozzi 2007.

6. Rudolph Dirks was not the only comics-author-cum-fine-artist in this period with reach into the emerging discourse of modernism. George Luks, another member of the ashcan school and author of *The Yellow Kid* (which was continued in Joseph Pulitzer's *The New York World* when Richard Outcault was hired by William Randolph Hearst's rival publication *The New York Journal*), also had works exhibited in the Armory Show of 1913. For the creative interplay between fine art and comics, see Zurier 2006, 181–245. Lyonel Feininger also straddled the two worlds of comics and artistic modernism, drawing the short-lived strips *The Kin-der Kids* and *Wee Willie Winkie's World* (in *The Chicago Tribune* between the years of 1906 and 1907), both of which are notable for a graphic experimentation that informed Feininger's artistic career. See the sections on Feininger in Carlin, Karasik, and Walker 2005, 37–41, 187–93.

7. Unless indicated otherwise, all quotations and figures are from this edition. Limitations of space and the cost of reproduction preclude reproducing this sequence in its entirety, and without this visual reference many of the claims I make here will lose their full force. As this volume is going to press, high-quality scans of these comics can also be seen at the "ACME Novelty Archive" website, an unofficial yet highly valuable treasure trove of Ware's work. See http://www.acmenoveltyarchive.org/item.php?item_no=556 [accessed 24 June 2008]. The entire series, minus "3mpir3stat3.jpg," has also been reprinted in Houghton Mifflin's *Best American Comics 2008*.

8. Ware himself has used Nabokov's interviews on literature as an analogue to his own theories of graphic composition. See the epigraphs to his introductory essay in *McSweeney's* #13.

9. See http://www.acmenoveltyarchive.org/item.php?item_no=316 [accessed 24 June 2008].

10. The most common etymology of "emo" is as a contraction for "emotional hardcore," a genre of brooding punk rock acts whose fans cultivate an introspective, angst-ridden aesthetic that conveys a similarly dissociative world view.

11. The focus on missed human connections, especially with respect to shared architectural spaces, can be said to be a leitmotif of Ware's entire oeuvre. *Jimmy Corrigan* turns at the end on the revelation, withheld from both the main characters and the inattentive reader, that the title character is genealogically related to the adopted daughter of his until-recently-absent father, a revelation that raises knotty questions of genealogy, race, and family history acknowledged only obliquely within the frame of the narrative. Similarly, Ware's novel-in-progress, "Building Stories"—published variously in the *Chicago Reader* (2002–2006), *The New York Times Magazine* (2005–2006), and *The ACME Novelty Library* #16 and 18—relates the interconnected lives of tenants in the same Chicago brownstone, yet refuses an acknowledgment of those connections to his characters.

12. Purchasers of "Upper East Side" are likewise reassured: "A 'street' version of this portfolio, in which the mass-produced images are carelessly folded and bent into a cardboard wrapper nowhere approaching the exquisite beauty and drawing room graciousness of this edition (to say nothing of being shrinkwrapped and made available to commoners in bookshops and kiosks with no eye toward protecting their patronage's investments or liquid assets) / {i.e., the 'Lower East Side' model} / is available to interested art students, layreaders and those who simply don't appreciate the finer things in life and whose interests are transitory, easily flummoxed or otherwise capricious."

13. That Ware's other novel-in-progress, "Rusty Brown," takes as its main characters two comics collectors indicates the degree of Ware's interest in laying bare the economic substrate of his chosen medium. See *The ACME Novelty Library* #16, 17, and 19. Ware himself is an avid and accomplished collector, the connections between his work and his collections serving as the organizing theme of his inclusion in the 2008 exhibition "ReSOURCE" at the Hite Art Institute of the University of Louisville. See Linn 2008.

WORKS CITED

Baetens, Jan, and Ari J. Blatt, eds. 2008. *Yale French Studies: Writing and the Image Today* 114.

Ball, David M. 2010. Chris Ware's Failures. In *The Comics of Chris Ware: Drawing Is a Way of Thinking*, ed. David M. Ball and Martha Kuhlman, n.pag. Jackson, MS: University Press of Mississippi.

Ball, David M. and Martha Kuhlman, eds. 2010. *The Comics of Chris Ware: Drawing Is a Way of Thinking*. Jackson, MS: University Press of Mississippi.

Bertozzi, Nick. 2007. *The Salon*. New York: St. Martin's Griffin.

Carlin, John, Paul Karasik, and Brian Walker, eds. 2005. *Masters of American Comics*. New Haven: Yale University Press.

Chute, Hillary. 2008. Comics as Literature? Reading Graphic Narrative. *PMLA* 123(2): 452–65.

Chute, Hillary, and Marianne DeKoven, eds. 2006. *Modern Fiction Studies Special Issue: Graphic Narrative* 52(4).

Clark, T. J. 2000. Origins of the Present Crisis. *New Left Review* 2: 85–96.

Cohen, Josh. 1998. *Spectacular Allegories: Postmodern American Writing and the Politics of Seeing*. London: Pluto Press.

Cummings, E. E. 2004. A Foreword to Krazy. In *Arguing Comics: Literary Masters on a Popular Medium*, ed. Jeet Heer and Kent Worchester, 30–34. Jackson, MS: University Press of Mississippi. Originally published in 1946.

Geyh, Paula, Fred G. Leebron, and Andrew Levy, eds. 1998. *Postmodern American Fiction: A Norton Anthology*. New York: W. W. Norton & Company.

Groensteen, Thierry. 2000. Why Are Comics Still in Search of Cultural Legitimization? Translated by Shirley Smolderen. In *Comics and Culture: Analytical and Theoretical Approaches to Comics*, ed. Anne Magnussen and Hans-Christian Christiansen, 29–41. Copenhagen: Museum Tusculanum Press.

Harvey, David. 1990. *The Condition of Postmodernity: An Enquiry into the Origins of Cultural Change*. London: Blackwell Publishing.

Inge, M. Thomas. 1990. *Comics as Culture*. Jackson, MS: University Press of Mississippi.

Jameson, Fredric. 1991. *Postmodernism, or, The Cultural Logic of Late Capitalism*. Durham, NC: Duke University Press.

Jason. 2006. *The Left Bank Gang*. Seattle: Fantagraphics.

Kidd, Chip. 1997. Please Don't Hate Him. *Print* 51(3): 42–49.

Linn, Bruce. 2008. *ReSOURCE: Artists Who Collect to Create or Inspire Their Work*. Hite Art Institute: University of Louisville.

Manghani, Sunil, Arthur Piper, and Jon Simons, eds. 2006. *Images: A Reader*. London: Sage Publications.

Mirzoeff, Nicholas, ed. 1998. *The Visual Culture Reader*. London and New York: Routledge.

North, Michael. 1999. *Reading 1922: A Return to the Scene of the Modern*. New York: Oxford University Press.

Prager, Brad. 2003. Modernism in the Contemporary Graphic Novel: Chris Ware and the Age of Mechanical Reproduction. *International Journal of Comic Art* 5(1): 195–213.

Seldes, Gilbert. 2004. *The Seven Lively Arts*. In *Arguing Comics: Literary Masters on a Popular Medium*, ed. Jeet Heer and Kent Worchester, 22–29. Jackson, MS: University Press of Mississippi. First published in 1924.

Stein, Gertrude. 1990. *The Autobiography of Alice B. Toklas*. New York: Vintage. First published in 1933.

Ware, Chris. N.d. *The New Yorker* Interview with Chris Ware. newyorker.com. http://downloads.newyorker.com/mp3/061127on_ware.mp3 [accessed 17 July 2008].

———. 2000. *Jimmy Corrigan: The Smartest Kid on Earth*. New York: Pantheon.

———. 2005. *The ACME Novelty Library: Our Report to Shareholders and Rainy Day Saturday Afternoon Fun Book*. New York: Pantheon.

———. 2006a. Richard McGuire and "Here": A Grateful Appreciation. *Comic Art* 8: 5–7.

———. 2006b. Cover illustration. *The Virginia Quarterly Review Special Issue: Writers on Writers*.

———. 2007. *The ACME Novelty Library* 18½. ["Thanksgiving"] Chicago: The ACME Novelty Library.

Ware, Chris, ed. 2004. *McSweeney's Quarterly Concern* 13.

Worden, Daniel. 2006. The Shameful Art: *McSweeney's Quarterly Concern*, Comics, and the Politics of Affect. *Modern Fiction Studies* 52(4): 891–917.

Zurier, Rebecca. 2006. *Picturing the City: Urban Vision and the Ashcan School*. Berkeley: University of California Press.

Interview

—JIM WOODRING

Jim Woodring was born in Los Angeles in 1952. His early work found print in various alternative publications such as *The Los Angeles Free Press*. During his time working in an LA animation studio, he self-published the first issue of *Jim* in 1980. This "illustrated autojournal" was a collection of images and comics that Woodring professes is based on the hallucinations of his childhood. The comics publisher Fantagraphics later published *Jim* as a comics magazine, the success of which led to Woodring leaving his job as an animator and becoming a full-time comics writer and artist. His work has since been printed in a variety of Fantagraphics comics, as well as in other publishers' comics, periodicals, and magazines, such as the *Kenyon Review*, *Heavy Metal*, and *World Art Magazine*.

Since 1991, his most notable creations have been the characters in his comic *Frank*. Frank inhabits a surreal and macabre world where parallel dimensions and physical laws bend and collapse, and a dramatic cast of animals, impossibly disfigured humans, and personifications of abstract concepts murder, eat, enslave, and love one another.

The following is a summary of an interview conducted by telephone on November 6, 2007.

Jim Woodring: Frank's world . . . is sort of a playground for simple forces and appetites . . . I like the image to come to me without explanation, sufficiently mysterious to inspire interest. I like the mystery, the struggle of bringing something into the light. The knowing that it means something without knowing what it means; that's the charge I want. That's what the best surrealism does. I like an image that harasses you a little bit, that worries you, tugs at you . . . *Frank*'s a simplified, vastly simplified to say the least, reflection of how I see the world. Even though the stories are easy to describe, what happens in them is open to interpretation. I'm astonished at what people see in *Frank*. Frequently they understand them, or see obvious messages in them, better than I do. I love a mystery. If the meaning of a story comes to me while I'm writing it I will usually abandon it as too obvious. If I have to understand, let the understanding come when the thing is finished. There are some stories I still don't understand, thank God.

Paul Williams: I wonder whether *Frank* attracts interpretations like a Rorschach blot?

JW: Oh definitely. There's a DVD of animations by Japanese animators [*Visions of Frank*, 2005]. And they have all made changes in the storylines, and one assumes these changes reflect their own interpretations of the stories and their own feelings about them; I like that.

PW: You seem very at ease with other creative people coming along and taking these characters and making them play out what they see in them.

JW: Completely. It makes me feel good and sort of proud that some people get so much out of Frank.

PW: Do you think *Frank* could be a suitable text to be studied in schools or universities? Is this something you've come across before?

JW: *Frank* stories have been used as subjects of study in some college courses, and not only in the context of comics study, or so I've been told. There have been some papers written on *Frank*, and at least one Master's thesis. I have a copy of it but I've never been able to bring myself to read it. Actually I haven't read most of the articles and reviews of *Frank* that I've collected. It sort of gets to me, seeing evidence that people are taking *Frank* that seriously.

But you know I have to say that these stories do express things that are very meaningful to me. I think there are concepts in those stories worth contemplating and discussing, though personally I would prefer to discuss them outside the context of *Frank*. Spiritual and personal forces and whatnot. I guess the question of whether or not they should be studied in school is settled by whether or not they *are* studied in school.

PW: In December 2006, you were awarded a United States Artists Fellowship: nearly a year on, has that award changed the way you look at your work? Generally, do you think awards and things like that change one's status within the comic industry?

JW: It hasn't changed the way I look at my work. It's an honor, obviously, but more importantly it's money. I can't really tell you how I make a living. I work, and the money comes from somewhere, from art sales, licensing, royalties, and the occasional windfall.

Being a USA Fellow hasn't affected my professional life, as far as fans and fellow creators are concerned. All they care about is whether the work—anyone's work—is good. Generally speaking prizes and honors help the individual recipients hook up with larger opportunities in the outside world . . . movie deals, lecture tours, that sort of thing.

PW: Are there other ways in which you recognize your work being acknowledged? Do you go into comic book stores, and if you do, do you look for where *Frank* is positioned and think about where your work sits within the industry?

JW: You know, when I set out to be an artist and tried to determine what I wanted to accomplish, I set my sights rather low. I wanted to be a cult artist, with a small but enthusiastic audience. Most of the artists I've loved have been intense individuals whose work had a limited but powerful appeal... Alfred Jarry rather than Hemingway. I guess I've succeeded at that. I have a small audience but they really get it. Letters and notes from these people are what make me feel I've done what I wanted. That and original art sales.

I don't know if you know the British television series *The I.T. Crowd* but the room where the geeks live is decorated with *Frank* posters and toys, among other cartoon ephemera. Chosen for their cult appeal, I guess. That sort of thing does give me a thrill. I have heard about things like someone going around Dublin stenciling Frank on walls; I guess I enjoy that sense that the work is out there.

I don't go into comic book stores very often, but I do look for whether they have my books, and they often aren't there. If they are, they are usually in the grim little corner most comics shops have reserved for "alternative comics."

I occupy exactly the niche I set out to: the cult artist.

PW: Do you think that the way the media looks at comic creators has changed since you have been working in the medium? Do you think this will remain constant?

JW: Boy, that's a good question. During the 1990s, we were all asking when would comics get the recognition they deserve? People were doing all this great work, and there was a cliché that every time an article on a good comic book came out the headline would be "Zap! Pow! Comics aren't for kids any more!" That was the sort of recognition they received. Comics were not being reviewed in *The New York Times*, they were not being taken seriously outside the comics field, except for *Maus* and maybe *Watchmen* and *Dark Knight*.

That's changed now: *The New York Times* does review collections of comics. Comics are seen as a type of literature, they are well represented in bookstores. Chris Ware was the one who made comics become prestigious as beautiful objects that could also be read. Right at the moment there is a glut of beautiful-looking new cartoon books, all thanks to Chris Ware.

I'm guessing that having become so established, comics, or graphic novels if you want to call them that, are here to stay as permanently as humor books and art books.

PW: Increasingly it seems that comic series are being released as graphic novels exclusively because that makes more financial sense than being distributed as a finite series of individual comic issues first. Do you think the fact that the graphic novel has become the dominant outlet for some of the most interesting comics will have a knock-on effect for the kinds of comics being produced?

JW: I think there is a growing resentment among comics readers of series that are designed to come out as pamphlets and are later collected into one book. People often skip the pamphlets and wait for the inevitable collection, and who can blame them? But it's tough on the cartoonist who has to somehow make a living while working for half a year on a single book which will not likely compensate them in sales revenue.

Most of the most prestigious graphic novels—I dislike that term—have been long and somewhat gloomy realist stories. I think some people set out to emulate that. Personally I seldom see new comics I am interested in: even though I am attracted by the handsomeness of the books on the shelf, the actual stories seldom capture my attention. I think comics haven't necessarily gotten better, they just look better on the shelf. Will great comics live like literature does? Cartoonists tend to be swallowed up by the sands of time.

PW: That's really interesting because as part of this "graphic novelization" of comics it is almost as if the archive is being brought to the surface: there is a lot of very lavish editions of certain key creators, especially key comic strip creators. Do you have a sense that there is an established body of "greats" that is solidifying, and that some creators are being left out of that story of comics in the twentieth century?

JW: I think there is always a large body of established greats. That they are obscure doesn't eradicate them. Lovers of cartoons will always find out about the great ones—Herriman, McCay, Segar, Barks, all those guys—even though they may be hard to find. Right now there seems to be a push to beatify Frank King for *Gasoline Alley*. There's a huge new collection of his Sunday pages. They're beautiful and they deserve to be preserved, but there is something deflating about it for me, as if this childhood pleasure were being taken from me and priced beyond my means, which it has.

PW: OK. You did mention that there are some creators you think are doing really good work that don't get recognized at the moment.

JW: Well, for example, Kim Deitch. He should be a lot more popular. Really, though, I feel the marketplace is the final arbiter. A lot of what I consider great work goes underappreciated, but there's usually a discernable reason for that. Some things are just too rarefied to be understood by everyone, like *Krazy Kat*. Some are too rough, like Ivan Brunetti's *Schizo*. I love Brunetti's work and I feel the world would be a better place if it were better appreciated, but I can see why it isn't.

PW: It's really interesting you should mention Kim Deitch, because he is someone whose work comic academics have been interested in (see Gardner 2006). And someone like Chris Ware, who is swallowing up a lot of attention in universities. Academics are writing about comics more than ever, and talking to people at conferences, there's a general feeling that sometime in the next five years [in the UK] we will see masters' degrees in comics, and we will see dedicated courses within undergraduate degree programs on the graphic novel. The history of comics often seems to have—you mentioned it before—its "next big thing" moment, that this is it, we're finally through the door to cultural acceptance—and as soon as you're through the door there is another one ten yards up the road. It will be interesting to see whether comic scholarship will do the same thing: a motley collection of scholars say in five years' time they'll be courses on comics, but will there be courses on comics? Or just a cycle of anticipation that is built in [to the study of the medium]?

JW: That is interesting. Are you aware of the controversy over David Hockney's suggestion that the Dutch Masters must have used optical projections?

PW: No, no I have to say I'm not.

JW: He wrote this book [*Secret Knowledge*, 2001] saying that he believes that European painters began using optical devices in the fifteenth century, which is when really photographic-looking art began to appear. The invention of optical drawing aids corresponds to a change in European painting [contro-versially, Hockney proposed that Jan van Eyck used optical devices to pro-duce *Portrait of Arnolfini and His Wife* in 1434].

This has started an academic firestorm and a lot of back- and-forth debates, arguments, and recriminations. But almost every artist I have talked to feels Hockney's interpretation has some credence to it: "Oh yeah, something hap-pened there." I feel the same way, but I can't defend this argument in the intel-lectual arena because I don't back up my impressions with scholarly research. But I trust my feelings as an artist more than I trust the clinical evidence that seems to refute Hockney.

I mention this because something similar happens with the over-intellec-tualization of comics. I think that the uninformed opinion of a practitioner can have a kind of validity that an impartial researcher can't reach. Some-times you don't get closer to the center of something the more you dissect it into tiny, tiny pieces. I can see students being turned off comics by having to delve into Scott McCloud's *Understanding Comics*, which is a fun read for people who already understand comics but which I think can bewilder and frustrate people for whom it is an introduction to the form.

Have you seen Ivan Brunetti's book on comics [*Cartooning: Philosophy and Practice*, 2007]? One of the things he says is that in order to be a good cartoon-ist you should be an interesting person with interesting things to say. It's self-evident but it needs to be stated. He also says you can destroy your work by being too professional. Brunetti's book on comics should be a "classroom standard."

PW: You have produced drawings for advertising agencies, PR companies, student films, animation studios, CD covers, as well as self-publishing. Do you need to swap heads for these roles, to use a *Frank*-style metaphor, or are there continuities in how you approach your various projects?
JW: At best there are continuities. I have done projects that required me to do things that I've never done before, and that required thinking in different ways that were alien to me, but that was when I was struggling to survive and would take any paying job that would allow me to draw. That's sort of in a dif-ferent category. Generally speaking, I won't do commercial artwork unless it's something I'm comfortable with and I can do exactly what I want. I'm no good at bringing someone else's vision into being.

PW: It does strike me that an enormous amount of comic book artists work-ing today, as it has been throughout the history of American comics, not many artists can afford "just" to be comic artists. The comic work they do is a real balancing act between what they want to do and what pays the rent.

JW: That's true. Making a living doing comics isn't easy. During the 1990s I'd spend three or four months doing a comic book and get fifteen hundred dollars for it. Real income had to be generated in other ways. I was lucky enough to get other jobs. We were able to hang on to our house by the skin of our teeth.

PW: There are not many cultural media where an artist might see his work being reviewed in *The New York Times* and still have to sell things just to pay the bills. Do you think comics are being read and reviewed like never before, but the economic status of creators is still pretty dire?

JW: Well, I get the feeling that cartoonists are finding it easier to make money now because there are more opportunities. Partially because of the academic interest, people can work around the country, they can give lectures; also they're in demand as minor celebrities. They can teach.

PW: So the renewed public status of comics does have a beneficial knock-on effect in that sense?

JW: Oh I think so.

PW: In an interview, you have said that it is "difficult to do high-falutin' stuff" in comics. "The best ones are the ones that 'say something' almost inadvertently." (Qtd. in Lanier n.d.)

JW: I do believe that. I think, take almost any comic strip that was popular in America between the 1930s to the 1950s, they were not "high-falutin"; they were the most populist kind of unpretentious slapstick. *Krazy Kat* got away with being poetic because that aspect was swaddled in daffiness. The original art had no value; it was thrown away.

The more grandiose comics, like *Little Nemo* or *Prince Valiant* are great achievements and it's wonderful that they were in the funny papers... but they both have a grandiosity that for me slightly mitigates their appeal as comics. Or Lyonel Feininger's *The Kin-der-Kids*, it's good, it's enjoyable, but it doesn't have that raw, yeasty, fun feeling you get in comics like, you know, *Krazy Kat* or *Moon Mullins* or *Bringing Up Father* or any of them.

PW: At the same time, some of the most well-known comics explicitly address the "big events"—the "high-falutin'" stuff. Do you think that sets out in advance who is going to read those comics?

JW: Well, firstly, could you name a few?

PW: *Maus* would be one example; *From Hell*; in some ways, *Jimmy Corrigan*.
JW: Well, those are "graphic novels." No, you have me there. I just have prejudices, I guess. There's something ironic about a big weighty slog of a comic book. And in many of them the cartooning is not very engaging. But I can't say a word against such achievements. I just have prejudices.

R. Crumb manages to be heavy and frolicsome at the same time.

PW: Do you think he's more appreciated by cartoonists and comic creators than comic readers more generally?
JW: Yeah. It's appalling how many comics enthusiasts don't know or care to know about R. Crumb.

I think books like *Persepolis* are going to appear more and more. Historically relevant personal accounts. Joe Sacco is a pioneer. There will always be an interest in that sort of thing. People will buy those books because of what they are about. If *Maus* had been about something other than the Holocaust, how successful would it have been?

PW: You talked about *Gasoline Alley*—
JW: *Gasoline Alley* is a great comic, and it has been rescued from obscurity in these beautiful new books. That's obviously a good thing, but somehow I still feel a bit deflated by the sumptuousness and costliness of those books.

PW: I can see that. It is strips like *Gasoline Alley*, *Krazy Kat*, and *Peanuts*, as soon as they get packaged in deluxe editions, you can't look at them in the same way, I think.
JW: Yeah. Comics are best enjoyed in their modesty and humility. A private joy. There is a pleasure in finding large pleasure in small things, and now, you know, you're shelling out a lot of money for these editions and the expectation is that much greater.

PW: That "pleasure in finding large pleasure in small things," in comics that used to be a profound part of the experience. They weren't in Borders, they were something you had to make a trip to the comic shop to see, or something you had to root around for, and as that changes maybe the pleasures we find in them changes too.
JW: Right. Pamphlet comics are disappearing and being replaced by $30 books. On the other hand this has revitalized the industry—and brought new levels of whining! Right now we've got what we wanted.

It was hard to imagine comics would come to be seen as a fine art form. Take Gilbert Hernandez and *Love and Rockets*. Back in the 1980s, it was mostly known to people who considered themselves in on something special and only they knew about it, not everyone did. People saw the Hernandez brothers filling magazines with fantastic work and I think cartoonists wanted to emulate their ability and artistic achievement. Now comic creators give lectures and talks, receive prizes, they are lionized and are enjoying rewards that are more like those successful fine artists have traditionally enjoyed. Young cartoonists think comics come with all these trappings, like gallery shows and trendy magazine articles. Years ago, people got into cartooning because they liked comics, and they thought they might have a knack for drawing them; I think there are new attractions now . . . the legitimization of comics is something that a lot of us have been hoping and working for for years, and I for one wasn't at all sure it would ever happen. In hindsight it seems inevitable that such a great medium would take its place in the real world. But will comics ever be the freewheeling, disposable, populist outbursts of creativity they once were? I doubt it.

WORKS CITED

Brunetti, Ivan. 2007. *Cartooning: Philosophy and Practice.* Booklet accompanying the journal *Comic Art* 9.

Gardner, Jared. 2006. Archives, Collectors, and the New Media Work of Comics. *Modern Fiction Studies* 52(4): 787–806.

Hockney, David. 2006. *Secret Knowledge: Rediscovering the Lost Techniques of the Old Masters.* London: Thames & Hudson. Originally published in 2001.

Lanier, Chris. N.d. Comics and the "Fine Art" Shuffle. *Chrislanier.com.* http://www .chrislanier.com/yerba_big.jpg [accessed 11 Nov. 2007].

Visions of Frank. 2005. Various directors. DVD. Presspop.

IV: Creative Difference: Comics Creators and Identity Politics

CHAPTER EIGHT

Questions of "Contemporary Women's Comics"

—PAUL WILLIAMS

In the graphic novel *The Sandman: A Game of You* (published as an edited collection in 1993), a young female character—provocatively named Barbie—ventures into a comic book store, where the adolescent male inhabitants stop to stare at her. When Barbie brings her purchase to the till she recounts, "There was a big *greasy guy* behind the counter who seemed *really* amused that I was like, female, and asking for this comic. He said it *wasn't* very collectable. Then he said they didn't normally see breasts as *small* as mine in his store, and all these guys laughed."

To start to appreciate the full meaning of this fictional incident depends upon understanding two related stereotypes surrounding comic texts and readership: first, that comics are dominated by the superhero genre, and women in this genre usually come with unfeasibly distorted anatomical features; second, as a "real" woman and not a fantastically large-breasted character, this female reader is out of place in the masculine realm of the comics store, whose "natural" denizens are the socially inept male readers of superhero comics. The writer of this scene, Neil Gaiman, understands there is dark humor in this unpleasant exchange; unfortunately, much of it is the rueful smirk of recognition. The popular *The Sandman* series was read by demographic groups askew to the adolescent male readership assumed in *A Game of You*, but this scene depends upon the assumption that comics, superheroes, and male readers are firmly interlinked for its humor (and its depiction of exclusion pivoting around gender) to work (Sabin 1996, 168).

In showing how women's comics form part of the field of contemporary North American comics, this chapter challenges such assumptions, and equally important, it illustrates that women's comics are not a radical innovation: they exist on a historical continuum of women's comics going back to the 1930s. However, this compels greater critical attention rather than finalizing "once and for all" the place of women's comics in the industry's history. The three questions structuring this chapter pick at the term "contemporary women's comics" and indicate the complexity of approaching comics creators and readers with the framework of gender: how "contemporary" are "contemporary women's comics"? Who are the "women" in "contemporary women's comics"? What are the material forms of these "contemporary women's comics" and how do different material forms imply certain reading communities?

The importance of these questions is as follows: they are not only relevant to contemporary women's comics but they encapsulate tensions in the field of North American comics more generally. This demonstrates the centrality of women's comics within contemporary comics culture, not as a peripheral presence to be "bolted on" to an understanding of the medium in a fallaciously inclusive gesture. In defining the terms of that centrality we begin to reevaluate our (invisibly male-centered) paradigm for comics history and the constitution of "women's comics" within that history (see related discussions in art history in Pollock 1988, 8–9). The icons and themes of women's comics in the early to mid-twentieth century have often been revisited since the 1980s, and a genealogy of comics articulating feminist political positions is outlined in the first section of this chapter.

In the 1970s, the political project of the women's movement could be discerned in the academic study of other forms of visual culture. John Berger's theorization of the gendering of spectatorship in *Ways of Seeing* (1972) was an early move in bringing the insights of feminism into the field of art history, a conjunction that percolated through the decade (Pollock 1988, 1–17). In film studies, Laura Mulvey's article, "Visual Pleasure and Narrative Cinema" (1975), became a foundational text in the critical interrogation of classical narrative cinema as offering a masculine heterosexual gaze that frames women as objects of pleasure and spectacle for the voyeur peeping into the diegesis. Unsurprisingly, the women's comics of the 1970s were inspired by the same questions of gender, politics, and visual representation—unsurprising because feminism already "regarded ideas, language and images as crucial in shaping women's (and men's) lives" (Kuhn 1985, 2). Annette Kuhn cites the demonstrations staged against the Miss America contest in 1968, which feminists protested "on grounds that it promoted an impossible image of ideal womanhood, and was complicit in the widespread idea that all women—not only participants in beauty contests—are reducible to a set of bodily attributes" (3).

In the 1990s the marginality of certain women's comics was identified by certain readers as a sign of liberation from mainstream commercial culture and its dangerous and constrictive construction of feminine identities. The same decade saw changes in the publication, marketing, and reception of comics that placed some female comics creators in central positions of cultural currency and legitimacy. This divergence of opinion on where women's comics can and should sit in relation to the cultural "mainstream" (however understood) has led to a reconsideration of the notion that feminist comics must angrily challenge the representational traditions of a medium dominated by male creators. The essence of women's comics as expressive of the women's movement remains, but as this chapter shows, the nature of that relationship grows in its permutations.

HOW "CONTEMPORARY" ARE CONTEMPORARY WOMEN'S COMICS?

The identification of female comics readers (and their targeting as consumers willing to buy comics) goes back to the 1930s and the invention of the comic book. A unisex readership was assumed for the early comedy and cartoon franchise comics; newspaper strips aimed at girls and women were eventually marketed in their own titles, with *Little Orphan Annie* and *Little Lulu* two of the most popular (Sabin 1996, 84–86). The long-running comic book, *Archie*, featuring the humorous and romantic exploits of American teens, was not only successful among young female readers, but it generated over a dozen spin-offs, and numerous other publishers launched competing titles. The targeted young female readership of these particular humor titles, with their almost unrelenting emphasis on courtship rituals, is discernable in the cut-out fashions and advertisements for dresses they featured. Aimed at a slightly older teenage female readership (although hosting letters seemingly from young housewives), romance comics boomed in the late 1940s, where the thwarted or hard-fought amorous quests of young working-class women filled the pages (89–90).

Female characters were also present in comics genres marketed at male readers, such as the scantily clad white women adventurers epitomized by *Sheena, Queen of the Jungle* (Wright 2003, 36–39). Following the popularity of superheroes in the very late 1930s, *Wonder Woman* was created in 1941 by William Moulton Marston. Her initial period of spectacular sales coincided with the entry of female labor into traditionally male jobs in order to permit mass enlistment by men into the armed forces during World War Two. Marston's emancipatory attitude towards women was compressed into this popular female character: Lillian S. Robinson has observed Marston held an eccentric feminism "marked by a belief in women's essential moral superiority, combined with a demand for the equality of opportunity that would permit physical strength and social power to become feminine attributes alongside that superiority" (2004, 45). Writing in the *American Scholar*, Marston bemoaned that the "feminine archetype lacks force, strength, and power" (1943–44, 42), and *Wonder Woman* came with the caption "fighting fearlessly for downtrodden women and children, in a man-made world." Nonetheless, numerous critics have commented on the exploitative visual language of sexual fetish at work in *Wonder Woman*: "stories were rife with suggestive sadomasochistic images like bondage, masters and slaves, and men grovelling at the feet of women" (Wright 2003, 21; see also Sabin 1996, 88).

The female underground comix creators of the 1970s and 1980s were inspired by these million-selling comics. That heritage of female characters was evident from the anthology which began the women's comix movement, *It Ain't Me Babe*: Olive Oyl, Little Lulu, Wonder Woman, and Sheena march across the cover with their fists held up militantly. *It Ain't Me Babe* was originally an underground feminist magazine from 1970, featuring cartoon covers and comic strips. Later that year, the collective behind the newspaper produced a comix anthology under the same title, subtitled "Women's Liberation." In one strip, various female comics characters inferior or peripheral in their original publication contexts (Daisy Duck and Supergirl, for example) rise up against their male counterparts. The potential for women's liberation that Robinson reads into Wonder Woman was realized by those preexisting female characters appropriated in *It Ain't Me Babe*.

This comic was marshaled by one of the artists from the newspaper, Trina Robbins, a founding member of the Wimmen's Comix Collective in San Francisco in 1972. The anthology they produced, *Wimmen's Comix* (1972–1992), featured many influential female creators working into the twenty-first century: Robbins herself, Lee Marrs, Melinda Gebbie, Aline Kominsky, Diane Noomin, and Roberta Gregory. Another women's comix publishing company—Nanny Goat Productions—produced a series of anthologies, including *Tits & Clits* (1972–1987) and *Abortion Eve* (1973). As with the majority of underground comics from this era, these titles depicted countercultural practices ("free love" and illegal drug-taking, for example), frankly represented taboo subject matter (such as abortion), and were distributed and sold at a distance from the newsstands (through the mail and in the "head shops" selling psychedelic merchandise and drug paraphernalia) (Robbins 1999, 87–92).

Advancing the militancy of *It Ain't Me Babe*, the women on Gebbie's cover for *Wimmen's Comix* #7 (1976) brandish knives and shotguns as a man lies dead beneath them. While Kominsky and Noomin contributed to the early issues of *Wimmen's Comix*, Noomin recounts that her last contribution to the anthology for ten years was in 1974. Why?

> I think maybe the *Wimmin's Comix* Collective took the path that many women's or political collectives do over the years and became a hot-bed of bickering and power plays. Aline and I found ourselves on one side of a power play and we decided. "Well, fuck you, we'll do our own comic." Basically, we felt that our type of humor was self-deprecating and ironic and that what they were pushing for in the name of feminism and political correctness was a sort of self-aggrandizing and idealistic view of women as a super-race. We preferred to have our flaws and show them (Noomin 2004).

Consequently, Kominsky and Noomin started their own title in 1976, *Twisted Sisters*, whose unselfconscious autobiographical openness (the first issue featured Kominsky's depiction of herself on the toilet) was shared by the 1990s comics memoirists discussed in section three of this chapter.

Wimmin's Comix ceased publication with #17 (1992), citing apathy on behalf of retailers towards women's comix. "What a waste of time and energy. Forget it" (Qtd. in Robbins 1999, 115). However, women's comics appeared to have entered a new period in the early 1990s, partly a result of an elective affinity with a kindred movement in popular music. The last twenty years of women's comics exist in dialogue with the history of women's comics preceding it: for instance, a national organization, Friends of Lulu, formed in the 1990s to "increase female readership of comics" and "promote the work of women in comics" adopted Little Lulu as its mascot. This organization does not espouse the militant, sometimes anti-male sentiment of 1970s women's comix. Its goal, as expressed on the website, is an "expanded female reader base" contributing to greater comics sales. This particular "women's movement" in comics is working in the interests of the medium as whole by repositioning it back at the center of North American reading habits: in this instance a residual sense of women's comics' marginality coexists with an interpretation of women's comics as (potentially) a "mainstream" commercial product.

WHO ARE THE "WOMEN" IN CONTEMPORARY WOMEN'S COMICS?

Scrutinizing the class, ethnicity, and sexuality of the "women" it spoke for, feminism has complicated the assumption that "women" are a monolithic, homogeneous whole (see Rich 1998). This new orthodoxy in the academic feminist movement has generated its own reflexive positions. If the project of women's emancipation has absorbed the key criticism that the first-wave feminist movement was dominated (politically, at least) by white, middle-class heterosexual women, what (if anything) links localized sites of activism against sexism, misogyny, and the subordinate status of women?

Studying contemporary women's comics with these issues in mind, for many creators this localization of gender roles underpins their graphic narrative. This is partly because the field of reception in North America has absorbed international successes in women's comics, notably Marjane Satrapi's *Persepolis* (originally published in France between 2000 and 2003, and now on numerous university reading lists). Satrapi was born in Iran in 1969 and grew up in Tehran (experiences on which *Persepolis* is based), and currently lives in Paris. She has written for *The New York Times* and *The New Yorker*, and her graphic novel *Embroideries* (2005) visualizes Iranian women's conversations about their sex lives. In a society where women are pressured to remain chaste until marriage, these conversations include advice on how to fake one's virginity: social convention and the self-representation of the female body converge in a way neatly illustrating the localized nature of this issue.

In conjunction with Satrapi's outlining of the self-policing of female sexuality in Iran is her avowed commitment to a universal humanism contesting masculine-orientated cultural codes determining female actions. In the following example Satrapi's position is questioned by journalist Deborah Solomon who argues the prescriptions of female appearance in Tehran are more heinous than in New York:

> SOLOMON: Your books denounce Islamic fanaticism, particularly as it
>   curtails the rights of women. Is that your main theme?
> SATRAPI: Oh, no, not at all. I don't consider myself as a feminist but
>   more a humanist . . .
> SOLOMON: Still, in your work, you are constantly contrasting your love
>   of food, smoking and sensual pleasures with the acts of self-denial
>   demanded by the mullahs, like wearing a chador.
> SATRAPI: It's a problem for women no matter the religion or the society.
>   If in Muslim countries they try to cover the woman, in America they
>   try to make them look like a piece of meat.

SOLOMON: Are you suggesting that veiling and unveiling women are equally reductive? I disagree.

SATRAPI: We have to look at ourselves here [the USA] also. Why do all the women get plastic surgery? Why? Why? (Solomon 2007)

For Solomon not all inequalities are equal, but through Satrapi's humanist lens there can be no prioritizing of female humiliation. This chimes with a universal humanism whereby the degradation of any human being is intolerable, and any strategic targeting of inequality is unethical because it starts from a position of cultural difference where there is only essential humanness. Matching Satrapi's disinclination to see herself "as a feminist," in *Persepolis* her character tries to put into practice the theory of postwar French feminist existentialist Simone de Beauvoir: if women urinated standing up like men their perception of life would change. "It ran lightly down my left leg. It was a little disgusting." This unsuccessful experiment in feminist consciousness leads Satrapi to conclude she is not yet liberated. In this instance the bold promises of feminism lose out to the humbling nature of the female body.

Theresa M. Tensuan has argued that, like Satrapi in *Persepolis*, the American comics creator Lynda Barry in *One! Hundred! Demons!* (2002) depicts a version of her adolescent self moving from "immaturity" to "maturity," and consequently readers are able to discern the imposition of a normative framework of social order. Opening up the tensions that lie between the two states, Barry questions the social codes and communal assumptions that engender "limiting" roles, perhaps especially for women (Tensuan 2006, 954). Tensuan considers the short narrative of "Girlness" in *One! Hundred! Demons!* and its exploration of why Barry was a "tomboy" and not a "very girlish girl." Barry hypothesizes that the answer lies in environmental influences: "clothes, toys, and hair. The Girlish Girls had a lot of these things. Even their dolls had pretty clothes, teeny toys, and long, combable, fixable hair. If I had these things, would I have been a girlish girl too?"[1] This suggests that in Barry's work the construction of gender lies in the processes of acculturation that often remain invisible, whereas in this (admittedly slender) example from *Persepolis*, biological determinants are crucial and potentially limiting.

One of the most memorable female comics creators of the contemporary era, Julie Doucet self-published her notorious *Dirty Plotte* as a mini-comic in 1987 while she studied at art school in Montreal (it would be published full-size by Montreal's Drawn & Quarterly). Her choice of title continues the theme of the localization of the experience of gender difference: "plotte" is French slang for "cunt," and in *Dirty Plotte* Doucet explains how the word's meaning is anatomical and offensive—offensive when men in the street use it casually to refer to Doucet as a sexual organ to be ogled. Doucet's character tells the reader, "plotte is a very dirty word . . . . ." and to use this term in the title of her comic implies that she is unconcerned it will besmirch her propriety. Doucet draws herself in fishnet stockings held up with safety pins, skin covered by plasters and tattoos, with red lipstick and fingernail polish dripping onto her skin.

Instead of seeing the dirtiness of "plotte" as a marker of disrespectability she revels in the unashamed pleasure of slovenliness, offering a "dirty version" of herself in *Dirty Plotte*. This maneuver disarms the potentially shocking encounter in the street with men who would shout "plotte" in her vicinity to impose their sexual attention on her—she cannot be shocked by the word when she already wears it as a gleeful badge of (dis)honor. If this interpretation of Doucet's comics abstracts her work into academic theorization, a visceral reading of *Dirty Plotte* as a rejoinder to domineering masculine sexuality is suggested by the dripping red lipstick and nail polish—and the razor blade Doucet's character plays with around her neck. As Sabin observes, "Doucet's fondness for knives, scissors, and razors was guaranteed to provoke recessed testicles in male readers" (1996, 211).

As another approach to feminist comics in affect rather than the politics of female roles, the character of Bitchy Bitch in Roberta Gregory's *Naughty Bits* may fit certain personae advocated by the women's movement. Everyday life incenses Bitchy to the point of apoplectic rage: one could construct a feminist reading of Bitchy as a character gleefully rejecting the "Angel of the House" type embodying self-sacrifice, deference to male authority figures, and domestic servitude as the model for female behavior, embracing instead its monstrous polar opposite (see Gilbert and Gubar 1979, 76). Scornfully referring to publisher Fantagraphics's line of Eros erotic comics, Gregory draws (in a *Naughty Bits* comic published by Fantagraphics) herself opening a comic and being prodded in the eye by a mammary proboscis. She recollects: "Anyhow, back at Porno- I mean Fanta-graphics, I got stuck with workin' on a lot of that EROS sh . . . I mean 'material' . . . So. I did what I USUALLY do in this situation . . . COMICS! . . . something to make MEN feel as queasy as all this sexist GARBAGE makes WOMEN . . . " (Rpt. in Robbins 1999, 123). Rather than a feminist celebration of womanhood unrestrained by outdated conventions of meekness, in Gregory's account it was the sickening experience of being a female comics artist working on the "sexist GARBAGE" of erotic comics that fueled her desire to create a counter-aesthetic. The production of Bitchy Bitch comics is a direct response to facile comics pornography, intended to reverse the gender of the assumed reader, revealing in the process the implicit masculine audience of Fantagraphics's Eros line (and its corollary, the exclusion of women readers). Also at stake are issues of art, alienation, and labor discussed elsewhere in this collection.

Gregory presents herself as the production-line comic-book worker operating under intrusive editorial pressure as regards "material" in the production of commercial texts that Gregory-as-proletarian finds creatively unrewarding and seeks to distance herself from as producer. Writing and drawing Bitchy Bitch is specifically the efforts of a worker in the sex comics industry to redeem the labor that sickens her, efforts that take comic book form in order to address the particularly gendered terms with which this worker understands the degradation of their alienated productivity, shadowing the theoretical position of feminist art history that "art objects" are commodities aimed at specific (perhaps gendered) consumers making meaning in the context of social practices (Pollock 1988, 6–7).

Returning to the question that began this section—is there a shared political agenda across these comics? Satrapi shrugs off being identified as a "feminist," and further complicating the "women" in contemporary women's comics, some women's comics have male creators, such as Jaime and Gilbert Hernandez's series *Love and Rockets* (1981–present). Both Hernandez brothers consider the role of women in their respective societies. Taking an example from Jaime's story, "House of Raging Women," the situation of female wrestlers Rena Titañon and Pepper Martinez is an explicit analogy for the degrading manifestations of those gender roles. Pepper comments on the abuse they endure in the ring from male spectators: "Rena's had to put up with it her whole career. I'm sure she's heard worse . . . . All female grapplers are treated shitty, villain or not. I mean, haven't you ever been walking down the street and a carload of guys drives by and shouts all kinds of stupid, obnoxious shit?" The abuse Rena suffers in the ring is the microcosm of a society where women are under the constant public judgment and surveillance of men.

There *does* seem to be a recurrent trend of bearing witness and refusing to allow violence, words, and exclusions directed against women to remain invisible. Drawing the experience of these barriers and prohibitions, whether the creators are male or female, may make all of the above "women's comics," part of what feminist bell hooks has termed "an oppositional gaze. By courageously looking, we defiantly declared: 'Not only will I stare. I want my look to change reality'" (hooks 1992, 116). It may be overambitious to make too great a claim for the common ground of experience between female workers in the sex comic industry and in the wrestling business, between U.S., Latina, Iranian, and French-Canadian women, but all of these comics visualize how women face legal, religious, cultural, and economic barriers because of their gender and sexuality. Many of these comics also celebrate female creativity and the strategies of physical and psychic survival women have fostered. If one is to retain the idea of "women's comics" and their contribution to the women's movement, it would have to accommodate the role of these comics in that witnessing process.

CONTEMPORARY WOMEN'S *COMICS*?
FROM MINI-COMICS TO GRAPHIC NOVELS

Contemporary women's comics range from photocopied and stapled mini-comics to lavish hardcovers. Such varying modes of production have, in certain instances, welded women's comics to a specific feminist subculture: the Riot Grrrl movement. The Riot Grrrl scene provides a case study of how women's comics shared a *material* affiliation with other feminist cultural texts in the 1990s; that material affiliation was understood to have ideological implications for the coherence and self-definition of this version of feminism.

The Riot Grrrl movement began with the arrival of female punk bands Bikini Kill and Bratmobile in Washington, D.C., during the summer of 1991. Reacting to a punk scene dominated by an atmosphere of male exclusivity, they first defined themselves as "angry grrrl" bands, which mutated into *Riot Grrrl* for the title of the pocket-sized fanzine produced by Bratmobile members Allison Wolfe and Molly Neuman. The appellation stuck as this permutation of the women's movement spread out from D.C. in 1991: the fanzine led to a weekly forum for girls, as well as music tours, high school and college networks, Riot Grrrl chapters around the country, and in July 1992 D.C. was host to the Riot Grrrl Convention (Klein 1997, 213–14). In addition to the music, conventions, and meetings, the Riot Grrrl movement was articulated by a network of fanzines and alternative comics, and many female comics creators worked in both: Ariel Bordeaux produced a comic (*No Love Lost*) and a fanzine (*Deep Girl*) that typified—in Robbins's words—"the mildly depressing autobiographical genre so often found in women's and grrrlz's zines and comics" (1999, 125–27).

The Riot Grrrl fanzines praised women's comics such as *Dirty Plotte* and Diane DiMassa's *Hothead Paisan*. An overlap of theme is evident: Doucet's representation of street harassment discussed above was mirrored in the Riot Grrrl fanzines, punk songs, and discussion groups that discovered ways to disarm the "exasperating and degrading" sexual appraisal of women walking in public. Doucet's imaginative remedy seems to fit the Riot Grrrl refusal to dress conservatively: "We do not want to give up our freedom to walk anywhere or to wear what we like" (Klein 1997, 218). Doucet's surrealist solution did not make it irrelevant in a community where discussion and inventiveness were seen as components of feminist activism. Klein recalls, "Many girls discussed guerrilla tactics [to retaliate to street harassment], and even if we never carried them out, we felt better for thinking about them" (218).

Riot Grrrl fanzines and comics alike drew on the ethos of the punk music scene where the Do-It-Yourself attitude encouraged non-professional creators to produce texts in small print runs using standard office equipment such as photocopiers. Existing icons (such as Wonder Woman) were appropriated with scant regard for copyright law. The most significant distribution and sales networks for the fanzines and comics were mail order and specialist book and music shops. Many Riot Grrrl bands withheld their interviews from mainstream media channels, protesting "what they saw as a 'patriarchically [sic] constructed' commercial" system, instead talking exclusively to their fanzines (Triggs 2000, 34–36).

While Riot Grrrl originated in a popular music subculture, comics played a powerful role in cultivating the sense of a "micro-community of dissent," to paraphrase Teal Triggs (2000, 35). Like the fanzines, the comics circulated in material forms where, put simply, readers were forced to seek them out—they were not part of an entertainment industry exploiting every opportunity to sell publications to as great an audience as possible to maximize profits. The creators of the fanzines and comics repeatedly express how important it was that they offered a personal perspective on womanhood unqualified by the commercial imperative of avoiding offense and controversy.

British Riot Grrrl fanzine writer Angel wrote, "I see comics as a visual version of what fanzines write. It's about free expression and personal viewpoints" (Qtd. in Sabin and Triggs 2000, 104). This sense of the "personal" was key: autobiography, memoir and confessional narratives characterized the fanzines and comics, which—with their distribution and reception materially differentiated from "mainstream" comics and women's magazines—encouraged readers to see themselves as participants in a community of like-minded young women. In this community, readers' skepticism about the representation of women (for example) would be listened to by those who had similar questions of their own about gender roles in North American (and British) society (and indeed elsewhere in the world). As one fanzine producer describes: "The point IS that the zine provides a forum in which to have your ideas put into print and distributed across the country to people who actually give a dam [sic] about what you're saying" (Qtd. in Triggs 2000, 36).

In the early 1990s, the loosely autobiographical work of Jessica Abel was one (very successful) example of the kind of mini-comics being produced. An avowed feminist, Abel's covers for *Artbabe* repeatedly show the character of Artbabe looking straight at the reader. One effect of this is to prevent the reader from thinking they are spying unnoticed on Artbabe's life as she unknowingly amuses us (and Artbabe does not feature inside the comics that bear her name). As Angel summarizes about the audience for her own fanzines, she writes for girls "who want something to call their own, where they're not treated as male entertainment slaves" (Qtd. in Sabin and Triggs 2000, 102). Rejecting a feminine identity based on being visualized as an object of pleasure for men to gaze upon (Berger 1972, 47, 51), Artbabe returns the reader's gaze. The cover of *Artbabe* #4 (1995, when this title was self-published) features Artbabe flexing an impressive bicep, offering an alluring image because of the strength and autonomy she conveys.

As well as fanzine work, Abel published 50 copies of the first issue of *Artbabe*, which was self-published as a full-size, professionally printed comic in 1996 and then published by Fantagraphics in 1997. Abel is best known for her graphic novel *La Perdida* (serialized 2001–2005, published as a collection 2006) (Ishola 2007, 31; see also Robbins 1999, 127–28). Abel's comics have traversed the spectrum of materiality, and in 1999 *Artbabe* took the optimal format for mini-comic distribution, the "missive device." These were comics designed to be sealed and sent in the mail, published by the UK small press company Slab-O-Concrete, saving even the cost of packaging. *Artbabe* in "Pigskin vs. Paintbrush!" was printed in this format, with Artbabe on the cover looking wryly at the reader, dressed in an American Football uniform, and held aloft by male football players. For postal workers handling this missive device, the cover encapsulates the "straggle-haired" attraction of *Artbabe*, immersed in life as it unfolds, with a stylized and stylish take on the action—after all, "She puts the "arty" in "Party" (Sabin and Triggs 2000, 26).

It is notable that Abel's literary credentials are sufficiently established for her to be the subject of an individual "Artist Profile" in a special edition of *World Literature Today* dedicated to Graphic Literature, published in 2007 by the University of Oklahoma. Discussed elsewhere in this volume, the ascendancy of the graphic novel as a function of the publishing industry has entailed a continuing repackaging of comics writers and artists as creators of literature: Abel's selected works in her "Artist Profile" lists collections and self-contained graphic novels, not self-published comics or missive devices. The fanzines and mini-comics containing her work had a particular material existence (photocopied and stapled) and an informal means of circulation (such as through the mail). For many Riot Grrrl readers, their community was structured through publications defined by similar physical parameters of production and reception. Far from being seen as limitations, these material conditions contributed to the sense that members of the movement belonged to a privileged community where women could express a personal perspective on womanhood. The same material conditions fostered the belief that such perspectives were "truly" individual because they were not solely driven by commercial imperatives. Furthermore, when the comic and fanzine creators located their personal narratives in wider social issues concerning the construction of gender (and how destructive they can be), they believed they would find encouragement within their "micro-community of dissent."

These material conditions for producing comics worked in synthesis with a grassroots feminist movement, but mini-comics produced in small print runs are less suitable for undergraduate reading lists or bookshop shelves. As a material form suggesting literariness and the extended development of thematic and structural principles, Abel's graphic novels invoke a different kind of reading experience (unquestionably the convenience of having her earlier work in one place is an incentive for her fans to purchase comics they already own a second time). Her brief "Artist Profile" implies this, repackaging Abel as a feminist novelist (albeit one who works in graphic literature) whose work enjoys sophisticated literary status, where she shares journal space with tributes to Pulitzer Prize-winning writers.

CONCLUSION

Not least because of continuity of creators, contemporary women's comics have continued a close connection with the women's movement. To use its own lexicon, the Riot Grrrl scene claimed its marginality as an alternative to the patriarchal, commercially driven entertainment industry. But exhibits of evidence such as the academic legitimacy of Satrapi and Abel and the organization the Friends of Lulu indicate how women's comics might (and are willed to) be published and read as works of literature sold to paying customers from more diverse and expanding demographic groups than ever before. If Riot Grrrl's celebration of marginality was successor to the (sometime) anti-male sensibility of the underground women's comix, the feminism of the Friends of Lulu seems avowedly inclusive and seeking institutional "mainstream" popularity. As discussed above, this need not be watered-down feminism—contemporary women's comics remain important vehicles of witnessing the roles women are asked to adopt or the specific forms of abuse and restriction they face in localized situations because of their gender. Every term in the phrase "contemporary women's comics" is unstable, but running throughout is a commitment to visualizing the experiences of women.

A panel from Diane DiMassa's comic *Hothead Paisan* (subtitled *Homicidal Lesbian Terrorist*) provides a structuring analogy. In three separate outbursts, the eponymous character says "FEH" "MUH" "NIST" (Rpt. in Robbins 1999, 141). Like Hothead, the contemporary women's comics discussed here are part of a rephrasing of feminism, just as the self-identification of third-wave feminism implied that the late twentieth century had not seen the women's movement of the late 1960s and 1970s achieve its goals of equality between the genders—third-wave feminism elongated and sought to revivify the women's movement (Klein 1997, 207–8). As Hothead's phrasing suggests, sometimes refreshing a set of ideas that have become well known means defamiliarizing them, so at first glance one pays particular attention because they do not appear to relate to anything we thought we knew. This investment of attention reveals that these ideas—FEHMUHNISM—were ones we were acclimatized to all along, but spoken now in a different accent. In Julie Doucet's sleazy French-Canadian surrealism, Bitchy Bitch's unrestrained rage, and the Hernandez brothers' empathetic soap operas, contemporary women's comics offer many accents of feminism to solicit one's attention.

NOTES

1. Tensuan links Barry to Alison Bechdel for their shared use of marginal figures to understand how gender and sexuality are formulated under the pressure of social convention (2006, 951). Bechdel's graphic novel, *Fun Home: A Family Tragicomic* (2006), meditates on the suicide of her father, a closet gay, a few months after Alison's coming out.

WORKS CITED

Anon. 2002–08. The Friends of Lulu. *Friends of Lulu.* http://www.friends-lulu.org/index.php [accessed 25 July 2008].
Berger, John. 1972. *Ways of Seeing*. London: Penguin / BBC.

Chute, Hillary. 2006. An Interview with Alison Bechdel. *Modern Fiction Studies* 52(4): 1004–13.

Gilbert, Sandra M., and Susan Gubar. 1979. *The Madwoman in the Attic: The Woman Writer and the Nineteenth-Century Literary Imagination*. New Haven: Yale University Press.

hooks, bell. 1992. *Black Looks: Race and Representation*. Boston: South End Press.

Ishola, Olubunmi. 2007. Artist Profile: Jessica Abel. *World Literature Today* 81(2): 31.

Klein, Melissa. 1997. Duality and Redefinition: Young Feminism and the Alternative Music Community. In *Third Wave Agenda: Being Feminist, Doing Feminism*, ed. Leslie Heywood and Jennifer Drake, 207–25. Minneapolis: The University of Minnesota Press.

Kuhn, Annette. 1985. *The Power of the Image: Essays on Representation and Sexuality*. London: Routledge.

Marston, William Moulton. 1943–44. Why 100,000,000 Americans Read Comics. *American Scholar* 13: 35–44.

Mulvey, Laura. 1975. Visual Pleasure and Narrative Cinema. *Screen* 16(3): 6–18.

Noomin, Diane. 2004. Wimmin and Comix. *ImageTexT: Interdisciplinary Comics Studies* 1(2). http://www.english.ufl.edu/imagetext/archives/v1_2/noomin/index.shtml [accessed 16 Mar. 2009].

Pollock, Griselda. 1988. *Vision and Difference: Femininity, Feminism and Histories of Art*. London: Routledge.

Rich, Adrienne. 1998. Notes Toward a Politics of Location. In *Literary Theory: An Anthology*, ed. Julie Rivkin and Michael Ryan, 637–49. Oxford: Blackwell. Originally published in 1986.

Robbins, Trina. 1999. *Girls to Grrrlz: A History of Women's Comics from Teens to Zines*. San Francisco: Chronicle Books.

Robinson, Lillian S. 2004. *Wonder Women: Feminism and Superheroes*. New York: Routledge.

Sabin, Roger. 1996. *Comics, Comix & Graphic Novels*. London: Phaidon Press.

Sabin, Roger, and Teal Triggs, eds. [2000]. *Below Critical Radar: Fanzines and Alternative Comics from 1976 to now*. Hove: Slab-O-Concrete Publications.

Solomon, Deborah. 2007. Revolutionary Spirit: Interview with Marjane Satrapi. *The New York Times*. http://www.nytimes.com/2007/10/21/magazine/21wwwln-Q4-t .html?ref=magazine [accessed 1 Aug. 2008].

Tensuan, Theresa M. 2006. Comic Visions and Revisions in the Work of Lynda Barry and Marjane Satrapi. *Modern Fiction Studies* 52(4): 947–64.

Triggs, Teal. [2000]. Liberated Spaces: Identity Politics and Anti-Consumerism. In *Below Critical Radar: Fanzines and Alternative Comics from 1976 to now*, ed. Roger Sabin and Teal Triggs, 33–42. Hove: Slab-O-Concrete Publications.

Wright, Bradford W. 2003. *Comic Book Nation*. Rev. ed. Baltimore: The John Hopkins University Press.

CHAPTER NINE

Theorizing Sexuality in Comics

—JOE SUTLIFF SANDERS

The study of representations of sexuality—even specifically the study of *visual* representations of sexuality—is nothing new. Clustered mainly around refrains such as liberatory potential through psychoanalytic models (Laura Mulvey, Mary Ann Doane) or agendas of self-representation (Vito Russo, Emmanuel Cooper), scholarship on the visual representation of sexuality already enjoys a rich tradition. Within this broader field, writers in the comparatively new field of comics studies have quickly begun to borrow theoretical structures from other areas of media studies to explore the representation of sexuality in comics.

Two common structures are represented, for example, by Joseph W. Slade's division of smut comics according to the economic class of the comics' consumers (in *Pornography and Sexual Representation: A Reference Guide*, 2001) and the handy tradition—which I have used in my own work—of talking about sexuality in comics by emphasizing the sexual orientation of the comics' creators and characters. One of the many attractions of these familiar theoretical structures is how easily they transfer between comics studies and other literary and cultural studies models: an emphasis on class, sexual orientation, or liberation as the critical criterion of a study can be found in virtually any current volume of any journal in any field of the humanities.

Nonetheless, there is an approach to sexuality in comics that relies on theoretical structures indigenous to comics, an approach with greater sensitivity to the history of comics than would be likely in a theoretical model borrowed from elsewhere. A careful understanding of the *dialectical nature of American comics addressing sexuality*, of the series of revolutions against the status quo that appear throughout the history of American comics, will develop the potential for thinking about sexuality in comics through a structure that takes for granted the national specificity of its development. A sharp understanding of the mission of American comics about sexuality must take into account how comics creators have pushed off against the mainstream and then pushed off against the alternative as they conduct their explorations of sexuality. To that end, I want first to sketch the broader history of sexuality in American comics, then to articulate and demonstrate a theory of sexuality in comics that focuses on the ideological camps in the ongoing debate about sexuality in American comics.

HISTORICAL OVERVIEW

The earliest concerted movements in American comics to deal explicitly with sexuality featured inventive modes of distribution and a focus on straight (if occasionally deviant) male sexuality. The underground form known as the Tijuana Bible, or "eight-pager," is a remarkable first example. Slade's history of pornography in comics starts here, saying the "term applied initially to stapled pages of fiction and then, more commonly, to little booklets of comic strip panels. The latter type . . . blossomed in the 1920s and 1930s" (2001, 59). Art Spiegelman, in his introduction to a modern collection of Tijuana Bibles, explains that "the standard format consisted of eight poorly printed 4"-wide by 3"-high black (or blue) and white pages with one panel per page and covers of a heavier colored stock," although some of the Bibles were considerably longer (1997, 6).

The Tijuana Bibles were therefore a decidedly inexpensive form to print, and their casual disregard for copyright—they famously depicted, for example, Disney characters coupling—allowed them to tell ribald stories that were more outrageous than titillating. These celebrity-centered and inexpensive forms transformed easily between 1930 and 1950 into a new industry of pin-ups and humorous sex cartoons (Pilcher 2008, 11, 52). They mutated further through the use of a mail-order, scheme of distribution that replaced the under-the-drugstore-counter distribution, and toward the middle of the century cheap but aesthetically informed fetish comics could appear in subscribers' mailboxes alongside men's magazines (see the discussion of Irving Klaw and Bettie Page in Pilcher 2008, 116).

But men were not the only ones catered to by comics in the period after the Second World War: girls' romance comics achieved a peak of popularity during this period that can scarcely be imagined today. John Benson reports that beginning in 1949 and continuing through 1955:

> Nearly 3600 issues of romance comics were published . . . encompassing over 200 titles from more than 35 publishers. They represented nearly one-quarter of the total comics market, easily outselling the more famous (or infamous) horror comics that competed for rack space. The total sales of romance comics during those peak seven years was, incredibly, in the range of one *billion* copies (Benson 2003, 6).

Trina Robbins tells a similar story of the explosive sales of mid-century romance comics: "The first issue of *Young Romance* sold ninety-two percent of its print run, and by its third issue the print run tripled. Within two years the comic was joined on the newsstands by *Young Love*, then *Young Brides* (1952), and *In Love* (1954). Simon and Kirby were selling well over one million copies of their romance titles every month" (1999, 52). These stories of young women caught up in the throes of heterosexual romance have been relegated to the corner of pop irony ever since Lichtenstein's famous paintings, but they were once a massive part of the discourse about sexuality in American comics.

Similarly massive but in no way ignored is the role of the superhero in American comics. These books "paved the path up to the portals of adulthood, offering sexy and dangerous fantasies in which the sex was present but still subliminal" (Kushner 1995, ii). Surface brushes with sexuality largely rotated around the eternally deferred longing of a hero's alter ego for a less interested member of the opposite sex—Diana Prince for Steve Trevor, Peter Parker for Mary Jane Watson, and so on and on. But at least as important is the form's fascination with idealized bodies, a less-than-subtle symptom of how the anxieties of sexuality saturate superhero symbolics. The fascination with these bodies was clear even from comics' early days, so clear that the 1954 establishment of the Comics Code mandated heterosexuality geared toward marriage if it was to tolerate the robustly sexy bodies of superheroes at all.

The turning point in the history of sexuality in American comics, though, was the alternative comix movement of the late 1960s and early 1970s, a movement that would grapple with every preceding aspect of sexuality in the history of American comics. The artists working in the comix revolution were knowledgeable about that history (Spiegelman 1997, 5) and driven to the underground marketplace by the Comics Code and the limitations of comics art produced to sell on the mass market. Although the conversation about sexuality between comics artists had been in effect for decades already—mainly through the borrowings of visual techniques and copyrighted images—it is with the comix movement that we can see the first clear instance of a group of cartoonists pushing off against what had come before. Mainstream comics, typified by the strictly controlled symbolism of sexuality in superhero titles, provided a firm idea of what comix would *not* be. To say that the comix creators of the late 1960s approached sexuality with wild abandon would not be precisely true: they approached sexuality with calculated, all-encompassing abandon, portraying rough sex, perversion, homosexuality, incest, autoeroticism, and nearly every other permutation they could conceive. The effects of these creators' works are still being felt today (Pilcher 2008, 152–3).

From the close of the comix movement, the discourse about sexuality in American comics has been relegated mainly to the sublimated texts of superhero stories and a new alternative press. In the alternative press, the prurient impulses of the Tijuana Bibles have largely been channeled into a "sophisticate" readership (Slade 2001, 61), appealing more to specialized markets, as did the fetish comics of the mid-century. Other treatments of sexuality in comics, including a burgeoning representation of queer characters, usually—but not always, as we will see—draw from a less caustic, more liberal sensibility focused on the values of acceptance and diversity. The argument about sexuality simmering beneath the surface of American comics has its roots in the freewheeling aesthetic of the Tijuana Bibles and the revolutionary spirit of the comix movement.

THEORIZING THROUGH HISTORY: MAINSTREAM (VERSUS ALTERNATIVE)

In broader literary studies, there is typically a nebulous sense of a mainstream and an alternative press. But in American comics, a sense of a mainstream and an alternative press has existed for more than 50 years in ways unseen elsewhere in the world. It is on the tension between the mainstream and the alternative—and the continuing revolutions within the alternative press—that I wish to concentrate now.

Two main factors have created the clear division between mainstream and alternative. The first is the longtime dominance of American comics by two companies, DC and Marvel, whose jealously guarded (and phenomenally lucrative) superhero properties and close relationship with the largest printers and distributors deliver enormous market shares every quarter. Such clear market dominance and reliable product similarity create a visible mainstream unparalleled in most of the history of poetry and prose.[1]

The second factor is the Comics Code, the censoring organization the industry inflicted upon itself to avoid public censure in the middle of the twentieth century. The Code was a tool for creating a mainstream, for defining the contents of the art form according to very narrow terms. And neither were these two factors exclusive. The Code functioned as a tool for shoring up the mainstream against public fears about the influences of comics even as it labeled the competition as potentially harmful. The result is that the culture of comics in America has a built-in idea of a mainstream and an alternative press with different artistic ranges and missions.

Sexuality is clearly one of the most significant terms in the distinction between mainstream and alternative press, but the distinction is not merely that sexuality is present in the latter and absent in the former. Neither is the distinction merely that sexuality is somehow more potent in the alternative press than in the mainstream. Instead, some interesting trends become obvious when the question of sexuality is approached with an emphasis on the tension between the mainstream and alternative presses.

For the most part, sexuality in the mainstream press—particularly as viewed from the alternative press—is blithely oppressive. Gilbert Hernandez, one of the most important creators in the alternative press, has made this point in his inaugural graphic novel for Fantagraphics's Eros line of comics—part of the alternative press's "sophisticate" sex comics profile mentioned above. *Birdland* is a freewheeling fantasy of beautiful people entangled in a series of overlapping liaisons, none of which are complicated by anything more than longing. In the final pages, though, the lisping bombshell Fritz turns to the audience and adds a pointed comment: "*Thome* people are more tolerant of depictionth of a man brutally athaulting a woman than they are of him making *love* with her. Go figure."

Hernandez repeats this point in an interview, saying that he conceived of his erotic comic specifically to combat "the old truism: You can stab a tit but you can't show someone kissing one" (Hernandez and Hernandez 1993, 106). This truism is not merely an edict handed down by conservative society, as Hernandez and other comics artists know. It is directly tied to the dominant mode of displaying sexuality in mainstream comics: sexuality in the mainstream is most often encoded into scenes of violence (see also Delany 1994, 117). And the conflation of violence and sex in comics has a long history in the mainstream. Maurice Horn has pointed to the mainstream comics of the 1940s and 1950s, showing how the costumed women were regularly "in situations of an undeniable sado-masochistic nature" (1977, 10). In a familiar strategy, then, sexuality in mainstream comics is certainly present, but sublimated, this time not through the idealized bodies of the costumed characters, but the violence it directs against its heavily fetishized women.

Not every mention of women in mainstream comics works quite this way, though, and there is one important mode of American comics that has used female characters in a very different way: romance comics. Romance comics are not precisely liberating, but they do relocate the pain that other mainstream comics connect with the image of women's sexuality. Rather than focusing on physical pain caused to female characters through the "undeniable sado-masochistic" plots, romance comics focus on the emotional pain of women's sexuality, pain that comes in the melodrama of heterosexual romance. There are two important results to this change.

First, it insists on the role of the woman as the subject, rather than the object, of the romantic situation, since the story is of her interiority, not the violence visited upon her body from outside. Such a story necessitates a viewpoint that emphasizes a young woman's character and therefore subjectivity. Second, it tells a repetitive story of a fairly narrow path through feminine sexuality. These codes of gender (how a girl should behave) tie to codes of sexuality (how a girl can find sexual fulfillment) in fundamental ways, as Valerie Walkerdine has shown.

Although romance comics—again, in accordance with the dictates of the Comics Code that allowed them to occupy the mainstream—stopped short of depicting sexual activity or the hint of alternatives to heterosexuality, the girls in the stories and the girls reading the stories were *"prepared* in certain important ways for current adolescent heterosexual practices which appear to offer a way out, a resolution to their victimization. That is, although heterosexuality is not an overt *issue*, the other features of femininity are so produced in the pages of the comics as to render "getting a man" the "natural" solution" (Walkerdine 1984, 175). Historically, then, whether they connected sexuality to violence or heteronormative development, mainstream comics have shown a decided propensity for conservative, even destructive visions of sexuality beneath the protection of a Comics Code that prohibited the image of deviant sexuality.

In the 1960s, a new comics culture developed in a cohesive enough form to present a persistent alternative to the mainstream. The comix movement, whose most famous practitioners sold their books on the streets of San Francisco, conceived of themselves from the beginning as the opposite of the mainstream. I have noted above how the Code was instrumental in the formation of the mainstream, but it was equally instrumental in the formation of the underground: the alternative press was alternative because it rejected the authority of the Code.

Without the approval of the Code, though, the comix movement had to reimagine who comic books were for and how they could be delivered. "The comix publishers were not in any way competing with Marvel or DC," Roger Sabin has said, "because they were going for an entirely different readership" (1993, 41), a readership who frequented not the newsstands of middle America, but the "alternative record shops, bookshops and, above all, headshops—hippie shops that sold fashionable clothing, joss-sticks, drug paraphernalia (pipes, reefers) and so on" (45). The comix movement therefore thrived because of the economic structures of the late 1960s available to a counterculture. Not surprisingly, the famously anti-bourgeois sexuality of countercultural America at the time was reflected in the books whose distribution depended on the specific organizational structures of that counterculture. The comix, as Slade has said, "combined political comment with sexually outrageous images" (2001, 60; see also Sabin 1993, 36). If the stratagem for dealing with sexuality in the mainstream was sublimation, the stratagem for dealing with sexuality in the underground would be the opposite.

At the center of the comix movement in San Francisco were Robert Crumb, S. Clay Wilson, Spain Rodriguez, Robert Williams, and the contributors to *Zap Comix*. Together, these cartoonists embodied a movement,[2] an alternative press whose explicit sexuality was the opposite of the sublimated sexuality of the mainstream press. Pilcher has spoken of a "smut revolution" that sprang up around *Zap*'s popularity (2008, 151), and Estren has said that "the Crumb sex books" set a tone for discussion of sexuality that still remains in sway (1974, 127).[3] In their collaborations, Crumb and the men who surrounded him struck out against the discourse of sexuality whose limits were defined by the Code. In this new vision of sexuality in comics, Crumb and his colleagues felt a vital liberation. Crumb says:

> I, too, became a rebel. I cast off the last vestiges of the pernicious influence of my years in the greeting card business. I let it all hang out on the page. Seeing what Wilson and Williams had done just gave me the last little push I needed to let open the floodgates. Blatant sexual images became a big thing, still happy and positive at first—a celebration of sex (Qtd. in Holm 2004, 88–89).

The comix movement was fertile ground for a collaboration that would address sexuality as exactly the opposite of the strategy used by the mainstream.

But the collaboration between Crumb and the *Zap* collective also inspired the next revolution. Most significantly, the new approach to sexuality in the comix community often left unexamined received ideas of the role of women. There is very little disagreement that the core of the comix movement was dominated by men whose liberated ideas about sexuality easily slid into misogyny, revealing "what was seen as the profound sexism present in many of the existing undergrounds (particularly the work of Crumb, Wilson and Spain)" (Sabin 1993, 41).

If it is true that sexuality was present in mainstream comics, sublimated there to be rendered explicit by the underground comix, it is also true that the sublimated violence attached to sexuality in the mainstream came screaming to the foreground in the comix movement—and again, that violence was directed at women. Crumb himself mocks his contemporary San Francisco comix creator, Trina Robbins, opining that, "As Trina says, I 'ruined' underground comics by encouraging all the younger boy artists to be bad and do comics about their own horrible sex fantasies. Ha ha!" (Qtd. in Rosenkranz 2002, 89). But again, Crumb was hardly alone. S. Clay Wilson's most recognizable stories, starring a character known as the Checkered Demon, are shot through with rampant rape and hard sex (Wilson 1998).

Although the women around him may initially protest the Demon's attentions, they soon make sounds that indicate they have been longing to be treated this way. The plot follows whatever path will allow the chopper-riding Demon to create the most mayhem, often stopping off for scenes of violence and degradation toward women that are otherwise unrelated to the plot. Scenes such as these and the (racist, in addition to misogynist) Crumb character Angelfood McSpade are often explained as rooted in the filthy unconscious of American culture, further evidence that this is another example of the underground rendering explicitly what the mainstream sublimated, but the male comix creators have made no attempt to distance themselves from the hatred evident in what they unearthed from America's unconscious.

Few female fans remained loyal to the movement,[4] and even fewer female creators—again, such as Trina Robbins—were allowed a central role in the movement. Rumors abound of intentional exclusion from the tidal wave of comix anthologies, and the explanation for that exclusion is always the same. Robbins has argued that the answer is simple. She was excluded, she says:

Because I objected from the very beginning to all the sexism, to the incredible misogyny. We're not talking about making fun of women. We're talking about representation of rape and mutilation, and murder that involved women, as something funny and I objected to that, so they objected to me. That was the major reason (Rosenkranz 2002, 155).

Therefore, within this group that defined itself as the opposite of the mainstream, a split occurred. It began—if the rumors can be believed—by male artists who would not tolerate women as creators in a comics form that concerned itself so explicitly with sexuality, but it continued, as the record clearly shows, with a new group of female artists who now defined themselves by their work on sexuality, work that was intentionally different from existing American comix about sexuality. As Sabin has said, "What was peculiar about the women's comix . . . was that they did not emerge as an integral part of the regular underground, but rather as a reaction to it" (Sabin 1993, 224).

The anti-misogynist movement began quickly and prolifically. In the early 1970s, female creators gathered to start their counter-movement to the counter-movement. *It Ain't Me Babe* appeared in 1970, and *Wimmin's Comix* began in 1972. Also in 1972, Nanny Goat Productions formed and published the first issue of *Tits & Clits*, "an answer to the overly macho nature of underground comix" (Rosenkranz 2002, 196). Over the following decades, the movement would ripen, even producing its own volume of women's erotica, *Wet Satin* (Robbins 1976). As Pilcher says, "Sex was an important part of these women's comix, but it was a very different type of sex than that portrayed by their male counterparts. The stories were about female sexual empowerment, not relying on men, reactions to sexual harassment, birth control, and periods" (Pilcher 2008, 162). In an important echo of the revolution that had started the comix revolution, the anti-misogynist revolution pushed off against the core of the comix crowd to define itself.

But the chain of reactions was hardly finished. Mainstream comics had their party line—one laid out clearly in the Comics Code—and alternative comix had their party line, the one against which the female cartoonists of the 1970s revolted. Yet another revolt came on the heels of the women's comix movement, and again, the defining term was sexuality. In Robbins's history of women's comics, she tells of how her own story in the first issue of *Wimmen's Comix* was a story about a lesbian. In the mid-1990s, Robbins reports, a new female cartoonist told of her first brush with Robbins's story. That cartoonist, Mary Wings, writes:

One day, tired from a night of leafleting and tribadism, thumbing through a *Wimmen's Comix* I came upon Trina Robbins' story "Sandy Comes Out." I remember feeling alienated and angry . . . Straight women are oppressing me all over the place—with their male identification and their nipples. Not to mention their boyfriends who—they mention—want to watch (Robbins 1999, 91–92).

The sentiment Wings's comment contained in the 1990s is the same as that expressed by Robbins herself in the 1970s: the revolution needs a revolution before its portrayal of sexuality can be acceptable. Jennifer Camper's anthology *Juicy Mother* (2005) is a sign of the continuation of that struggle. In her introduction, Camper says, "Where are the comix by and about women, people of color and queers? I want an alternative to the alternative, but there are few venues for these stories" (2005, 7). In the same paragraph, she bemoans the absence of comix such as Robbins's, but as Wings's comment reveals, the 1970s women's comix were not fully geared to fill the need Camper feels. Today's alternative press, Camper argues, needs an alternative.

APPLICATION: *HOTHEAD PAISAN: HOMICIDAL LESBIAN TERRORIST*

I have been arguing for an understanding of sexuality in American comics that is grounded in the particular to-and-fro of the industry's odd history of revolutions, first against the mainstream, and then against the alternative press. In the interest of brevity, I will now focus on just one book, Diane DiMassa's *Hothead Paisan: Homicidal Lesbian Terrorist* (collected in 1999), that takes place late enough to respond to the anti-misogynist movement and early enough to anticipate the new wave of alternative comics exemplified by *Juicy Mother*. DiMassa's book is best understood through the series of arguments over sexuality that have marked the history of American comics.

Hothead Paisan is, first of all, in dialogue with the mainstream. From mainstream romance comics, for instance, the book borrows the strategy of focusing on a female protagonist's subjectivity as represented through her emotional turmoil. Hothead's rage at men and oppressive, patriarchal consumer culture is a constant topic of the book, but so are her despair and loneliness: she writes in her diary about the people she loves and the many aspects of life she hates (1999, 198–99), confronts the terrible weight of her anger and self-loathing (358), and even engages in a touching courtship in the final chapters. The result of this psychological realism in a book of hyperbole is a strong sense of subjectivity for the book's protagonist. But part of that subjectivity is Hothead's stubborn resistance to efforts by television, advertising, movies, and men on the street to punish her for her sexual deviance and cajole her into a safely straight and highly gendered sexuality. Whereas romance comics offered subjectivity at the cost of compulsive heterosexuality, Hothead mocks and resists what a voice from her television calls "the constant onslaught of white heterosexism" (16). By retaining emotional depth and therefore subjectivity but resisting dissolution in the narrative of heterosexuality, *Hothead Paisan* carefully chooses from the legacy of mainstream comics.

The book is also in provocative dialogue with the alternative press. Specifically, DiMassa is reacting against the comix movement that saw itself as alienating so many women readers. She reacts to it most specifically through a subtle but important argument with S. Clay Wilson. Wilson's Harley-riding, unkempt demon remains as one of the clearest symbols of the movement's misogyny, and it is through this image that DiMassa engages with him. The first brush she makes with the Checkered Demon is Hothead's own set of demons, visible only to Hothead and her Buddhist friend Roz. The demons foster Hothead's rage and encourage her to ever greater feats of destruction, but Roz works against them tirelessly, helping Hothead escape the confusion and despair that her rage masks (358–60). The second encounter Hothead makes with Wilson's legacy is through her own fantasy about what she would be if she were a man, even though she hates men:

> The stinking truth is . . . if I was born a testosterone container, I would be a mean, nasty, live to ride-ride to live, die hard, I-love-my carburetor, dirty BAD BIKER! I'd like to be disgusting with missing teeth, and I'd say things like 'Shovelhead.' I'd be hairy and scary. I'd be a violent alcoholic who works as a diesel mechanic. Nothing would bother me! Of course I'd be a white male and I'd clomp everything down and take everything I saw. Nobody would dare fuck with me! I wouldn't give a shit about anyone! (371).

Taken together, these brushes with Wilson's Checkered Demon demonstrate a continued struggle with the inheritance of the comix movement that provided a community for the alternative press but left a conflicted legacy for women working in the medium. When Hothead's demons cling to her and she assumes the role of the "dirty bad biker," she is able to express her rage, but she is no longer able to address her sexuality. The demons encourage her to smash and destroy, but never to feel loving, which is hardly a surprise, but they never even encourage her to feel sexual arousal. Because a major component of the Checkered Demon's bad biker persona is his endless, violent sexual appetite, it is remarkable that in Hothead's entire fantasy of becoming a male biker herself, there is no mention of sexuality. This is a significant absence, considering the running theme of Hothead's loneliness and sexual longing through the rest of the book. The rage and even machismo that Hothead inherits from Wilson's Demon is, for DiMassa, incompatible with sexuality. What *Hothead* expresses in its allusion to Wilson, then, is the field's ongoing argument, its distaste not only for the limitations of the mainstream, but also for those of the alternative.

Reading DiMassa's text as part of the dialectical history of American comics focusing on sexuality lays bare the specific arguments it is undertaking. As a descendant of mainstream romance comics, it can borrow a strong sense of female self if it divorces itself from the heteronormative encoded in that tradition; as a descendant of the comix movement, it is free to engage in an explicit conversation about deviant sexuality, but it must struggle with the demons of misogyny and self-loathing that have clouded that very same conversation.

CONCLUSION AND FUTURE DIRECTIONS

My goals have been to sketch the outlines of sexuality in comics through its history and major arguments and to articulate a way of approaching it that will add to the growing field of comics studies.

It is my hope that the structure I have proposed will be extended further than space in this chapter has allowed. For instance, the distinctions I have made between the mainstream and alternative press use the Comics Code as a major touchstone, but the Code was created and indeed seemed to target the horror comics of the mid-twentieth century. Those comics regularly connect violence against women to sexuality, as I have argued was typical of the superhero books of the day—why then did one survive and not the other? Was one kind of violence easier to sublimate than the other? To bring this history closer to today, we might also ask what role the alternate press sees for itself in the discussion in comics of sexuality now that the mainstream has, on the one hand, developed imprints to allow it to join that conversation and, on the other hand, showed less and less respect for the once-almighty Comics Code Authority?

I also hope for inquiries into another surprisingly fruitful alternative to the alternative press, namely the mainstream . . . or at any rate eddies within it. DC in particular has found a way to borrow a page from the counterculture to publish extraordinary and relevant work about sexuality. Under the imprints of Paradox (the descendant of Piranha, another DC imprint) and Vertigo, DC has published, for example, Howard Cruse's magnum opus, *Stuck Rubber Baby* (1995), a powerful graphic novel about growing up gay in the American South during the Civil Rights movement. One of Vertigo's early titles was David Wojnarowicz's *Seven Miles a Second* (1996), a hard-hitting story about gay teen sex, loss, and living with HIV. Paradox and Vertigo, however, would have been inconceivable as imprints of a major press during the 1960s; they are a product of a mode of distribution that targets specialist comics shops rather than newsstands, enabling distribution on a scale necessary for a major publisher but specialized enough to shield the publisher from public awareness of its dabblings in edgier material. This approach to distribution is the clear descendent of comix distribution during the 1960s: the paraphernalia being sold alongside the comics has changed, but the model is the same.

My real goal has been to suggest an approach to sexuality in American comics that is grounded in the particular realities of American comics. With this history of rolling revolutions in place, I believe we can build a discussion about sexuality that is more relevant to this field than it would be if conducted only using tools borrowed from other aspects of the humanities.

NOTES

1. On the other hand, this stark division between mainstream and alternative is paralleled in American film, where a "Hollywood movie" is a certain kind of film with a likely budget, cast type, and distribution.

2. It is necessary to point out that Crumb himself has often resisted being identified with a movement (as Holm reflects in his Introduction, ix), but usually his complaints are at being grouped with the hippy movement—of which he is clearly no part—rather than being grouped with his fellow artists at *Zap* and *Snatch*.

3. For further speculation on the scope of the *Zap* influence in comics about sexuality see Horn (1977, 189–90) and Pilcher (2008, 142).

4. There are any number of exceptions to this generalization, but the perception that such was the case is also shared by Crumb, who says, "the very sight of all those sweaty, bulbous cartoon characters fucking and sucking immediately drove away most of the female readers" (Qtd. in Rosenkranz 2002, 89).

WORKS CITED

Benson, John. 2003. Introduction. In *Romance without Tears*, ed. by John Benson, 6. Seattle: Fantagraphics Books.

Camper, Jennifer. 2005. Introduction. In *Juicy Mother Number One: Celebration*, ed. Jennifer Camper, 7. Brooklyn: Soft Skull Press.

Cooper, Emmanuel. 1986. *The Sexual Perspective: Homosexuality and Art in the Last 100 Years in the West*. London: Routledge.

Cruse, Howard. 1995. *Stuck Rubber Baby*. New York: HarperCollins.

Delany, Samuel R. 1994. *Silent Interviews: On Language, Race, Sex, Science Fiction, and Some Comics*. Hanover: Wesleyan University Press.

DiMassa, Diane. 1999. *The Complete Hothead Paisan: Homicidal Lesbian Terrorist*. San Francisco: Cleis Press.

Doane, Mary Ann. 1991. *Femmes Fatales: Feminism, Film Theory, Psychoanalysis*. New York: Routledge.

Estren, Mark James. 1974. *A History of Underground Comics*. San Francisco: Straight Arrow Books.

Hernandez, Gilbert. 1992. *Birdland*. Seattle: Eros Comix.

Hernandez, Gilbert, and Jaime Hernandez. 1993. Interview. *The Comics Journal* 178: 106.

Holm, D. K., ed. 2004. *R. Crumb Conversations*. Jackson, MS: University Press of Mississippi.

Horn, Maurice. 1977. *Women in the Comics*. New York: Chelsea House Publishers.

Kushner, Tony. 1995. Introduction. In *Stuck Rubber Baby*, by Howard Cruse, ii. New York: HarperCollins.

Mulvey, Laura. 1989. *Visual and Other Pleasures*. Bloomington: Indiana UP.

Pilcher, Tim. 2008. *Erotic Comics: A Graphic History from Tijuana Bibles to Underground Comics*. New York: Abrams.

Robbins, Trina, ed. 1976. *Wet Satin: Women's Erotic Fantasies*. N.p.: Kitchen Sink Press.

———. 1999. *Girls to Grrrlz: A History of Women's Comics from Teens to Zines*. San Francisco: Chronicle Books.

Rosenkranz, Patrick. 2002. *Rebel Visions: The Underground Comix Revolution: 1963–1975*. Seattle: Fantagraphics Books.

Russo, Vito. 1981. *The Celluloid Closet: Homosexuality in the Movies*. New York: Harper & Row.

Sabin, Roger. 1993. *Adult Comics: An Introduction*. London: Routledge.

Slade, Joseph. 2001. *Pornography and Sexual Representation: A Reference Guide*. 3 vol. Westport, CT: Greenwood Press.

Spiegelman, Art. 1997. Those Dirty Little Comics. In *Tijuana Bibles: Art and Wit in America's Forbidden Funnies, 1930s-1950s*, ed. Bob Adelman, 6. New York: Simon & Shuster Editions.

Walkerdine, Valerie. 1984. Some Day My Prince Will Come: Young Girls and the Preparation for Adolescent Sexuality. In *Gender and Generation*, ed. Angela McRobbie and Mica Nava, 175. London: Macmillan.

Wilson, S. Clay. 1998. *The Collected Checkered Demon*. Vol. I. San Francisco: Last Gasp.

Wojnarowicz, David. 1996. *Seven Miles a Second*. New York: DC Comics/Vertigo.

CHAPTER TEN

Feminine Latin/o American Identities on the American Alternative Landscape: From the Women of *Love and Rockets* to *La Perdida*

—ANA MERINO
(translated by Elizabeth Polli)

The fall 2007 volume of the academic journal *MELUS*, which discusses multiethnic literatures in the United States, was dedicated to graphic narratives and featured essays and reviews of comic works and graphic novels by such authors as Adrian Tomine, Ben Katchor, Will Eisner, Ho Che Anderson, Gene Luen Yang, and the Hernandez brothers. Gilbert, one of the Hernandez brothers, created the cover for this particular edition (volume 32, number 3), which played with the border iconography of his world and offered a multi-ethnic vision of the reality of the United States. Professor Derek Parker Royal, editor of the volume, interviewed him about the meaning of his work within the context of the Hispanic community.

Gilbert said his main objective was to tell stories that connected and entertained a general audience; however, he wanted his story lines to humanize Latinos and break the stereotypes Anglo-Saxon popular culture imposed on them (Parker Royal 2007, 223). In this discussion, Gilbert defined his comics as resisting any type of narrow ethnic classification. When Parker Royal asked him if he considered himself to be "an ethnic writer in the field of comics" or if he opposed that type of designation, Gilbert responded, establishing a distinction between how he is perceived by others, how he perceives himself, and what the characters he created were like:

> I feel that's how I'm looked at, perhaps, but I don't think of myself that way. I'm just writing stories. I forget they're Latino. I write a carácter with a Hispanic name, but sometimes he looks like a black person, sometimes he looks like a blond-haired, blue-eyed guy. That's the thing about the mix of Latinos around the world. The skin color ranges from the palest to the darkest . . . (227).

The discourse relating to the "Latino" that Gilbert elaborated upon winks at the academy and gently mocks its tendency to compartmentalize and define every style that concerns any work: "I don't really think about it as an ethnic thing too much. Maybe I should, because the more ethnic I am, the more attention I get" (227).

Irrespective of Gilbert's sarcastic tone as to what his work means and the way the academy perceives it, it is indisputable that the oeuvre of both Hernandez brothers is a milestone in the articulation of feminine identity and Latino-ness within the world of alternative comics. Jaime, Gilbert and Mario entered the field in 1981 with their self-published comic *Love and Rockets*, in which each one developed his own strips. They sent a copy of the first issue to Gary Groth, editor of *The Comics Journal*, for review purposes—both Groth and his partner Kim Thompson saw the creative and commercial possibilities of *Love and Rockets* and offered to publish it through their recently created publishing house, Fantagraphics, in 1982.

Unfortunately, and in spite of his unquestionable talent, the oldest brother Mario abandoned the project after the third issue, continuing to work on a few small strips and collaborations. By the end of the 1980s, Jaime and Gilbert's comics had evolved and solidified into two separate established narrative and aesthetic styles. Jaime's initial stories flirted with science fiction tropes before settling into a realist style set in a barrio in southeast Los Angeles referred to as "Hoppers 13" in which he reproduces his own experience with the 1980s Latino punk music scene. Meanwhile, Gilbert's stories took place in and around Palomar, a fictitious town in an unnamed Latin American country relatively close to the border with the United States. Gilbert reveals that in Palomar he wanted to reflect "a more general Latino culture," even though it is true that:

It looks closer to Mexico, but I really wanted any Latino from anywhere to feel like they belonged there. That's why I never located it specifically in the real world [. . .] It's all mythical, and I think that the readers of all Latino backgrounds could place themselves there . . . (Parker Royal 2007, 228).

Gilbert and Jaime were the first to represent the Latina voice in the context of U.S. comics for the adult audience, and they rejuvenated alternative comics by breaking with the autobiographical trends of the countercultural comix. The brothers, sons of a Mexican father and a Texan mother, grew up in California in the 1960s and 1970s, and were steeped in the multiethnic intensity of those times. In 2004, Fantagraphics published a 704-page volume titled *Locas* by Jaime Hernandez, which compiled the stories of Maggie, Hopey, Isabel, Penny, and their friends. It was a striking vision of Latina femininity during the punk rock 1980s and the questions of identity that followed in the 1990s.

The year prior, Gilbert's volume *Palomar* had appeared, containing 522 pages of stories from the fictional town of Palomar and a cast of characters including Ofelia and Luba, Sheriff Chelo, aspiring starlet Tonantzín, and the boys growing into young men: Heraclio, Jesús, Vicente, and Israel. Accustomed to narratives celebrating exaggeratedly masculine superheroes or the hedonistic visions of the underground comix, the first generation of Anglo readers who discovered the Hernandez's stories were introduced to social milieus rarely seen in human terms in American comics. Jaime and Gilbert created stories in which protagonists were Latina women whose decisions and actions drove the narratives. Thus Gilbert and Jaime connected with a female reading public that felt an intense affinity with these characters, whose social roles seemed credible and were represented without idealization. Emerging alternative female comics creators such as Jessica Abel claimed the brothers' narratives as inspiration for her own.

Conscious of the weight and importance of Jaime and Gilbert's comics, Abel also attempted to articulate feminine identity within the parameters of a fictional comics narrative in her work, *La Perdida*. Published by Fantagraphics, *La Perdida* appeared as five separate comic books between 2001 and 2005 and was later collected as a complete graphic novel by Pantheon Books in 2006. *La Perdida* tells the story of Carla, a young North American woman who travels to Mexico City in the attempt to find her Mexican roots. In contrast to the female characters of the Hernandez brothers, Carla represents a more recent generation, who, in spite of her paternal Latino origins, has not lived the multiethnic experience of being Latino/a in the United States.

Carla's voyage is transformed, thus, into an effort to define the contradictions of her origins.

La Perdida pays homage to the Hernandez brothers, and like many of their remembered narratives, it assembles a story from the near past whose events were seminal in the construction of the characters' present. Abel's graphic novel is voiced in the first person by the protagonist Carla, who reflects upon the consequences of that coming-of-age journey to Mexico City. The recent recollection (only two years have passed) plays, therefore, a key role when defining her existential condition at the moment of remembering. Significantly, even though Carla is capable of articulating the desires behind the trip two years earlier, she recognizes from her role as narrator in the present that those desires have become estranged: "What I was thinking when I decided to go—it's no longer all clear to me. / That is, I can remember, but it's like peering into the mind of a stranger. I had all these ideas and plans that seem now to be entirely based on misconceptions . . . / . . . of Mexico, of living abroad, of myself" (Abel 2006, 11).

Her desire is constructed around the idea of searching for the Latino roots that challenge her daily Anglo existence and that she hoped would liberate her from the void represented by her absent Mexican father: "I thought that I went because I was sick of the USA, sick of everybody. / I wanted to find my Mexican roots. Somehow it seemed I would like them better than my Anglo ones, which makes no sense when you think about it. I'd spent most of my life resenting my disappearing Mexican dad" (11). Carla's existential voyage maps on to the evolution of her attitudes towards stereotypes and her opinions regarding "otherness" and "authenticity."

Abel herself explained certain aspects of the character in a 2005 interview with The Comics Journal. On the one hand, it is true that her initial idea was to focus her work on the relationship between Carla and Harry, her American boyfriend, a member of a privileged class who typifies "frat-boy" attitudes. Nevertheless, the story transforms into what Abel describes as "Carla's relationship to Mexico and Mexicans and the naiveté of her attitude and how that causes distortions in her own behavior and understanding" (Stump 2005, 87).

The Hernandez brothers' work has many aspects in common with La Perdida—both brothers use the Spanish language in a figurative fashion, inserting Spanish words, but they comment as well as on the circumstances of bilingualism. Notably, Jaime Hernandez constructed a tale between 1984 and 1985 titled "Las Mujeres Perdidas" ("The Lost Women"), his first attempt at a longer narrative. The plot revolves around the central character Maggie, who was working as a Prosolar mechanic on the island of Chepan. Throughout this story, Jaime experimented with the possibilities of the medium and began to define the plethora of female characters that would mark his artistic trajectory.

Maggie, the young punky mechanic, escapes a terrorist attack against her place of employment, a robot warehouse. At the moment of the explosion she was with Rena Titañon, an older, mature woman known as the queen of the wrestlers. The two escape by walking through a maze of sewer tunnels running under the industrial park, through the desert and to the ocean.

Here, Jaime plays with parallel time: the two women are given up for dead and Jaime begins to define Hopey, Penny, and Isabel, the other protagonists of his choral repertoire, by means of the affection they felt for Maggie. This adventure, which initially appeared in six episodes in the comic book *Love and Rockets*, presented as "Mechanics," concludes in its last episode with a final panel in which "Las mujeres perdidas" is written in Spanish—"The Lost Women," where Maggie is in the street after having just gotten off a bus with her suitcases. This closing title in Spanish sums up the importance of the plot and will give the name to volume three of the recompilation, an importance only signaled and offered to Spanish-speaking readers.

In the 1980s, Gilbert and Jaime were not conscious of the narrative potential of their work. The recompilations of *Locas* by Jaime or *Palomar* by Gilbert are the result of decades of work where the universes of their dramatic ensembles take shape. Nevertheless, Abel is conscious of the malleability of the medium and its potential within the publishing market, thus she planned *La Perdida* as a stand-alone book right from the start. Jessica's character Carla is very different from Maggie or any of Jaime's other protagonists. We are no longer in a period marked by the energy and iconoclasm of the 1980s punk sensibility, and Abel's Carla is ill at ease in her twenty-first-century world. Carla is deeply insecure and her desire to define and identify authenticity makes her profoundly vulnerable and easy to manipulate. She is incapable of establishing a solid network of female friends who might give her their support and she lets herself be carried away by circumstances and by her own prejudices.

Reading *Love and Rockets* during her freshman college year was fundamental to Abel. She hails the work of Jaime Hernandez as "the largest influence" on her comics because she felt his work was compelling and she "wanted to do something like that" (Stump 2005, 80). She felt her own biographical context could generate comics narratives—she could evoke the experience of Jaime's punk-rockers from the perspective of her own generation.

Abel's "Perdida" traveling to Mexico is tied to a story called "Flies on the Ceiling" from Jaime's graphic tale of Isabel in Mexico, created between 1988 and 1989. The events of "Flies on the Ceiling" had been alluded to years before in a brief four-page episode titled "Locos" that appeared in *Love and Rockets* in 1984. Speedy, Izzy's brother (Isabel is referred to as Izzy in her family), was talking about his sister's life to a friend. According to Speedy, Isabel was at one point in time the epitome of the living dead. Mixed up in a sinister punk movement, she spent all day locked up in her house, only to leave at night to walk around the neighborhood dressed up as a vampire. What had happened to Isabel?

In high school she was one of the founders of the female gang The Widows. In spite of her violent attitude, Isabel respected herself, at least in her brother's opinion. When she turned eighteen she was arrested and spent time in jail with the group of Mexican-American girls called the "Southside chucas." This experience affected her so much that when she was released, she went back to high school, got her diploma, and received a scholarship for college. In jail, Isabel discovered how limiting the territorial worlds adolescent Latinas had invented were. They had fabricated their universe around the idea of respect as a sign of identity, appropriating the barrio from the margins of provocative and violent gang life.

In college Isabel realizes she wants to write mystery stories. At the same time she begins standing up to her father who is pressuring her to become a schoolteacher. The confrontation becomes more intense and results in Isabel marrying Jack Ruebens, her college English professor, a white man twice her age. This attempt to disassociate herself from her own environment by means of a marriage far removed from her own roots does not end well—one year later Isabel is divorced and trying to concentrate on her writing, which by then has transformed into a rhetoric of "dead babies and dancing skeletons" (Hernandez 2004, 173).

She continues to go by her married name and publishes a few stories into which she pours her existential anxieties. Meanwhile, no one knows anything about a trip to Mexico. Her brother Speedy tells his friend that his mother received a postcard from Isabel that simply said, "Mom, I'll come home when you rid of the vermin. —till then. I love you and the kids" (174). She returned home for the wake of her father looking haggard: "She looked half dead, and started dressing like a borracho (drunkard). Like she didn't care about nothing no more. Before Mexico she would a never gone out in a tore up robe an' slippers, no matter how bad things got! / You think maybe something happened in Mexico, 'ey? / I dunno, maybe . . . " (174). The mystery of what happened on that trip turns into a recurrent theme. In 1986 in an episode of "Locas," Hopey accidentally finds the fifth volume of Isabel's dairy and secretly reads it, fascinated upon discovering a reference to Izzy's trip to Mexico on the last page: "That was that. There was nothing left for me here. I had no other choice but to go to Mexico" (246).

The story of Isabel in Mexico consists of numerous mute panels where the reader interprets the grief and guilty feelings that are asphyxiating the protagonist. In three tiers of three panels each, page one narrates Isabel's anxieties after her failed marriage, the confrontation with her father, and the extremely difficult decision to have an abortion. The next page is a single full-page illustration in which Isabel is depicted from the waist up, her half profile revealing a serious gesture, her eyes closed, and her skin sweaty, all on a black background—and a diabolic masculine silhouette, drawn with white traces, borders Isabel's profile. The profile projected around the frontal image of Isabel is the representation of the Devil customarily employed in popular Hispanic iconography. With a trace of chalk Jaime wrote the title of the tale, "Flies on the ceiling," and adding an explanatory subtitle in smaller letters, just under his signature, "The story of Isabel in Mexico." The dates appear drawn in the devil's genitals, intensifying the masculinity of this sinister character.

On the following page the first panel shows Isabel's legs, drawn from above. This panel contrasts with the previous illustration where her body was cut off from the waist down. Next we see her standing, contemplating the gigantic footprints of a bird. This moment of silence, where we see Isabel absorbed, is interrupted by the voice of a man who from the modest wall that surrounds his house nearby calls Isabel and asks her to help him convince his small son to eat something. Isabel has experience taking care of her younger siblings and soon convinces the boy to eat.

The man realizes that Isabel is itinerant and he offers her a room and money if she will stay and cook and take care of his son, Beto. On the following page we see Isabel adapting to daily life in the village—cooking, cleaning, going to the market, and taking care of Beto. At the request of the father and the son, she even sits down to eat with them. It appears Isabel is integrating into the community, and that she has established an ever-deepening relationship with the boy and his father.

One day she asks Beto where his mother is, and he tells her that "she ran away." Isabel feels comfortable with the man and the boy, but the tranquility she desires is a mirage, as one night while returning home she crosses paths with an old woman embracing a rooster who tells her that she knows who Isabel is. When she arrives home, Isabel gives her diary to the man so that he can read it and understand what she has been through. He, nevertheless, clearly explains his posture: "Isabel, I'm not here to judge you. I couldn't if I wanted to. What I mean to say is . . . / I would love you if you were the devil himself" (Hernandez and Hernandez 1991, 6). The man's words offer her a degree of security and Beto tells one of his playmates that Isabel will soon be his mother. This desire to form a family and be happy is thwarted by the weight of her guilt that has reached diabolic proportions. When Isabel realizes that darkness is at her doorstep, she abandons the boy and the father as they sleep, believing that as such she will protect them and they will not suffer the consequences of her own condemnation.

The manner in which both Isabel and Carla relate to Mexico and the patriarchal and phallocentric reality that surrounds them is interesting. Isabel leaves for Mexico and remains there hoping that the emotional weight of her confrontation with her father in the U.S. will become easier to bear. This is impossible, however, as she carries such a terrifying feeling of guilt she comes to believe that the Devil is after her.

The sequence retelling Isabel's encounter with the Devil is full of symbolic imagery. After leaving the man and boy, she rents a modest room. A crucifix hanging on the wall suddenly falls to the floor, face down, and large cracks begin to slowly grow in the wall. Isabel asks why this is happening to her—she is not the first person to get divorced, to have had an abortion, or to have attempted suicide. A voice emanates from one of the cracks in the wall and tells her that it is not her sins, but her feelings of guilt that have brought this on.

Though Isabel is not the first person to feel the weight of one's guilt, her vulnerability is marked by fear and this allows the diabolic being to accost her. The traumas she has suffered arise in the conversation she holds with the voice, but her capacity to resist and her ability to confront fear do as well. Isabel associates the diabolic voice that springs from the wall with masculinity and the patriarchal and phallocentric order that has marked her existence:

ISABEL: You'got all the answers, don't you mister satanico?
VOICE FROM THE CRACK: Mister? What makes you think I'm a he?
ISABEL: You sound like my father. You of all . . . should know how
    much I . . .
VOICE FROM THE CRACK: . . . Hate your father? No, it's not just him.
    You hate the entire male race. So chalk up another for my side, eh?
    (Hernandez and Hernandez 1991, 9).

Isabel challenges the voice to show itself: "Show your real self if you are so big and bad!" (9). When Isabel leaves the room, the sinister voice whose physical form has not yet materialized has the last word: "Who knows? One time I may come to you as your own baby?" (9). It is with this type of hallucinating encounter with fear and guilt that her mental world begins to collapse.

Isabel mails the postcard to her mother and later realizes she does not want to see the evil force accosting her. She seems to be stronger and prepared to confront her anxieties, but then she begins to have convulsions and vomits up lizards. Many of these sequences, in which we see Isabel dragging herself through the street suffering terrible stomach pains, surround her with elongated and diabolic masculine shadows.

The face of the evil entity fills one whole panel, but the next sequence is two girls pretending they are making their first communion in a bedroom next to a dresser filled with religious images. One of the girls opens the top drawer and she finds the votive offering of the head of Christ suffering with the crown of thorns. In the next panel Isabel wakes in a bed while a young woman and the old woman who was holding the rooster earlier help her in a type of diabolic birth in which deformed beings with lizard tails are born.

After this hallucinating episode, Isabel seems liberated and goes back to the man and the boy, only to discover soon after that it is impossible to escape from her diabolic guilt. Then, visibly aged from the pain, Isabel abandons the man and the boy once again and returns to the United States. In the last panel, in chalk on a black background the words "the end" are drawn. A silhouette of the man affectionately embracing his son curled up in his lap is also seen. In a frame to the left a crucifix appears to protect them from their despair.

In *La Perdida*, Carla visits Mexico to try and recover the essence of the absent father. Her memory is of a childhood of rejecting her origins and of trying to recall what her father represented. When her younger brother Rod comes to visit, the emotions she has found for what it meant for both of them to grow up half Chicano come together. In Rod's case, his Mexican identity was much more defined because he was under his father's care for several years and thus he maintained the Spanish he had learned. The character of Carla is ashamed now of having lost her "Mexican ness" that her brother knew how to hold on to.

As she explains in the narrative texts in the panels, she deeply hated being Mexican-American and her father for not having taken her to live with him. When he chose to take her brother and not her, it was clearly discriminatory: the father considered his son more important due to his masculine gender and wanted to transfer his values to him—and was basically unconcerned with his daughter's cultural upbringing. Carla reacted by underestimating

Rod and perceiving him from a highly prejudiced point of view: "I thought my brother was a totally embarrassing little wetback" (111). Even though her father does not share his knowledge or time with her, Carla cannot disregard what he meant to her, no matter how much she hated him:

> I hated being 'different' / In seventh grade, I even changed my name in my school records to say 'Carla Oliver,' instead of 'Olivares.' / By the time I got to high school, I was ready to be me again. But it took me years to get all the records changed back. I blame the whole thing on my mom. I think I even believed it was her fault for a little while there . . . (110).

Reclaiming her Latina identity during adolescence meant confronting the Anglo space represented by her mother. Not only does Carla need to find her father in order to redefine her identity, but as an adolescent she rejects her mother and blames her for the cultural and emotional void left behind by her father. Unfortunately her trip to Mexico does not seem to free her from blaming her mother or from her guilty feelings of being of mixed heritage.

Carla projects her rage against her ex-boyfriend Harry only to later find herself unwillingly involved in a plot in Mexico to kidnap him. She suffers great disappointment when she eventually realizes she is surrounded by false male friends who scorn or exploit her. Even though Carla is the narrator of her own story, the weight of cultural norms that privilege masculinity are at work in the unfolding of the plot: the kidnappers neither respect nor value Carla and they project onto her the misogynist and machista discourse of their culture. They take over her apartment in order to hide Harry in the rooftop bedroom, they order her to cook for them and threaten her—when she travels to give her English classes they follow her so she will not give them away. For the kidnappers, she is simply a woman and therefore available to be beaten, ordered around, and humiliated with impunity.

Her world crumbles around her when she discovers with horror how the kidnapping has spread into her home, and that Memo and Oscar, whom she thought to be her best Mexican friends, are involved. Oscar himself, the Mexican boyfriend she took up with after Harry, goes to her bedroom to get her, pretending everything is the same as always: "Oscar came to get me to make lunch. / It looked like they expected me to cook for them too . . . to put me in the position of a subservient Mexican housewife" (201).

Due to the situation imposed on her, Carla has suffered a silent kidnapping, but in contrast to Harry, she is worth nothing to the kidnappers. She is to keep quiet and act as if nothing is happening. Ricardo, one of the kidnappers, becomes aggressive when Carla resists and tells them to get out of her house, believing she still has the power to change the situation: "Listen bitch! We'll stay where we want to! You're in OUR country!" (201). Ricardo makes it clear that she is doubly powerless, as a woman and as a poor foreigner: "You aren't rich enough to be worth keeping around if you're going to be trouble, you read me? / I know a lot of ways to hurt you that won't show on the outside" (205).

From a phallocentric point of view, Carla exists vulnerably in the borderline space of lawlessness that the very kidnapping signifies. Everyone, including Harry, blames her for what is happening. On the one hand Harry is convinced she is involved, and on the other Memo reminds her that she hates Harry obsessively. Memo cynically tries to explain to her that the hatred she feels for what her "ex" represents should be transformed into material actions: "You hate him. You hate him with passion and fire...But you lack the courage of your convictions. You think it's enough to hate him for his arrogance and money. You don't ACT to make things right" (203). Carla questions the cynicism implicit in Memo's argument: "What are you talking about? I should kidnap him because I don't like him? That's the solution?" (203).

Even though Carla is not responsible for what happens, she is, without realizing it, the catalyzing agent. She never imagined her harsh public criticism against Harry and his social position as a rich, white, North American boy could provoke his kidnapping in Mexico. In the end, when Carla reflects on what occurred, she blames herself: "It wouldn't have happened without me" (254). After she returns to Chicago, the phallocentric rhetoric that positioned her as socially peripheral is now incorporated into her self-image—she did not find the identity she sought in Mexico and has carried back a burden of guilt. She thus marginalizes herself as someone who has lost the strength to change her life, someone unable to be the center of her own being:

> I look at her, the girl I was. Her head full of plans and hopes for what might lie in her future. / And I watch her. I watch her take one step, two steps. / And then she takes a turn down an obscure and unmarked path. I struggle to keep track of her as she fades from view. Before I know it, she's gone from sight, from understanding. / She's lost . . . (255).

Jaime Hernandez and Jessica Abel's narratives illustrate the journeys of two women traveling across the border to Mexico, both of whom undertook those journeys to reinterpret their personal pasts and reposition their identities in the present. Hernandez employs a more surreal and explicitly symbolic style than does Abel: his expressive form is as important for conveying meaning as the events they represent. Jaime intimates Isabel's intense emotional experiences by means of mute panels charged with semiotic richness.

La Perdida constructs a story whose meaning depends far more on the events in the narrative and how they change the characters' relation to each other: the fictitious autobiographical voice that constantly narrates events sometimes takes over the rhythm of the visual representation. These differences may be attributable to the contexts of publication, with *La Perdida* produced with the intention of being a single narrative, and "Flies on the Ceiling" intended as a short impressionistic piece published alongside other stories of varying length from which the grander tableau of the Locas characters and their lives can be constructed.

The Hernandez brothers established a reputation for creating female comics characters open to historical change, whose representation can be sexual without being sexist or stereotypical, whose identities are polyvocal and seen from a variety of perspectives, and aren't simply stock characters. Abel's *La Perdida* adapts the scenarios and characters of their work in comics, building up a female character subject to contradictions and touched by innocence. Whereas the ongoing "soap opera" genres of *Love and Rockets* made a degree of "open-ended-ness" a requisite component of the characters created by the Hernandez brothers (and ghosts and the memories of the dead are powerful recurring motifs in their work), in Abel's graphic novel Carla was conceived as a closed character where redemption is only a nostalgic sigh. Abel and the Hernandez brothers also attempt to represent the plethora of possibilities for constructing characters at the point where Latina femininity crosses the boundaries of gender and nationhood. These creators depict the expectations and limitations their characters struggle against as women in societies privileging men and masculine experience: those proscriptions of gender are arguably the most potent borders of all.

WORKS CITED

Abel, Jessica. 2006. *La Perdida*. New York: Pantheon Books.

Davis-McElligatt, Joanna. 2007. *Locas: The Maggie and Hopey Stories* by Jaime Hernandez. *MELUS: Special Issue. Coloring America: Multi-Ethnic Engagements with Graphic Narrative* 32(3): 267–270.

Gaiman, Neil. 1995. Jaime and Gilbert Hernández Interview. *The Comics Journal* 178: 91–123.

Glaser, Jennifer. 2007. *Palomar: The Heartbreak Soup Stories* by Gilbert Hernandez. *MELUS: Special Issue. Coloring America: Multi-Ethnic Engagements with Graphic Narrative* 32(3): 264–267.

Groth, Gary, Robert Fiore and Tom Powers. 1989. The Hernández Bros. Interview. *The Comics Journal* 126: 61–113.

Hatfield, Charles. 1997. Heartbreak Soup: The Interdependence of Theme and Form. *Inks: Cartoon and Comic Art Studies* 4(2): 2–17.

———. 2005. *Alternative Comics: An Emerging Literature*. Jackson, MS: University Press of Mississippi.

Hernandez, Gilbert. 2003. *PALOMAR The Heartbreak Soup Stories*. Seattle: Fantagraphics.

Hernandez, Gilbert, and Jaime Hernandez. 1991. *Flies on the Ceiling*. Vol. 9 of The Complete Love & Rockets. Seattle: Fantagraphics.

———. 1990. *Las Mujeres Perdidas*. Vol. 3 of The Complete Love & Rockets. Seattle: Fantagraphics.

Hernandez, Jaime. 2004. *Locas: The Maggie and Hopey Stories*. Seattle: Fantagraphics.

Parker Royal, Derek. 2007. Palomar and Beyond: An Interview with Gilbert Hernandez. *MELUS: Special Issue. Coloring America: Multi-Ethnic Engagements with Graphic Narrative* 32(3): 221–46.

Stump, Greg. 2005. The Jessica Abel Interview. *The Comics Journal* 270: 68–106.

V: Authorizing Comics: How Creators Frame the Reception of Comic Texts

CHAPTER ELEVEN

Making Comics Respectable: How *Maus* Helped Redefine a Medium

—IAN GORDON

Over the last twenty years comic books have undergone a substantial change in terms of types and content available and in their critical reception. The genesis of this shift can be traced to certain events in the production and distribution of comics. For fans of superhero comic books the key moments include Alan Moore and Dave Gibbons's *Watchmen* (collected in 1987) and Frank Miller's *Batman: The Dark Knight Returns* (collected in 1986). For others, including the great mass of non-comic-book readers, the publication of Art Spiegelman's *Maus* (collected in 1986 and 1991) and the critical response to it, is the singularly most important phenomenon in the reevaluation of comic books.

As Joseph Witek prophesied in 1989, *Maus* has changed forever "the cultural perception of what a comic book can be and what can be accomplished by creators who take seriously the sequential art medium" (97). This chapter discusses this process with particular emphasis on public and academic discourses on the status and nature of comic books in the wake of *Maus*. *Watchmen* and *The Dark Knight Returns* reinvented comic books for superhero fans—*Maus* reinvented comic books for non-comic-book readers.

One reason comic books enjoy a newly found respectability is that they are no longer a mass medium with numerous genres of stories printed on cheap paper sold in pamphlet form. Superhero comics are virtually the sole survivor of the vast array of comic book genres available from the late 1930s through to the 1980s—and the characters in these titles are probably more familiar to mass audiences through movies and computer games than comics. In search of respectability, at the end of the 1980s the industry and the media heralded the transformation of comics into graphic novels—books sold in bookshops rather than on newsstands.

As indicated in the introduction, scholars have taken issue with the periodization of the term and even whether it is semantically accurate; many graphic novels, of which *Maus* is the prime example, are simply not novels at all. But *graphic novel* is the catch-all designation given to a range of innovative work, perhaps not generally associated with comic books, that have received critical attention from academics and the quality press. Indeed, to complain about the term graphic novel as applied to a comic book, say like *Maus*, on the basis that they lack the qualities of novels is akin to noting that not many comic books, *Maus* included, are funny.

This shift in terms is rather mild when compared to the shifts in form experienced by comic book characters most likely to appear in movies today. For every blockbuster superhero film there seems to be a quirky, offbeat independent film based on a comic book. Academics studying comics have mostly gone beyond earlier studies that labeled them worth studying for providing a funhouse mirror on American culture or somehow being representative meta-narrative texts. An array of scholars now account for the formal properties of comics, their impact on national and international cultures and societies as constituent and active phenomenon, and as a literary genre. In short, the medium has been transformed and artists receive critical acclaim.

This chapter unpacks this development in four sections: an overview of the development of comics that led to the production of *Maus*, a discussion of why *Maus* had such an impact, an analysis of the changing view of comics in the press, and an examination of the blossoming of academic work on comics art.

FROM WERTHAM TO *MAUS*

In the 1950s, Fredric Wertham and others attacked comic books as a cause of juvenile delinquency and other behavior deemed abnormal. Wertham's campaign promoted the view that comics were for children, though he specifically excluded comic strips from his onslaught because he said their presence in newspapers ensured they were subject to editorial control and thus primarily aimed at adults. To be sure, newspaper readership surveys supported Wertham's view of comic strips as material read by adults—but then why were comic books seen as children's material rather than as a form with readership among all ages?

Viewing comic books as a children's genre lumped together Archie comics, superhero comics, Harvey comics, Dell comics (including the licensed Disney characters), and the horror and crime comics that EC and other companies produced. Viewed by critics as a genre, rather than as a medium with many genres, comic books were reduced to a childish level just at the time the medium showed potential to develop critical new forms. It was their unsuitability for children that made many of the EC titles stand out as examples of the potential of the medium. The imposition of the Comics Code then delayed the maturing of the form alongside the maturing of the great mass of comic book readers: adolescents and service personnel from the war years. It is also fair to say that broad social transformations such as the baby boom, the suburbanization of America, and the advent of television mitigated the appeal of a form born in the Depression and that found its widest popularity during the hardship of war. But these developments also contained the seeds of a transformation of comic books that occurred in the 1960s.

The rebirth of superhero comics is a familiar enough story to comic book aficionados—and there are two versions of the tale, depending on one's allegiance to which publisher: Marvel Comics or National Periodical Publications (later DC Comics). In the DC version, in 1956 Julius Schwartz introduced The Flash, a new version of the 1940s character, and started a superheroes revival. In the Marvel version, Stan Lee, facing the impending closure of Timely/Atlas/ Marvel in 1961, or perhaps his own departure from the industry, decided to do the sort of story he really wanted to do. Copying the success of DC's The Justice League of America, Lee created the Fantastic Four with Jack Kirby.

The history of superhero comics is important to understanding the changing attitudes to comic books for numerous reasons including the role of organized fandom, the longevity of the characters and their appeal across generations, and the political economy of the industry. But the tale of comic book history and the long march to respectability requires some acknowledgement of the immense popularity of other comic books. In the absence of longitudinal studies of comic book (and comic strip) readership it is difficult to offer an overview of the impact and role of particular comics in shaping comics readers, but as John Jackson Miller has shown, for many years the leading comics by sales figures (at least as reported by the companies in their annual statement required for special mailing rates) were Dell Comics's *Uncle Scrooge* (1960 and 1961) and Fawcett's *Dennis the Menace* (1963). In 1969 *Archie* sold more than any other comic book. The point here is that comic book reading was more likely than not an eclectic enterprise with the same people reading a range of comic books no doubt cycling through different types and genres and gradually leaving behind younger genres for perhaps the relatively more mature superhero comic books of Marvel and DC, or other comic-type fare.

The original *Mad* comic book, with its satires of comic book superheroes, and other subjects, illustrated that comics were a medium. The sort of satire in *Mad* and the later magazine version took the comics art form back to the satirical and caricature forms from which it in part derived. It put the *comic* back in comics art. *Mad*'s place in a historical narrative of the developing respectability of comics might at first seem odd. I think my own experience of a broad diet of comics material that included *Uncle Scrooge*, Harvey Comics, Archie, DC, Marvel, *Beano*, *Dandy*, *Mad*, and many other titles may have been atypical, but only for Americans by the inclusion of the two British titles. In any case *Mad* founding editor Harvey Kurtzman drew an association between *Mad* and the underground comix that began in the 1960s at the level of creators (Kurtzman 1991, 58–59; see also Witek 1989, 45).

It is more than likely that readers too followed a similar trajectory. Comix played with the form in ways that comic books simply did not. To be sure comix contained virulent racist and sexist images, such as Robert Crumb's Angelfood McSpade, which was both. Crumb has described this work as humorously poking "at the spot people are most uncomfortable with" and suggested that such images stemmed from a consciousness broken from its "social programming" by LSD (Crumb 2005). Whatever Crumb's explanation for his work, the underground comix broke through all sorts of programming and opened spaces for experiments with the form.

Art Spiegelman responded to the "flaming promise of Underground Comix." He contributed work to several comix, including one of the funniest, *Young Lust*, a parody of romance comic books. With fellow *Young Lust* artist Bill Griffith, the creator of Zippy the Pinhead, Spiegelman tried to realize the potential of comix in a more professional publication, *Arcade: The Comics Revue*, which Print Mint published for seven issues between 1975 and 1976. By 1980, though, that moment had "fizzled" out, and as Spiegelman puts it, comix "were stereotyped as dealing only with sex, dope, and cheap thrills . . . [and] got stuffed into the back of the cultural closet along with bong pipes and love beads."

Spiegelman moved back to New York City in 1976 where he met Françoise Mouly, and in 1980 they published the first issue of *Raw*, a graphix magazine. *Maus* first appeared in serialized form in *Raw*, commencing with the second issue in December 1980. Pantheon published volume one of *Maus* in book form in 1986. For the book Spiegelman reworked his illustrative style, reducing his more elaborate looking art in the serialized form to the deceptively simple appearance of funny animal comics (Spiegelman and Mouly 1987, 6–8).

THE POWER OF *MAUS*

The infantilization of the form between Wertham's campaign and the advent of comix lasted fourteen years or so, about the time for a generation of comic book readers such as Spiegelman to reach a maturity of sorts (he was twenty in 1968). Spiegelman's trajectory from suburban Rego Park, through youthful rebellion, to a hard-won adult relationship with his father is present in *Maus* and that narrative, especially the latter part, drives the story forward. As Witek suggests, *Maus* is as much autobiography as biography. Indeed the publisher denoted the work as Holocaust/Autobiography on the inside cover of the second printing of the first edition of volume one, but this categorization may well refer to the father's story.

Whatever the case, it is in this intersection of autobiography and biography that *Maus* becomes history, and not just a history of the Holocaust. Looking at *Maus* in 2008 it seems to me that one reason it resonated so well with Spiegelman's contemporaries, alongside Spiegelman's creative allegorical and metaphorical forms of Nazi/Cats and Jews/Mice, was that it offered the possibility for those of the generation who participated in a youthful rebellion of the 1960s to reconcile themselves with the world of their parents. Trying to understand a parent by recovering their experience of war has become somewhat of a calling for Americans who in the years since *Maus* have anointed their parents, in the words of Tom Brokaw: "The Greatest Generation." A comic book about the horrors of the Holocaust and its effects on survivors such as Vladek and his son Art provided a symbolical form through which to patch up generational conflict. That may seem a lot of freight for a comic book to carry, but no more than bearing the weight of the Holocaust on the backs of comic mice.

Maus is, as Joshua Brown noted in his insightful review, "an important historical work" with "a unique approach to narrative construction and interpretation." It is a work based on oral history and a work that reveals the processes of creating history from oral accounts (Brown 1988, 98). Moreover, *Maus* appeared at a moment when interest in the Holocaust as a topic of historical inquiry and memorialization was at a crescendo in America that translated (for example) into the creation of the United States Holocaust Memorial Museum, which opened in Washington, D.C. in 1993.

Maus as history is wonderful because it literally shows us how history is produced in a dialogue with the past and how historical narratives and interpretations are created through processes of selection and editing to convey the best sense of what happened. It deals with the issues of memory as a reliable source of evidence. Brown finds *Maus* "a successful work of history because it fails to provide the reader with a catharsis, with the release of tension gained through the complacent construct of 'knowing' all" (98). But *Maus* gained attention initially because of Spiegelman's representational strategies.

Adam Gopnik in a long essay in the *New Republic* remarked that people knew of *Maus* as the "Holocaust Comic Book" and its fame rested on drawing characters as animals. Gopnik labeled Spiegelman's choice as "a peculiar, idiosyncratic convention" suggesting that "there isn't any allegorical dimension in *Maus*, just a convention of representation." Gopnik took issue with those who saw *Maus* as trivializing the Holocaust through these representations and also with those who saw Spiegelman as overthrowing the tyranny of comics in favor of comix.

For Gopnik, Spiegelman had reconnected with and resurrected "the serious and even tragic possibilities of the comic strip and cartoon," a form that in Gopnik's account could be traced back to about 1600 or so in Italy. Gopnik argues that Spiegelman draws his characters more as though they are wearing animal masks, rather than anthropomorphic characters. And he argued that *Maus* drew "its power not from its visual style alone, but rather from the tension between the detail of its narration and dialogue and the hallucinatory fantasy of its images" (Gopnik 1987, 29–34). Some of *Maus*'s impact lay in the way readers had to confront the issue of how we look at and depict race/ethnicity/nationality visually; describing just how this process worked engaged many early reviewers of the book.

Joshua Brown thought readers of *Maus* would decipher the characters as humans wearing animal masks (metaphorically if not literally in the illustrations) and that Spiegelman had been purposively disruptive in this representation. Hitler described Jews as a different species and Spiegelman forces us to confront that particular racial rhetoric by recognizing his cats, mice, and pigs as humans. Joseph Witek understood *Maus* as firmly in the tradition of funny animal comics, starting with *Felix the Cat* and most famously Disney's animated characters. For Witek the animal metaphor worked simply "as a premise to be absorbed and then put out of mind," or in Spiegelman's words, "shucked like a snakeskin" (Witek 1989, 112). Writing in the *American*

Quarterly in 1991 I saw Spiegelman's technique as more allegorical in that the metaphor was not so easily "shucked." I read the Nazi/Cats as cats who dressed like humans and who had forced the Jews to live like mice (Gordon 1991, 341–46).

Fresh from working as a teaching assistant to Rabbi Abraham J. Karp in his History of the Holocaust class at the University of Rochester, my reading Nazis as cat-like came easily and I think I was probably not alone in that reaction. On the other hand, reading the Jews as having the characteristics of mice did not come so easily. For a start the central protagonists, the characters whose stories we follow and by the author's intention are meant to identify with, are Jew/Mice. But the metaphor is more easily shucked because *Maus* is biography and autobiography and the reader is constantly pulled back to a narrator represented as a mouse.

Cats play with their prey. It is in their nature, just as it was in the nature of Nazis—being a Nazi required a commitment to an ideology that denied some humans their humanity. The most basic of human instincts is to survive, just as Jews did everything they could to survive the genocide unleashed by the Nazis. Gopnik says the cat metaphor lets the cats, the Nazis, off too easily, from the question of how could they do it? But I think the binary at work here—the Nazis were cats and the Jews were struggling to survive as people—suggests the simple answer to the question: cats are amoral and Nazis were amoral, which is to suggest that evil is often as Hannah Arendt wrote: banal.

Gopnik wondered if perhaps such horror could only be presented in masks (Gopnik 1987, 33). For his part Spiegelman drew his masks in an extraordinarily simple fashion avoiding a "cute pudgy little mouse character with big, round, soulful eyes" because he wished to avoid unnecessary pleas for sympathy (Spiegelman qtd. in Brown 1988, 108). The power of *Maus* lay then not in pleas for sympathy, but in the depiction of the struggle for survival against an amoral, methodically brutal killing machine and in showing the cost of surviving for Vladek and those around him.

A quick guide to the impact of *Maus* can be had from doing a search of the Lexis database. From the publication of volume one in 1986 to 1997 the book has 772 citations. For the next ten years to January 2007 there are 2053 hits. From January 2007 to September 2008 there are 445 mentions. The book has only grown in reputation and any mention of graphic novels (just call them what they are: comic books) is incomplete without a tip of the hat to *Maus*.

For instance, a long piece in the *Washington Post* in August 2008 extolled the virtues of comic books through self-described lifelong prose guy Bob Thompson's discovery of their many virtues—and he duly gave *Maus* credit for starting a graphic novel boom. Moreover, the article was accompanied by a three-page comic (retrievable as jpg files from the website), one of which depicted Thompson's visit to Spiegelman and Mouly's loft residence, where *Maus* was born (Thompson 2008). On September 18, 2008, the *Wall Street Journal* ran an item including a short interview with Spiegelman about his reissued book *Breakdowns*, and over half the piece concerned *Maus* (Trachtenberg 2008). Two days earlier *The Times* (of London) carried an article by Ken Russell, the director of such films as *Women in Love* and *Tommy*, on a forthcoming festival of comics at London's Institute of Contemporary Arts under the heading "How the mighty *Maus* fuelled my flights of fantasy." To be sure the mouse of the title was Mickey, but Russell in his 1,000-word brief about the importance of comics dutifully gave two paragraphs (about twenty percent) to *Maus* and labeled Spiegelman a genius (Russell 2008, 18).

MUSEUMS AND THE MEDIA

In the first ten years after Pantheon published the first volume of *Maus* it was not immediately apparent it represented a transformative moment. To many critics and commentators it indeed looked like the exception that proved the rule that comics were not only (by and large) junk: only a rare genius like Spiegelman could pull off a work of quality in the medium. Writing in the massive catalog to accompany the High & Low: Modern Art and Popular Culture exhibition at the Museum of Modern Art in Manhattan (MoMA) in 1990, Adam Gopnik (with Kirk Varnedoe) described *Maus* as a "singular" achievement (Varnedoe and Gopnik 1990, 385).[1] Singular though Gopnik thought Spiegelman's work in the 1980s, the exhibition and the catalog contained a section on comics that examined the form from the Swiss originator Rodolphe Töpffer to Robert Crumb.

"Comics," a seventy-two-page chapter in the catalog, gave comics the sort of respect they seldom receive at the hands of art critics. Gopnik described them as "not a precursor of modern art but another kind of modern art" and one that shared "many of the same motives, forms, and dreams" (Varnedoe and Gopnik 1990, 152). Gopnik stressed both the accomplishments of outstanding artists such as George Herriman, Winsor McCay, and Crumb, but also pointed to the broader relevance of comics as an important optimistic counterbalance in modern art to the tendency to present modernity's destructive and alienating side.

Gopnik wove a tale showing the common response to modernity and artistic sensibilities of (say) Herriman and Juan Miro, the rise of comic books, the delirious ride they took through grotesque and kitsch stylings, and the impact this had on modern artists like Andy Warhol and Roy Lichtenstein. In Gopnik's hands the pleasure given by comics alleviated the mass commercial nature of the form and the tendency to leveling kitsch. His argument is enlightening and one not much examined by those who study comics. But in the exhibition, which I viewed in early 1991, placing comics side by side with, for example, Miro and Lichtenstein, tended to reduce the complexity of Gopnik's argument to "gosh gee these comics must have something going for them since great artists were either inspired by them or copied them more or less wholesale."

The interpretation tended to wash out and comics became curios of childish popular culture that somehow touched more rarefied levels of culture. Spiegelman responded to the exhibition with a scathing pictorial review, "High Art Lowdown," published in *Artforum International* (Spiegelman 1990, 115). Spiegelman took the curators to task for their "myopic choices," exclusions, and arbitrary organizational principles. In a 2002 interview Spiegelman recounted that these comments, which he regretted were all negative, led to MoMA contacting him, resulting in an exhibition of his work there in 1992 and eventually in the 2005 Masters of American Comics exhibition at the Hammer Museum and the Museum of Contemporary Art in Los Angeles.

The Masters of American Comics exhibition was curated by John Carlin and Brian Walker with an accompanying volume from Yale University Press. Although this exhibition and volume greatly improved on the MoMA effort, it still valorized the efforts of a few creative geniuses, all of who were men. In a complex and difficult media like comics, which sometimes is produced by individuals and other times by collaborative teams, singling out individuals in some ways engages in the same sort of marketing of artists as name brands that many art critics such as Graham Bader have criticized MoMA for doing in the High Low exhibition (Bader 2004, 109–12). But to be fair, the exhibition dealt with the complexity of comics as an art form, a creative medium, and a commercial undertaking in ways that no previous major exhibition had even broached (Fischer 2007, 730–32; Rhode 2007, 732–38).

Treating comics as childish remains the most common media trope. As comics researcher Gene Kannenberg, Jr. writes, journalists and/or sub-editors often seem incapable of producing a story on comics without a condescending headline along the lines of "Pow! Zap! Wham!: Comics Aren't just for Kids

Anymore" (Kannenberg 2008, 8). Two types of articles tend to appear under these sorts of headlines: pieces that track the rise of graphic novels and pieces that discuss the increasing number of superhero-comic-book-based movies and the lucrative profits to be had. The first usually start with *Maus* and track through a series of graphic novels such as Marjane Satrapi's *Persepolis*, Chris Ware's *Jimmy Corrigan*, and for good measure something by Will Eisner and Ben Katchor.

The second type approaches comics as idea generators for blockbuster movies, generally starting with Tim Burton's 1989 *Batman* (which incidentally does not hold up as well as Richard Donner's 1978 *Superman*) and work their way forward. In these accounts comics get some respect through backhanded compliments. The bottom line for respect in such articles is, well, the bottom line.

"Comics Boom!: Magazines earn megabucks through TV, film, retail sales," a cover story by David Liberman that ran above the fold in the Money section of *USA Today* in July 2008 is fairly typical of the way the press reports the business of comics. Replete with a dramatic splash headline featuring the Hulk crashing through a wall, the comic and boom of the headline are rendered comic-book style. But the report is all business, noting that the second Batman movie directed by Christopher Nolan, *The Dark Knight*, took a record $158 million in box office receipts in its opening weekend in the USA.

Overall comic book-based movies were on track in 2008 to best the 2007 record of $925 million in ticket sales, which amounted to ten percent of that year's box office receipts. Time Warner licensing resulted in retail sales of $6 billion for products carrying images of Superman, Batman, and other non-comic-book characters in 2007. Marvel characters did $5.5 billion worth of licensing sales. Against these figures the $700 million sales of comic books in 2007—up about $60 million from 2006—makes the other efforts look like a tail that is wagging the dog.

The article offers the now standard interpretation of comic books' role in this generation of profit in a succinct sound bite-worthy quote: "'Comics are a low-cost laboratory, with instant feedback, for what's happening in pop culture,' says Milton Griepp, publisher of ICv2, a website that tracks comic publishing." There is nothing particularly new about this sort of reporting since such articles have appeared regularly in the press since the success of the 1989 *Batman* movie and the accompanying licensing bonanza (see Kleinfield 1990, 1). The April 27, 1992, edition of the television show *Entertainment Tonight* reported Batman merchandise from the first film garnered sales of over one billion dollars worldwide by spring 1992.

Comics, then, fit into a corporate business plan as generators of licensed characters that produce super profits. Time Warner President Jeffrey Bewkes may have told the *Wall Street Journal* that the notion of synergy was "bullshit" but as far as comics goes, synergy has fertilized a rich vein of profit (Karnitschnig 2006, A1). And as both Connie Bruck and Gerard Jones have shown, the profitability of licensing comic book characters was part of the appeal to Steve Ross when he put together the Warner side of the Time Warner corporation between 1967 and 1969 in part through the purchase of DC (then National Periodical Publications) in 1967 for $60 million, a deal which included the associated company, the Licensing Corporation of America (Anon. 1967 and 1968; Bruck 1994; Jones 2004). It is a simple enough equation: with greater profitability comes greater respectability.

ACADEMICS AND COMICS ART

Much of the early quality academic work on comics can be traced back to Austrian-born and British-based art historian E. H. Gombrich, whose 1960 book, *Art And Illusion: A Study in the Psychology of Pictorial Representation*—derived from a series of lectures for the Smithsonian Institution in 1956—called for a critical inquiry of the form. Ellen Weise's 1965 edited volume, *Enter: The Comics*, which brought together the Swiss Rodolphe Töpffer's *Essay on Physiognomy* and one of his comics albums, *The True Story of Monsieur Crépin*, for the first time in English, was an initial response to Gombrich. David Kunzle, self-consciously following Gombrich's call, published the first of his two-volume history of the comic strip, *The Early Comic Strip Narrative Strips and Picture Stories in the European Broadsheet from c. 1450 to 1825* in 1973 (Kunzle 2007, ix). The second volume, *The Nineteenth Century*, followed in 1990. Kunzle's work set a benchmark in analytical and descriptive depth, but for a good many years Americans interested in comics did not take up his work or his methodology, which carefully placed technical and stylistic developments within a broad cultural matrix and offered a history of the form that explained why these developments happened.

But America did produce some early scholarly work of comics criticism. Arthur Asa Berger published his *Li'l Abner: A Study in American Satire* and followed up in 1973 with a series of essays in *Comic-stripped American*. Berger's work focused on how comic strips demonstrated American traditions of satire and caricature. Much of his argument was a plea to take comics seriously since they mirrored society's concerns and interests.

Other early academic work included Ariel Dorfman and Armand Mattelart's 1975 *How to Read Donald Duck: Imperialist Ideology in the Disney Comic*. Originally issued in Chile in 1971, this volume's highly polemical analysis of the Chilean versions of Disney comics made the none-too-subtle observation that comic book stories, even satires like Scrooge McDuck, proffered ideological positions. The book presaged a debate that became familiar enough among scholars of comics and other media about just how a cultural form infused its readers with a particular ideology. Elsewhere in academia around this time (circa the early 1970s) Donald Ault, a Blake scholar, was making waves through his courses at Berkeley that examined comics as part of a literature curriculum. Other academics with an early interest in comics included the Temple University communications professor, John Lent, and Faulkner specialist M. Thomas Inge.

In the late 1980s, Seetha Srinivasan at the University Press of Mississippi set up the Studies in Popular Culture Series with Inge as the general editor. Witek's *Comic Books as History* was the first book in this series that focused on comics (Heer 2008). In an essay for the *American Quarterly* I discussed Witek's book side by side with Kunzle's second volume. It may seem at first an odd juxtaposition, a work on twentieth-century American comic books with a foot in the comix camp, and a volume decidedly about nineteenth-century European comics art. But as it turns out, not so much so, because such a discussion marked a stage in the development of a comics studies field.

I hasten to add that the review editor of the journal, Charles Bassett, proposed the essay to me as I was searching for an opportunity to review Kunzle's book. Though not giving Witek nearly enough credit for the merits of his work I concluded the *American Quarterly* piece by suggesting that the comics form after a century of mass acceptance might be "about to receive the critical attention it deserves" (Gordon 1991, 341–46). Witek's book marked the beginning of some respectability, however attenuated, for academics who first and foremost study comics. Witek too was probably the first academic to build a successful career mostly around the study of comics, moving his way from a PhD under Ault at Vanderbilt through to being a full professor at Stetson University.

The somewhat older David Kunzle had been a working academic since the mid-1960s when he arrived at UCLA in the Art History Department and was perhaps protected from lowbrow accusations by the reach of his learning, his British accent, and Gombrich's reputation. As far as respectability went, Kunzle had the advantage of studying comics art unencumbered by associations with mass media or popular culture. At the same time Kunzle demanded that the material he studied be viewed as comic strips, which called into question the then popular and accepted notion of comics as a distinctively American art form.

I mean no disrespect to either of my colleagues, nor to suggest fundamental disagreement between them, when I say that they represented positions around which a field of comics scholarship grew. The University Press of Mississippi has continued to bring out a steady stream of works on comics and, as Jeet Heer has written, transformed "comics studies, hitherto and [sic] inchoate body of critical writing, into a coherent field" (Heer 2008). In addition to the many fine books published by Mississippi, other academic presses such as Duke, Chicago, Yale, and the now defunct Smithsonian Institution Press also published works on comics.

CONCLUSION

Given the boom in academic work on comics it is surprising that there is no English language single authored monograph on *Maus*. Pierre-Alban Delannoy published a work in French in 2002 and Ole Frahm a work in German in 2006. In 2001 the Belgian Leuven University Press published the English language volume *The Graphic Novel*, edited by Jan Baetens from papers delivered at a conference of the same name, and many of its chapters dealt with *Maus*. In 2003 the University of Alabama Press published *Considering Maus: Approaches to Art Spiegelman's "Survivor's Tale" of the Holocaust*, edited by Deborah R. Geis. These few volumes suggest a paucity of works on *Maus*, but there are, however, numerous journal articles and book chapters that discuss *Maus* in the context of the Holocaust, History, memory, trauma, and the formal properties of comics. The issues to hand in most of these pieces, even in two of the best by James E. Young and Marianne Hirsch, mostly expand on the concepts raised by Brown, Witek, and Gopnik in the 1980s (Young 1998, 666–99; Hirsch 1992–93, 3–29).

Maus may have shifted many attitudes toward comic books, but much of the academy still drags its heels. The March 2008 issue of *PMLA* contained an article by Hillary Chute titled "Comics as Literature?" that begins:

> Comics—a form once considered pure junk—is sparking interest in literary studies. I'm as amazed as anybody else by the comics boom—despite the fact that I wrote an English department dissertation that makes the passionate case that we should not ignore this innovative narrative

form . . . The field hasn't yet grasped its object or properly posed its project (Chute 2008, 452–65).

Chute's tone in framing her article belies much of the work that has shaped scholarship of comics and the quality and thoughtfulness of her own writing. Her piece goes on to discuss much of the scholarship on comics, but she overlooks several key scholars such as Witek and—surprisingly—Charles Hatfield, whose book, *Alternative Comics: An Emerging Literature* (2005), conveys in the title its importance to an author trying to discuss comics as literature. But she does of course discuss *Maus* at length. Indeed Chute is working with Spiegelman on his forthcoming *MetaMaus*.

Maus has made comics respectable. Those who study comics are slowly being admitted to the academic party, but sometimes comics scholars have to suitably humble themselves before being accepted in the VIP lounge of journals like the *PMLA*.

NOTES

1. The authors divided the chapters and Gopnik was responsible for the chapters cited here.

WORKS CITED

Anon. 1967. Kinney Plans to Acquire National Periodical in Exchange for Stock. *Wall Street Journal*, 24 July.
———. 1968. Kinney National Acquisition. *Wall Street Journal*, 27 Mar.
Bader, Graham. 2004. "High and Low." *Artforum International* 43(2): 109–12
Brown, Joshua. 1988. Of Mice and Memory. *Oral History Review* 16: 98.
Bruck, Connie. 1994. *Master of the Game: Steve Ross and the Creation of Time Warner*. New York: Simon & Schuster.
Carlin, John, Paul Karasik, and Brian Walker, eds. 2005. *Masters of American Comics*. New Haven: Yale University Press.
Chute, Hillary. 2008. Comics as Literature? Reading Graphic Narrative. *PMLA* 123: 452–65.
Crumb, Robert. 2005. "I'll never be the same." *The Guardian*, 10 Mar. http://www.guardian.co.uk/books/2005/mar/10/robertcrumb.comics [accessed 10 June 2008].
Fischer, Craig. 2007. Masters of American Comics—Two Reviews. *International Journal of Comic Art* 9.1: 730–32.
Gopnik, Adam. 1987. Comics and Catastrophe. *New Republic*, 22 June, 29–34.
Gordon, Ian. 1991. "But Seriously, Folks . . . ": Comic Art and History. *American Quarterly* 43: 341–46.

Hatfield, Charles. 2005. *Alternative Comics: An Emerging Literature*. Jackson, MS: University Press of Mississippi.

Heer, Jeet. 2008. The Rise of Comics Scholarship: the Role of University Press of Mississippi. *Sans Everything*, 2 Aug. http://sanseverything.wordpress.com/2008/08/02/the-rise-of-comics-scholarship-the-role-of-university-press-of-mississippi/ [accessed 30 Aug. 2008].

Hirsch, Marianne. 1992–93. Family Pictures: *Maus*, Mourning, and Post-Memory. *Discourse: A Journal for Theoretical Studies in Media and Culture* 15(2): 3–29.

Jones, Gerard. 2004. *Men Of Tomorrow: Geeks, Gangsters, and the Birth of the Comic Book*. New York: Basic Books.

Kannenberg, Jr., Gene. 2008. *500 Essential Graphic Novels*. New York: Collins Design.

Karnitschnig, Matthew. 2006. That's All Folks: After Years of Pushing Synergy, Time Warner Inc. Says Enough. *Wall Street Journal*, 2 June, A1.

Kleinfield, N. R. 1990. Cashing in on a Hot New Brand Name. *New York Times*, 29 Apr., 1 [Section 3].

Kunzle, David. 2007. *Father of the Comic Strip: Rodolphe Töpffer*. Jackson, MS: University Press of Mississippi.

Kurtzman, Harvey. 1991. *From Aargh! To Zap!: Harvey Kurtzman's Visual History of the Comics*. New York: Prentice Hall.

Rhode, Michael. 2007. Masters of American Comics—Two Reviews. *International Journal of Comic Art* 9(1): 732–38.

Russell, Ken. 2008. How the mighty *Maus* fuelled my flights of fantasy. *The Times*, 16 Sept., 18.

Spiegelman, Art, 1990. High Art Lowdown. *Artforum International* 29(4): 115.

Spiegelman, Art, and Françoise Mouly. 1987. Raw Nerves. In *Read Yourself Raw*, ed. Art Spiegelman and Françoise Mouly, 6–8. New York: Pantheon.

Thompson, Bob. 2008. Drawing Power. *Washington Post*, 24 Aug. http://www.washingtonpost.com/wp-dyn/content/story/2008/08/22/ST2008082201503.html [accessed 1 Sept. 2008].

Trachtenberg, Jeffrey A. 2008. King of Cartoons. *Wall Street Journal*, 18 Sept. http://www.wsj.com/article/SB122166625405548219.html [accessed 18 Sept. 2008].

Varnedoe, Kirk, and Adam Gopnik. 1990. *High & Low: Modern Art and Popular Culture*. New York: Museum of Modern Art.

Witek, Joseph. 1989. *Comic Books as History: The Narrative Art of Jack Jackson, Art Spiegelman, and Harvey Pekar*. Jackson, MS: University Press of Mississippi.

Young, James E. 1998. The Holocaust as Vicarious Past: Art Spiegelman's *Maus* and the Afterimages of History. *Critical Inquiry* 24(3): 666–99.

CHAPTER TWELVE

"A Purely American Tale": The Tragedy of Racism and *Jimmy Corrigan: The Smartest Kid on Earth* as Great American Novel

—PAUL WILLIAMS

Q. [Jimmy Corrigan: The Smartest Kid on Earth] *is billed as "a new humorous fiction"—but many readers find it more tragic than humorous. Is this more of a tragicomic book than a comic book?*
A. When I started making comics that weren't self-conscious garbage, I wanted to make something that was *empathetic*. Something that is humorous can divert the reader, but something that is tragic is empathetic. I wanted to do both.
—(Ware 2000b)

In the last ten years, few comics have garnered enthusiastic critical attention equal to Chris Ware's graphic novel *Jimmy Corrigan: The Smartest Kid on Earth* (2000). In his book, *Chris Ware* (2004), Daniel Raeburn hails Ware as a "luminary" who has won "every award a cartoonist can win: Eisner, Ignatz, Harvey and Rueben" (9). Raeburn overlooks the comics prizes of the non-Anglophone world, but he is right to emphasize Ware's star status. Ware's accolades extend beyond the comics industry, winning the British *Guardian* newspaper's First Book Award in 2001 for *Jimmy Corrigan* (Brockes 2001, 4).

In the U.S., his work has been exhibited in the Whitney Museum of American Art's 2002 biennial (Raeburn 2004, 16), the Smithsonian's design triennial (Ware 2000b), and at the Cooper-Hewitt National Design Museum (Thomson 2001, 14). 80,000 copies of *Jimmy Corrigan* had been sold by 2004 (Raeburn 2004, 9). One is struck by the sheer variety of broadsheet acceptance and promotion of *Jimmy Corrigan*, included in the end-of-year appraisals and summer reading lists of the British newspapers *Daily Mail* (Anon. 2003, 56), *Sunday Herald* (Anon. 2001c, 34), *Scotsman* (Anon. 2001a, 2), and *The Independent* (Anon. 2001b, 9–13).

The transformation in comics culture this collection explores has often been linked back to *Jimmy Corrigan* and the star persona of Chris Ware; Andrew D. Arnold stresses how Ware has "vastly increased the prestige of the medium" (Arnold, 2001; see also Shaar Murray 2001, 9). This chapter understands *Jimmy Corrigan*'s success in relation to the construction of comics as graphic novels by critics and reviewers, and the associated interpretation of the comics creator as an author comparable to literary writers. Francophone scholars André Gaudreault and Philippe Marion offer a relevant model for situating *Jimmy Corrigan*'s reception in North American comics history. Gaudreault and Marion argue that sequential art has had two births: the first is the *appearance* of the comics medium in the early nineteenth century, with Rodolphe Töpffer at the forefront of this birth. Töpffer pressed the existing technology of autolithography into the production of a new "means of transmission, the picture book," and a new means of narration, telling stories with "an analytical cutting of the action" and "a syntagmatic montage of the fragments" that had not been achieved before (2005, 5–11). The second birth is the *constitution* of a media institution, the baptismal recognition of its specificity and autonomy, which conceptualizes it in relation to coexistent media. This second, "*distinguishing birth*" is bound up with the "process wherein an institution assumes control of the medium, establishes its internal consensus, and regulates it" (5, 13).

Between the two births is a phase Gaudreault and Marion conceive of as a "period of emergence" in which the new medium is "subordinated to adjacent cultural practices" even though early institutional structures may have formed around it (8). Gaudreault and Marion argue that comics went through this period of emergence at the turn of the twentieth century, when its most significant "intermedial synergy" was with the "popular press": "In its interaction with this press the comic strip and graphic novel became accepted and popular culture industries" (11). Out of this interaction, comics' second birth—its constitution "as a singular medium" (11)—took place in the first half of the twentieth century.

In France, comics are recognized as one of the nine arts (Gaudreault and Marion 2005, 9): Gaudreault and Marion's evaluation of comics' full and healthy second birth is therefore understandable, but the independence they proclaim for the medium is questionable in the Anglophone context. In stressing how the reception of *Jimmy Corrigan* unfolded under the aegis of the field of literary production, this chapter nuances Gaudreault and Marion's assertion, perhaps indicating that the institutional autonomy characterizing the second birth of a medium has yet to be completed for North American comics. Certainly, their own repetition of the term "graphic novel" registers lexically how the perception of comics—or the perception of a certain type of comic, published in a certain form and directed at certain teenage and adult consumers—remains entangled with literary publishing.

Several aspects of *Jimmy Corrigan* have attracted praise: its self-conscious engagement with the superhero genre that dominates the comics medium, its witty self-deprecation, its formal virtuosity, and its high production values. The emotive charge of *Jimmy Corrigan* is remarkable: abandoned as a child by his father and brought up by his domineering, interfering mother, Jimmy has become a lonely Chicago office worker. He receives a plane ticket from his father and an invitation to spend Thanksgiving with him, Jimmy's stepsister Amy, and Jimmy's grandfather, also called James. The book follows the father and son's awkward meeting in small-town Michigan, brought to an abrupt conclusion by Jimmy's father's death as a result of an automobile accident. Interwoven with these events is Jimmy's grandfather James's childhood recollections of 1890s Chicago, particularly life with *his* father, William Corrigan, a glazier working on the 1893 World Columbian Exposition. Resentful of his wife's death in childbirth, William's morning pedagogical encouragements indicate his general demeanor towards his son: "Get up you goddamn little son of a bitch."[1] Eventually William abandons James, on his ninth birthday, at the Exposition.

This distressing genealogical narrative is emblematic of a major phenomenon in the publishing industry since the late twentieth century, the exponential rise in popularity of traumatic life stories (Gilmore 2001, 2–7). Accordingly, while conceding that the characteristics cited in the above paragraph were all factors in *Jimmy Corrigan*'s favorable reception, this chapter insists that the conceptualization of Ware as an author and *Jimmy Corrigan* as a novel is the motor behind the praise it received from reviewers and critics. Further, I argue that *Jimmy Corrigan* has been aligned with a long tradition in publishing and literary criticism: the perpetual hailing of the Great American Novel, a canonical book condensing the tensions, experiences, hopes, tragedies, and triumphs of the American republic and its peoples (as one example of scholarship among many, see Buell 2008).

Preexisting trends in book publishing and Chris Ware's position in relation to the wider construction of comics creators as literary figures facilitated the interpretation of the text as literature. Roger Sabin observes that since the late 1980s it has been the *novel* element of graphic novels that reviewers and critics have emphasized most prominently: "graphic novels were invariably reviewed in the book section rather than the general arts pages, writers were profiled rather than artists, and on the whole the quality of writing in a work was held in higher esteem than the art" (Sabin 1993, 247). One could add the (inconsistent) increase in shelf space dedicated to graphic novels by bookshops; Johanna Drucker observes that "Ware's books are competitive in a mass market, selling for prices that make them part of a regular hardcover fiction niche" (2008, 41). Chris Ware's interpolation as a literary author is not simple, and (unlike many of his peers) the design of *Jimmy Corrigan* is frequently commended (see Heller 2002 and Raeburn 2004, for example), but he has also received prestigious literary prizes and the presence of the graphic novel on those end-of-the-year reading lists demonstrate that in the press the company Chris Ware is most likely to keep is with prose fiction writers. This accords with his other publishing interests: Ware guest-edited #13 of Dave Eggers's literary periodical *McSweeney's Quarterly Concern* and has contributed work to *The New Yorker* (see David M. Ball's chapter in this collection), a magazine that has published prose by authors such as F. Scott Fitzgerald and Truman Capote (both closely associated with the Great American Novel). *Jimmy Corrigan*'s reception was informed by and is further evidence of the "transition of part of the comics industry from a 'comics culture' to a 'book culture.' [The co-option of comics by the book trade] served to remake comics in prose literature's image" (Sabin 1993, 247).

In addition to these publishing contexts exterior to the text, several aspects of *Jimmy Corrigan* invite one to read it as a "Great American Novel." *Jimmy Corrigan*'s kinship with this privileged literary mode (and the cultural capital it enjoys) was referred to by many reviewers, who observed a "bleak depiction of the dark side of the American dream" (Wynne 2003, 16) and "a small-scale history of America's last one hundred years" (Ware 2000b). Press accounts celebrated *Jimmy Corrigan* for representing "the Great American novel in comic book form" (front dustjacket, Raeburn 2004; see also Blackburn 2002, 5).

Interweaving the characters' lives with a handful of seminal events from U.S. history enhances the sense that the Corrigan family's exploits operate as a synecdoche for the fortunes of the national family since the Civil War. William Corrigan's involvement in the battle of Shiloh is the earliest meaningful scene to be represented in the graphic novel's non-linear narrative, and the Civil War's legacy of uneven race relations is central to the personal and national story that follows. Similar constructions of personal and national identity during and after modern mass conflict recur in other texts hailed as Great American Novels, such as Stephen Crane's *The Red Badge of Courage* (1895), Joseph Heller's *Catch-22* (1961), and Thomas Pynchon's *Gravity's Rainbow* (1973), which share with *Jimmy Corrigan* a visceral presentation of war's losses and a skepticism towards its glorification.

F. Scott Fitzgerald's *The Great Gatsby* (1925) epitomizes the "state of the nation" quality that reviewers have used as a criterion for selecting candidates for the Great American Novel, specifically the sense of purposelessness and emotional barrenness also featured in *Jimmy Corrigan*. Reviewers repeatedly commented on the graphic novel's representation of a USA whose citizens are left disorientated and lonely by their unrewarding work, their malnourished leisure activities, and the barren built environment (such as Nissen 2000; Nadel 2001, 13; Prager 2003, 197). Those settlements north of Chicago that Ware based Jimmy's father's town on are described by the writer as the bleakest of places: "Human beings: they are living out the grand dramas of their lives in these horrible areas that just seem to mock them at every turn. The modern world seems to make fun of people in a lot of ways" (Ware 2000b).

Both these sets of tropes from the Great American Novel tradition feed into the third theme, also depicted in *Jimmy Corrigan*, and the one discussed in detail here. What Ware's text shares with the novels *Adventures of Huckleberry Finn* (1884), *Absalom, Absalom!* (1936), and *To Kill a Mockingbird* (1960) (to name but three) is a preoccupation with the psychological and physical damage racism wrecks on individuals and families. Lusi Siroy's praise for *Jimmy Corrigan* implies the entwinement of racism and the Great American Novel, calling the book "a purely American tale that involves as many generations as Alex Haley's *Roots*" (2003, 18). Paradoxically, Ware identifies *Jimmy Corrigan*'s discussion of race as "a fundamental American thread" while insisting that the book was not planned as "any sort of grand opus or meditation on the American experience" (Ware 2000b).

Nonetheless, *Jimmy Corrigan* connects racism to the national consciousness and identity in a striking and lyrical way. The remainder of this chapter explores its projection of racism as a personal and national tragedy, one overlapping with the aforementioned representation of contemporary angst. It seems that meaningfully, honestly, and tolerantly connecting with each other could salve America's existential ennui. Irish-American Jimmy is "paralyzed by his own inability to decide or act, and a fear of being disliked" (Ware 2000b), but developing a relationship with his African-American stepsister Amy could provide the interpersonal bond that overcomes his impoverished, transient upbringing, and the "paralyzed" person his childhood produced. America's history of racism is an obstacle to Jimmy and Amy's sense of belonging to the same family: as Jimmy makes a gesture defying the notion that he and Amy cannot be kin because of their different skin color, a series of coincidences separate them and return Jimmy to his grey office. The tragedy of racism in *Jimmy Corrigan* is that it quashes the human contact that would redeem alienating modern life, and when Jimmy is ready to rise above it, happenstance and mistiming squander the opportunity.

JIMMY CORRIGAN'S CRITIQUE OF AMERICAN RACISM

Jimmy Corrigan tracks American racism from the postbellum period to the 1980s; on the inside back cover Ware provides a brief history of the "Draft Riots," intended to set the scene for the hostility between Irish America and African America in the wake of the Civil War:

> The "Civil War Draft Riots" occurred in New York City, Boston, and other large metropolitan centers in July 1863. At that time, persons who were able to pay a $300 "substitution fee" (i.e. the richer classes) were freed from the responsibility of Union Army service, leaving the poor classes (particularly Irish immigrants) especially vu[l]nerable to the draft. Afro-Americans were, ironically, inelligible [sic] for active army service, and so by default were positioned to take over the mostly menial jobs which would be vacated by the Irish. Angry mobs (reportedly composed of primarily Irish citizens) murdered nearly one thousand Afro-Americans and caused over two million dollars worth of property damage over a period of four days.

The 1890s narrative bears out that hostility. Returning from a magic lantern show featuring a "pickanniny" (an offensive African-American stereotype characterized by foolishness and overreaction [see Bogle 1994, 7–8]) struck on the head while attempting to steal a pie from a windowsill, William Corrigan is still laughing at the sight of "poor old 'Jim Crow.'" Buying a newspaper from an African-American boy, William feels in competition with an elderly man attempting to make a purchase at the same time. William scrambles with his change in a rush to buy the boy's attention and—the narrative title informs the reader—"secure himself in the elderly man's opinion as the more preferred of the two customers." Before William finalizes how much to give the boy, the elderly man has passed on his money and moved away. Since William's charity was motivated by self-image, he sees no reason to give the boy any money now, and he tries to inflate himself by putting the boy down with a single, "carefully aimed" word of abuse: "Niggers."

William drives his buggy through an area of the city primarily inhabited by African-Americans—in the words of the narrator, "neighborhoods that most of the town goes out of its way to forget." The compassion of the narrator is not shared by William, resentful of the sacrifices of the Civil War: "We give them their freedom and look at how they waste it." He takes "a little detour towards the lake. Conveniently then he can forget it all exists," and the forced nature of William's forgetting is conveyed by the way the word "Conveniently" flourishes across a whole panel in theatrical script.

It is important to note the Corrigan family is enmeshed in a network of racial and ethnic prejudices. In a position of power over African-Americans, with William able to fire the black maid May with impunity for challenging his authority, initially it seems Irish Americans are safely incorporated into American society—to the extent that they can denigrate more recent immigrant groups. At one point, James and Miss McGinty run away from Antonio, an Italian-American boy they had been playing with. Miss McGinty calls him "a little wop," a word whose offensiveness is conveyed by John Fante's short story "The Odyssey of a Wop" (1933). James uses the same language when he describes Antonio to the Corrigan family horse, and he ignores the Italian-American boy at school.

Predictably for schoolyard politics, the balance of power shifts when Miss McGinty and some other boys are impressed by the lead figurines Antonio's father makes, and which he allows visitors to the family home to make too. When James's horse comes out of the mould misshapen, his peers mock him with ethnic slurs: "Little Micky Leprechaun" and "Go find yer pot o'gold!" Irish-American stereotypes are inflicted upon James, echoing the magic lantern slides belonging to James's father that depict a wild-eyed looter with a chin-curtain beard during the Great Fire of Chicago. Along with low angled faces and "simianized" physiognomic features, these visual characteristics were part of a broader, historically specific vocabulary of images often deployed across the Anglophone Atlantic when the Celtic Irish were being represented. Such images summon up the political immaturity, lawlessness, and brutishness of the Irish and Irish Americans—and their occupancy on a lower rung of the evolutionary hierarchy than Anglo-Saxons (Curtis 1997, 58–67; see also Soper 2005, 263–64).

When the narrative returns to the twentieth century, the question of family belonging across the lines of "racial difference" suggests that racial prejudices have endured. James Corrigan bridges those two eras, and his upbringing among 1890s prejudices are apparent in his attitude to his step-granddaughter. Amy was adopted from Oswaga County Adoption Services by the white woman that Jimmy's father would eventually marry. In the 1980s, Amy explains to Jimmy, "Mom never thought she'd get married and have kids so she adopted me." Interviewing James for a Family History Project about the World Columbian Exposition, a fourth-grade Amy wishes she could have seen it. James replies: "Hm? Oh . . . Well they only let coloreds in for one day or so I think . . . "

The lack of compassion underlined by his choice of language is further demonstrated as James and Jimmy's father argue afterwards, Jimmy's father asking why James brought up the issue in the first place. After a pause, James begins, "Well, I still don't see why you would wanna have a," with Ware obscuring the end of his sentence with Jimmy's father's speech bubble. Jimmy's father does not want to hear the language his father will use to describe his stepdaughter—James has effectively communicated that his son's actions, marrying Amy's mother and bringing Amy into the family, are incomprehensible to him.

After Jimmy's father is hospitalized in a car accident during Jimmy's visit, his children feel they must confront their own racial identity in order to claim membership within his family. Amy is anxious that the white authority figures she continually encounters will question her kinship with her stepfather, while Jimmy's typical unease is heightened by his stepsister's blackness (Prager 2003, 198). Having only seen his sister in an old photograph, Jimmy first hears her voice as he squats inside a toilet cubicle and the sound of her footfalls—"step step step"—onomatopoeically reinforce his stepsister's presence. Acutely aware of the difference in their skin color and what he believes that signifies, Jimmy reaches for stereotypically black hairstyles (dreadlocks and cornrows) as he imagines what she looks like. Conscious of the political incorrectness of reacting with fear or anger, Jimmy wonders if he should greet her with "Whassup? I'm *Jim!* I just don't want you to think I'm afraid of *black people!*" The ridiculousness of this image—its incongruity with Jimmy's public persona and its patronizing inappropriateness—signifies that Jimmy is planning to react to the color of Amy's skin and not her personality.

Inside the hospital, the orderly refers to Jimmy as Amy's husband, assuming this black woman must be related to the older white man through his son. As Amy waits, she imagines a mistake has been made by the police officer who ascertained the status of her father before she arrived: realizing there is a male African-American patient called Corrigan at the hospital, Amy wonders if the officer insisted that the staff find a black man named Corrigan to check up on. Amy fears that her stepfather really is dead, and the police officer's insistence on black children having black fathers has created confusion and false hope. In Amy's daydream, a Dr. Smith comes to talk to her about her father, but like the police officer, is incredulous about her status as "Mr. Corrigan's closest relative."

Jimmy and Amy make forced attempts at bonding, with two main difficulties: her frustration at his reticence and awkwardness, and his fear of retribution for what Jimmy perceives as his betrayal of his mother by visiting his father. Amy tries to defuse the awkwardness by making a joke about the difference between their skin colors as they look through old photographs—which Jimmy fails to understand. Aggravated by Jimmy's vague, uninterested answers, Amy tells him, "Y'know I'm not going to bite you . . . I'm just curious about you, y'know?" The next panel is enlarged to show in more emphatic terms the pool of silence they are sitting in. Amy then asserts the bond that *should* exist between them—"I mean we're practically related, right?"—yet her choice of language implies she accepts they are not related in actuality. This is the central tenet of the tragedy of racism running through *Jimmy Corrigan*: the misconception that kinship depends, among other factors, upon the shared color of a family's skin.

Jimmy expects disapproval from his mother once she discovers the family her son has contacted, and her racism is one reason for this. Jimmy imagines her responding to his defense of "curiosity" with the words "Curious? About what? That man? [Pause] And that colored girl? I don't approve of this . . . " Jimmy is probably right to expect a racist reaction, as she rushes to anger and offensive stereotyping when Jimmy, his mother, and her fiancé Mr. Johnson return to her room at Sunnyvale Courts Retirement Health Care Facility:

JIMMY'S MOTHER: God . . . *damn* that woman . . .
MR. JOHNSON: What? What is it?
JIMMY'S MOTHER: Oh . . . it's that . . . *colored* maid . . . if I've asked
   her *once* I've asked her a . . . *hundred* times . . . not to *move* anything
   around . . .

MR. JOHNSON: Well, maybe it wasn't her . . . it's a holiday, you know . . .
  maybe it was a fill-in . . .
JIMMY'S MOTHER: No, no, it was *her* . . . I can *smell* her . . .

The pause before Jimmy's mother spits out *"colored* maid" implies she is taking her time considering a range of abusive possibilities. Because of her centrality in Jimmy's life, his desire to get closer to Amy, his "real sister" (Jimmy's
words), must negotiate his mother's racist reaction. Jimmy interprets Amy's
questions about his leisure interests as evidence that "she do like me . . . But
. . . if Mom won't like <u>her</u>? but <u>I</u> like . . . " Jimmy indulges in a melodramatic
fantasy in which his father recovers, and despite Amy's barely concealed love
for her stepbrother, Jimmy returns to his mother in Chicago, whereupon he
pines in his armchair for (presumably) Amy.

Jimmy gets married, has a family, and choking back his tears for his lost
love Amy, continues to be a satellite to his mother's caprices. Turning to wish
fulfillment, Jimmy's wife and new family are lost at sea and his mother dies,
freeing the way for Jimmy's return to Amy, and the romantic contact of fire-
side handholding. When Amy interrupts his daydream, Jimmy looks at her as
lover and wife; Amy is dazed with tiredness, Jimmy is dazed by longing. Amy
retires to bed, and Jimmy resumes his fantasy with an atomic explosion.

He and Amy become "the only people left on Earth," and the stepsiblings
become a couple, bringing up baby in a log cabin. With all other human life
extinct, the obligation to propagate the species legitimizes their union. Traditional gender roles are extended by this scenario: Jimmy becomes protec-
tor and provider, Amy becomes child-bearer and nurturer, played out in the
wholesome setting of a new frontier made possible by civilization's disap-
pearance ("everything is g-gone"). This fantasy suggests Jimmy's willingness
to join his father's family is partly attributable to his interpretation of Amy as
sexual and romantic figure. A slightly earlier panel, focused on Amy's breasts
in profile under her sweater, perhaps offers Jimmy's point-of-view as he looks
lustfully at his stepsister. His belief that the two could start a family of their
own is a challenge to the racist taboo on "miscegenation," but the fact this
only takes place in his post-apocalyptic fantasy gives some sense of how far
Jimmy thinks this is viable.

THE TRAGEDY OF RACISM

It is in *Jimmy Corrigan*'s most revelatory moment that the tragic nature of
racism is illuminated. As Amy drives herself and Jimmy to the hospital where

they will be told their father died in the night, Ware sets up their hopes and fears in a virtually symmetrical double-page spread. On one page, Jimmy confronts a "NUMBER #1 DAD" T-shirt, reminding him that on the other side of his abandonment by his father is the attention and compassion Jimmy's father showed Amy. Jimmy reevaluates the "HI" his father spelt out in bacon when Amy remembers, "On holidays he'd fix breakfast and make the bacon spell words . . . I used to love that . . . " Breakfast now symbolizes how Jimmy's father is belatedly extending to Jimmy the thoughtfulness Amy has enjoyed. Amy fears her father will be so badly injured he can communicate only through the wave of a hand so weak that it is conveyed by subtle, easily missed movement lines. As Jimmy approaches an unusual point of calm, smiling and thinking aloud, "I bet they will serve dinner there," Amy's restlessness with her stepbrother grows.

At the hospital, Jimmy and Amy are kept waiting until Dr. Wilson enters. The reactions Amy has been experiencing and imagining—that she cannot belong to this Irish American family because she is African American—are quieted as Dr. Wilson automatically refers to them as brother and sister. Their familial bond is most bruised and most required at this moment; Jimmy momentarily triumphs over the forces of racism running through his family line by outstretching his hand to brush his stepsister's as she shakes from the news of their father's death. Ware elongates this movement over the course of seven panels, heightening the high personal stakes in Jimmy's action and its significance as a culmination of his reconcilement with his father. "Swamped by a succession of tragicomic disasters, a man who has never quite come to terms with his own humanity must recognize the humanity of an Other (black, female) in order to cope with the humanity of the father whose absence had blighted his life" (Shaar Murray 2001, 9).

Despite defying the racism of (most notably) his mother by affirming his kinship with Amy through fraternal gesture, Jimmy is rebuked. Amy shoves him off his chair: "Get away from me!" Amy is stunned, and the nurse leads Jimmy outside before closing the door. Stood rigid outside the consultation room, Jimmy replays the scene in his head, imagining Amy's face to be more pained and grotesque than it first appeared: Jimmy places tears on her cheek. Mistakenly hailed by a cab driver, Jimmy gets in, crying too, and is driven away. When Amy is ready to apologize, no one is there when she opens the door.

Circumstance has intervened and divided this embryonic offshoot of the Corrigan family before it had the chance to grow together, especially poignant given the obstacles of "racial difference" and racism Jimmy has struggled against and seemingly overcome by reaching out to his stepsister. With Amy standing in the open doorway, Ware silently underscores the tragic quality of their dispersed family bond in a diagrammatic series of panels tracing Amy's genealogy back to the 1890s, back to Amy's great-grandmother, an illegitimate child picking flowers on land close to the Corrigan family home. Amy's great-great-grandmother was raped by her employer, Jimmy's great-grandfather William Corrigan. Looking back to the preceding 1890s narrative and May's "violation of my father's authority (however innocent)," one rereads James's following euphemism with horrific knowledge: "The next morning my father gave our maid her 'notice.'" Raeburn comments that the "way that Ware shows the events linking Jimmy and Amy by blood—using neither words nor action—is something that can be done only in comics" (2004, 78): the spatial economy with which Ware allows Amy's genealogy to unfold over two pages challenges the reader to follow, and compounds their horror.

This biological familial bond is not known to the characters in the 1980s, and metaphorically acts out the failure of the American national family to cohere, the USA's failure in letting itself be divided by the perception of race. If the country excavated its history, the myth of separate racial groups could be challenged—this requires the nation to exercise the imagination necessary to reconceptualize its history and ontology. Appropriately, it is this imaginative task readers of *Jimmy Corrigan* must traverse in order to track the genealogical connections Ware makes through the comic form at this moment. Ironically, this microcosmic coming together and irrevocable breaking apart of the Corrigan family takes place during the country's foremost celebration of national and family unity: the Thanksgiving holiday.

Like other critically awarded texts in recent years such as the film *Crash* (2005), *Jimmy Corrigan* laments that life in modern America is existentially impoverished, with racism a key component of that alienation. As a key component, it is commonly shared: Irish-Americans abuse African-Americans as "niggers," Italian-Americans abuse Irish-Americans as "Micky," Italian-Americans are abused as "wops." Racism appears as a common affliction preventing Americans of all colors coming together in friendship and understanding, but the ubiquity of stereotyping in *Jimmy Corrigan* blunts one's attention to the less obvious structures of racism:

The facile catch-all invocation of "stereotypes" elides a crucial distinction: stereotypes of some communities merely make the target group uncomfortable, but the community has the social power to combat and resist them; stereotypes of other communities participate in a continuum of prejudicial social policy and actual violence against disempowered people, placing the very body of the accused in jeopardy (Shohat and Stam 1994, 183).

The depiction of every ethnic group as victims of racial stereotyping fuels a moral imperative to empathize with racism's victims, while avoiding the radical economic, social, and political transformations necessary to restructure American society. Jimmy's success in straining against racism brings no reward; where racism fails to tear African-American and Irish-American apart, the little accidents of everyday life succeed. *Jimmy Corrigan*'s depiction of racism stresses its tragic quality as a corrosive presence obstructing the kind of human contact that could comfort Americans disorientated by personal loss and modern alienation. The framework of tragedy prioritizes empathy as an appropriate response, reflected in this chapter's epigraph, but the demands of empathy may defuse any further political exertion.

Against the ennui, reviewers keep finding moments of redemption in the text. For Poniewozik and Arnold, the "anomie" of modern life is partly alleviated by "the meaning and even beauty in every glimpse from a highway . . . that may be this melancholy book's uplifting message: even in the most emotionally barren settings, there is still something not to deaden us but to make us stronger" (2000, 116). For Shaar Murray, despite the absence of a "feel-good ending . . . what prevents the bleakness of Ware's vision from overwhelming the reader in a flood of cosmic pessimism is the sheer craftsmanship, imagination, inventiveness and compassion with which it is realised" (2001, 9). Perhaps the very act of trying to make a familial history of racism, miscommunication, and abandonment comprehensible consoles readers with a "drive of narrative" redeeming the book's "melancholic, pained, and painful view of humanity" (Jamieson 2003, 8).

Appropriately enough, literary scholar Marcus Cunliffe observes that in the 1890s American literary critics were "calling" for the Great American Novel to appear, and that such a book should be "uplifting" (1987, 239). In its aesthetic beauty, and the final scene in which Jimmy may have found an ally in his new office neighbor Tammy, the comic holds on to an optimism that suggests hope can unexpectedly pay off. The end of *Jimmy Corrigan* leaves the reader not sunk in depression but musing on its final image, with Jimmy reprotected by the wonder of youth symbolized by Super-Man.

CONCLUSION

As a dust-jacketed hardcover, early collected editions of the *Jimmy Corrigan* narrative conveyed a material sense that this comic was also a graphic novel, a text that could appropriately sit alongside prose novels. Its materiality stressed the kinship between graphic novels and literary fiction assumed in the arts media at the turn of the twenty-first century, an assumption that made it commonsensical for reviewers to understand Ware's text in literary terms. Accordingly, many writers venerated *Jimmy Corrigan* as a new arrival in the firmament of American literature, and it captured the allegiances of award-givers and reviewers in the literate broadsheets and weeklies.

As noted by some reviewers, it was particularly amenable for assimilation into the cultural apparatus of the contemporary arts media because in addition to capturing the length and narrative complexity of many prose fiction publications, it shared many of the tropes of the Great American Novel. The particular trope explored in this essay is *Jimmy Corrigan*'s representation of American racism as a personal and national affliction, preventing Jimmy and Amy Corrigan from bonding as family members. This is not necessarily tragic, though.

What makes racism tragic in *Jimmy Corrigan* is twofold: when Jimmy finally understands Amy as his sister, circumstance conspires to prize them apart. Their potential relationship as siblings, nurturing and sustaining each other through bereavement and derisive modern life, is confounded. At this moment, the tragic quality of their failure to form a family bond is raised to further dramatic heights by the unfolding visual map of their shared genealogical heritage: Jimmy and Amy remain ignorant that they *were* related biologically. This tragedy is alleviated slightly by the graphic novel's enigmatic conclusion, whose redemptive quality returns us once more to consider the Great American Novel tradition as a framework for understanding *Jimmy Corrigan*'s successful reception.

NOTES

1. *Jimmy Corrigan: The Smartest Kid on Earth* deploys a series of fonts and typefaces, upper and lower case letters. For ease of reading, whenever quoting from the comic I have used a uniform font and followed standard grammatical rules for upper and lower case. Quotations from the comic are not given page references because they are not printed in the text.

WORKS CITED

Anon. 2001a. Writing Worth Reading in 2001. *Scotsman*, 29 Nov., 2.

————. 2002b. Books of the Year. *Independent*, 1 Dec., 9–13.

————. 2001c. Under the Covers. *Sunday Herald*, 2 Dec., 34.

————. 2003. The Sun'll Come: Summer Books. *Daily Mail*, 23 May, 56.

Arnold, Andrew D. 2001. The Depressing Joy of Chris Ware. *Time*. http://www.time.com/time/columnist/arnold/article/0,9565,185722,00.html [accessed 4 Apr. 2007].

————. 2003. A Mouse; A House; A Mystery. *Time*. http://www.time.com/time/columnist/arnold/article/0,9565,477842,00.html [accessed 4 Apr. 2007].

Blackburn, Julia. 2002. Shelf Life. *Scotland on Sunday*, 14 Apr., 5.

Bogle, Donald. 1994. *Toms, Coons, Mulattoes, Mammies, and Bucks: An Interpretative History of Blacks in Americans Films*. 3rd ed. Oxford: Roundhouse.

Bredehoft, Thomas A. 2006. Comics Architecture, Multidimensionality, and Time: Chris Ware's *Jimmy Corrigan: The Smartest Kid on Earth*. *Modern Fiction Studies* 52(4): 869–90.

Brockes, Emma. 2001. I Still Have Overwhelming Doubt about My Ability. *Guardian Online*. http://books.guardian.co.uk/Print/0,3858,4315150,00.html [accessed 19 Dec. 2006].

Buell, Lawrence. 2008. The Unkillable Dream of the Great American Novel: *Moby-Dick* as Test Case. *American Literary History* 20(1–2): 132–55.

Crane, Stephen. 1975. *The Red Badge of Courage*. Charlottesville: UP of Virginia. Originally published in 1895.

Crash. Dir. Paul Haggis. Lions Gate, 2005.

Cunliffe, Marcus. 1987. *The Literature of the United States*. 4th ed. Harmondsworth: Penguin.

Curtis, Jr., L. Perry. 1997. *Apes and Angels: The Irishman in Victorian Caricature*. Rev. ed. Washington, D.C.: Smithsonian Institution Press.

Drucker, Johanna. 2008. What is Graphic about Graphic Novels? *English Language Notes* 46(2): 39–55.

Eggers, Dave. 2005. Chris Ware. In *Masters of American Comics*, ed. John Carlin, Paul Karasik, and Brian Walker, 308–17. Los Angeles: Museum of Contemporary Art and the Hammer Museum; New Haven: Yale University Press.

Fante, John. 1933. The Odyssey of a Wop. *The American Mercury* 30(117): 89–98.

Faulkner, William. 1995. *Absalom, Absalom!* London: Vintage Classics. Originally published in 1936.

Fitzgerald, F. Scott. 1994. *The Great Gatsby*. Harmondsworth: Penguin. Originally published in 1925.

Gaudreault, André, and Philippe Marion. 2005. A Medium is Always Born Twice . . . *Early Popular Visual Culture* 3(1): 3–15.

Gibbons, Fiachra. 2001. Graphic Novel Wins Guardian Book Award. *Guardian*, 7 Dec., 9.

Gilmore, Leigh. 2001. *The Limits of Autobiography: Trauma and Testimony*. Ithaca: Cornell University Press.

Heller, Joseph. 2004. *Catch-22*. London: Vintage. Originally published in 1961.

Heller, Steven. 2002. Chicago's Comic Book Hero has a Finely Tuned Gift for Hand-Lettering. *Eye: The International Review of Graphic Design* 45(12): 18–25.

Jamieson, Teddy. 2003. Outstripping the Best. *Herald*, 22 Nov., 8.

Kidd, Chip. 1997. Please Don't Hate Him. *Print* 51: 42–49.

Lee, Harper. 1989. *To Kill a Mockingbird*. New York: HarperCollins. Originally published in 1960.

Nadel, Daniel. 2001. Rev. of *Jimmy Corrigan: The Smartest Kid on Earth* by Chris Ware. *Graphis* 57: 13.

Nissen, Beth. 2000. A Not-So-Comic Comic Book. *CNN.com*. http://edition.cnn.com/2000/books/news/10/03/chris.ware/ind ex.html [accessed 4 Apr. 2007]

O'Keeffe, Alice. 2005. Strip Lit is Joining the Literary Elite. *The Observer*, 20 Nov., 16.

Poniewozik, James, and Andrew Arnold. 2000. Right Way, Corrigan. *Time*, 11 Sept., 116.

Prager, Brad. 2003. Modernism in the Contemporary Graphic Novel: Chris Ware and the Age of Mechanical Reproduction. *International Journal of Comic Art* 5(1): 195–213.

Pynchon, Thomas. 1973. *Gravity's Rainbow*. New York: Viking.

Raeburn, Daniel. 2004. *Chris Ware*. London: Laurence King Publishing.

Sabin, Roger. 1993. *Adult Comics: An Introduction*. London: Routledge.

Shaar Murray, Charles. 2001. Comic Tragedy for the Last of a Line. *Independent*, 16 June, 9 [Features].

Shohat, Ella, and Robert Stam. 1994. *Unthinking Eurocentrism: Multiculturalism and the Media*. London: Routledge.

Siroy, Lusi. 2003. Rev. of *Jimmy Corrigan: The Smartest Kid on Earth* by Chris Ware. *Times*, 7 June, 18 [Features].

Soper, Kerry. 2005. From Swarthy Ape to Sympathetic Everyman and Subversive Trickster: The Development of Irish Caricature in American Comic Strips between 1890 and 1920. *Journal of American Studies* 39(2): 257–96.

Thomson, David. 2001. The Antique Rude Show. *Guardian*, 4 Sept., 14 [Features].

Twain, Mark. 1994. *Adventures of Huckleberry Finn*. Harmondsworth: Penguin. Originally published in 1884.

Ware, Chris. 2000a. *Jimmy Corrigan: The Smartest Kid on Earth*. New York: Pantheon Books.

———. 2000b. Interview with Andrew Arnold. *Time*. http://www.time.com/time/nation/article/0,8599,53887,00.html [accessed 4 Apr. 2007].

———. 2000c. Interview with Beth Nissen. *CNN.com*. http://edition.cnn.com/2000/books/news/10/03/chris.ware.qanda/ [accessed 4 Apr. 2007].

———. 2006. Interview with Todd Hignite. In *In the Studio: Visits with Contemporary Cartoonists*, ed. Todd Hignite, 228–59. New Haven: Yale University Press.

Wynne, Frank. 2003. Out There. *Times*, 21 June, 16 [Weekend].

CHAPTER THIRTEEN

"That Mouse's Shadow": The Canonization of Spiegelman's *Maus*

—ANDREW LOMAN

On May 26, 1985, *The New York Times* published an important docu-
ment in the history of the American comic book. In "Cats, Mice and History—
the Avant-Garde of the Comic Strip," Ken Tucker discussed early chapters of
Art Spiegelman's Holocaust narrative *Maus*, published serially at the time in
the comics anthology *Raw* and as yet uncollected in a single volume. "Perhaps
because of *Raw*'s limited circulation," Tucker suggested, "few people are aware
of the unfolding literary event *Maus* represents." Were they only to see it,
Tucker argued, they would recognize a major work of art, "an epic story in
tiny pictures."

More than twenty years later in October, 2008, Spiegelman published *Portrait of the Artist as a Young %@§*!.*[1] Part memoir, part introduction to his early
experiments in comic-book narrative, *Portrait of the Artist* also characterizes
Maus's influence on his subsequent life. "That's a monument I built to my
father," he says, pointing behind him to a massive statue of a bespectacled
mouse. "I never imagined it would grow so big." Now it looms over him. "No
matter how hard I run," he complains, "I can't escape that mouse's shadow."

Maus casts its shadow far, and not just over Spiegelman—the book's success has precipitated a broad reassessment of the artistic potential of the
comic book. No longer deemed the effluent of mass culture, it has become
respectable and it is normal now to see comic strips published and books
reviewed in magazines that self-consciously declare their sophistication. In
this decades-long elevation of the form, Spiegelman's career has been pivotal.

Raw, which he co-edited with Françoise Mouly in the early 1980s, nurtured the American comics' "avant-garde" and introduced American readers to translated works from Europe and elsewhere.

When *Maus* was published in two volumes in 1986 and 1991, the American media were collectively astonished that comics have as much potential for intellectual and artistic sophistication as any other art form. Through the 1990s Spiegelman was an ambassador of the medium, writing on comics in *The New Yorker* and elsewhere, though he did not single-handedly elevate the reputation of the form. In the late 1980s when the news media were discovering the aesthetic potential of comics, their focus was wide enough to include the Hernandez brothers' *Love and Rockets* (1981–present), Frank Miller's *Batman: The Dark Knight Returns* (1986), Alan Moore and Dave Gibbons's *Watchmen* (1986–87), and others. But of these books, *Maus* was the boldest departure from popular assumptions about comics: if its aesthetic techniques were not necessarily more daring than those of many other works, nevertheless its rejection of the most pervasive comic-book genres of the time was far more complete, its subject matter more obviously serious. As such it was celebrated not just as a literary event, but as the greatest achievement of the form.

Within the decade, *Maus* began appearing in the anthologies published by W. W. Norton, Inc. Excerpts from *Maus* were published in *Postmodern American Fiction: A Norton Anthology* (1st ed., 1997), *The Norton Anthology of Jewish American Literature* (1st ed., 2001), and *The Norton Anthology of American Literature* (7th ed., 2007). Because Norton's anthologies are widely used in university literature departments, its editorial decisions govern much of what is read on university survey courses. One may reasonably point to a work's inclusion in these anthologies as evidence that it has become "great"—which is to say that it has achieved literary eminence, however provisional and temporary. *Maus*'s presence in these anthologies, and its promotion up the ranks within them from postmodern American literature to American literature, *tout court*, is therefore an important sign of *Maus*'s emergent canonicity.

What justifies the presence of *Maus* in such anthologies is the attention literary critics have devoted to it. Articles on *Maus* began appearing in 1992 and the pace of scholarly publication has not slackened—a phenomenon unprecedented in the form's history and as yet unmatched. There exist dozens of journal articles on *Maus*, a number of dissertations, and a collection of essays (but so far, however, there are no book-length scholarly studies in English devoted solely to Spiegelman). In stark contrast to this torrent of interpretation, only six articles on *Watchmen* are currently listed in the

MLA Bibliography, three on *Love and Rockets*, and just one on *The Dark Knight Returns*—a rivulet, a trickle, and a drought.[2] The extravagant divergence in critical attention to these various works has consolidated *Maus*'s eminence.

But criticism has also often set *Maus* in contexts having little to do with comics. This circumstance is not in principle a cause for regret: *Maus* can be productively situated in many contexts, and *Maus* criticism has been in most respects extraordinarily good. Still, *Maus* is linked fundamentally to the history of American comics, and ignoring this circumstance is akin to reading the novels of Nathaniel Hawthorne with no understanding of the history of American fiction. It is not unusual for critics to write brilliantly about *Maus* in relation to one context while making surprisingly simplistic remarks about it in relation to comics.

This circumstance must bemuse Spiegelman, not only because he is intimately familiar with the history of the form, but also because in the decade and a half since the completion of *Maus* he has been the form's preeminent ambassador, champion, and historian. His production of book-length comics has slowed since *Maus*—between 1991 and 2008 he published only two—but he has published articles and short strips discussing both well-known figures such as Charles Schulz and Theodor Geisel (Dr. Seuss), and also Winsor McCay, Jack Cole, and Harvey Kurtzman—remembered chiefly by comics *cognoscenti*. Uprooting *Maus* from the soil in which it germinated—American popular culture—has been the basis for its elevation to the status of Literature, but it risks re-inscribing the high art/low art binary that *Maus* has so often been said to blur, and, what is worse, has distorted understanding of the text itself.

MAUS IN THE NORTON ANTHOLOGIES: THE PRICE OF CANONIZATION

When instructors teach courses in American literature using one of the Norton anthologies that include excerpts from *Maus*, they join in declaring—perhaps in spite of themselves—that it is a significant work in the American tradition. Undergraduates who have not already encountered *Maus* in high school or elsewhere discover it monumentalized here. But in what sense, according to Norton's editors, is *Maus* great? How do they "frame" *Maus*? In what aesthetic networks do the editors situate it, and in what larger cultural or political contexts?

Predictably, each of these anthologies has a different answer, according to the individual anthology's priorities. *The Norton Anthology of Jewish American Literature* will not necessarily be concerned with demonstrating

Maus's postmodernity, nor will it necessarily be urgent for *Postmodern American Fiction* to compare Spiegelman's treatment of the Holocaust with that, say, of Claude Lanzmann (director of the testimony project *Shoah*) or other Holocaust representations. *The Norton Anthology of American Literature* must cast *Maus* as a work of art comparable to others in the American canon. But whatever their individual editorial priorities, each of the Norton anthologies characterizes Spiegelman's work and the medium in which it originated in perplexing, often profoundly flawed ways. While comics scholars can take pleasure in the status the anthologies accord *Maus*, they may nevertheless feel chagrin at the ways these anthologies frame the extracts.

The earliest Norton anthology to include excerpts from *Maus*—*Postmodern American Fiction*—is also the only one that includes the work of other graphic novelists.[3] The editors include excerpts from Lynda Barry's *Come Over, Come Over* (1990) and Paul Karasik and David Mazzucchelli's comic-book adaptation (1994) of Paul Auster's novel *City of Glass* (1985). The anthology thereby shows that Spiegelman did not conjure *Maus* out of the ether: the work emerged alongside other ambitious graphic narratives.

But if the editors are—from the perspective of a scholar of the form—engagingly broad-minded, the editorial apparatus is nevertheless deficient in its approach to *Maus* itself. Including *Maus* in an anthology of fiction is a major provocation. When the second volume of *Maus* was released in 1991, *The New York Times* placed *Maus* on its best-seller lists as a work of fiction, prompting Spiegelman to write the following letter:

> I'd like to thank *The Times* for its recognition and support of my book *Maus II*. I was delighted to see it surface on your best-seller list (Dec. 8). [. . .] Delight blurred into surprise, however, when I noted that it appeared on the fiction side of your ledger.
>
> If your list were divided into literature and nonliterature, I could gracefully accept the compliment as intended, but to the extent that "fiction" indicates that a work isn't factual, I feel a bit queasy. As an author I believe I might have lopped several years off the 13 I devoted to my two-volume project if I could only have taken a novelist's license while searching for a novelistic structure.
>
> The borderland between fiction and nonfiction has been fertile territory for some of the most potent contemporary writing [. . .]. [But] I shudder to think how David Duke—if he could read—would respond to seeing a carefully researched work based closely on my father's memories of life in Hitler's Europe and in the death camps classified as fiction.

I know that by delineating people with animal heads I've raised problems of taxonomy for you. Could you consider adding a special "nonfiction/mice" category to your list?

The Times responded by moving *Maus II* to the non-fiction list, pointing to Pantheon's classification of the book as memoir and the Library of Congress's classification of it as biography. The decision on the part of the editors of *Postmodern American Fiction* to reproduce *The Times*'s original thinking is therefore all the more troubling. And unfortunately, in the editorial scaffolding around the *Maus* excerpts, they do not register that their taxonomical calculus is problematic. "Spiegelman's work," they assert in a prefatory note, "moves between past and present, fact and fiction, and low and high culture with vertiginous intensity" (291). But ultimately, the anthology's title itself renders a taxonomical judgment: *Maus* may well move with vertiginous intensity between fact and fiction, but ultimately it is presented as fiction.

To be sure, *Maus* is a strange discursive creature, one using representational strategies commonly associated with fiction and adopting, as Spiegelman suggests, a "novelistic structure" in the service of Holocaust memoir. In the beast allegory *Maus* uses a different symbolic mode than conventional histories do (to put it mildly), and certain scenes in the present action of the book—exchanges between Art and Françoise, for instance—comment explicitly on how life differs from art. The initial placement of the book in *The New York Times* fiction lists is thus an understandable response to the eccentricity of *Maus* itself.

In this eccentricity it has affinities with postmodern fiction. As many literary critics have observed, postmodern fiction tends to play in the "fertile territory" between fiction and non-fiction. The literary theorist Linda Hutcheon has denominated postmodern historical fiction "historiographic metafiction," which, she asserts, "asks us to recall that history and fiction are themselves historical terms and that their definitions and interrelations are historically determined" (Hutcheon 1999, 105). Such fiction, she asserts, "acknowledges [. . .] the *reality* of the past but its *textualized accessibility* to us today" (114). *Maus* resembles such fiction: as Hutcheon writes elsewhere, it

> always reminds us of the lack of transparency of both its verbal and visual media. Its consistent reflexivity, pointing to the utter non-objectivity of the historian or biographer, here raises precisely the issues that have obsessed theorists of historiography for several decades now [. . .]. [S]elf-conscious narratives like *Maus* enact critical commentaries on the

very "making" of history, from what Hayden White calls its "narrativiz-ing" to the nature of its documentary archive (Hutcheon 1988, 11).

As Hutcheon notes, *Maus* "fictionalizes as it narrativizes, [and] imagines as it recounts actual, remembered events" (13). She argues that "'Literature' and 'history' [. . .] are not separate or separable categories of discourse today [. . .], and [. . .] hybrid works like *Maus* [. . .] have shown the cre-ative possibilities of cross-border activity between [. . .] seemingly differ-ent genres of discourse" (13). But here Hutcheon is opposing not *fiction* and history but rather *literature* and history, a crucial distinction.[4] The other eight excerpts included in the "Revisiting History" section of the anthology are from works whose authors all explicitly characterize the works as novels and stories; by contrast, Spiegelman denominates *Maus* "a survivor's tale," which implies not a fictional narrative but testimony.

Many of the other works conform to Hutcheon's definition of historio-graphic metafiction; none would be confused with works of history. In short, if the works in the "Revisiting History" section are hybrids of fiction and history—according to the logic of the metaphor, the offspring born from the union of these discourses—then *Maus* more closely resembles one parent and all the others more closely resemble the other. Including excerpts from *Maus* in *Postmodern American Fiction* raises taxonomical problems the editors decline to acknowledge, and to my mind amounts to an unfortunate mistake.

The taxonomical problem does not complicate *Maus*'s inclusion in *Jewish American Literature: A Norton Anthology*, since (as Spiegelman himself observes) "literature" is a more capacious term than fiction. The editors focus on *Maus* as Holocaust memoir, situating the narrative in relation to the Holocaust's chang-ing status in American culture (as Peter Novick and others have observed, the status of the Holocaust in American discourse has changed dramatically since World War II); they place Spiegelman alongside other American children of Holocaust survivors publishing second-generation Holocaust narratives since the 1970s. The questions they pose are historical rather than formal.

The editors' brief evocation of Spiegelman's career as a comic-book artist is punctuated by a peculiar characterization of the milieu in which Spiegelman's work was first published. They claim that "[before] the publication of *Maus I*" Spiegelman's work was published in "'zines,' underground publications on specialized topics. Circulated through informal networks, zines were enthu-siastically embraced by many subcultures, notably teenagers and 'Generation X-ers' who felt alienated from mainstream culture" (Chametzky et al. 2001, 1093). Using a term such as "zine" to describe the underground comics of the

1960s and 1970s is eccentric—intimating that *Raw* was favored by a disaffected, adolescent subculture borders on insult.

This characterization of the alternative comics scene amounts to a grievous missed opportunity. North American Jewish comics creators invented the superhero and the Jewish-American Will Eisner's *A Contract with God* (1978) was massively influential in popularizing the term "graphic novel." In light of the pivotal Jewish contributions to American comics, the editors' focus on alienated teenagers and "Generation X-ers" is disappointing. There are also minor but embarrassing errors of fact. The editors call the short but crucial strip about Anja Spiegelman's suicide "Prisoner *of* the Hell Planet" rather than "Prisoner *on* the Hell Planet" and wrongly state that it was first published in a comic book called *Funny Animals* (Spiegelman published his three-page proto-version of *Maus* in *Funny Aminals* [sic], a comic book published in 1973; he first published "Prisoner on the Hell Planet" in *Short Order Comix* in 1972).

A similar emphasis on Spiegelman's emergence from the mass-cultural margins informs the treatment of *Maus* in *The Norton Anthology of American Literature*. *Maus* is the only comic book excerpted in this anthology, thus by the standards of Norton the only one that can be denominated "American literature" without further qualification. One may hope that future editions of the anthology will include additional representatives of the form. But the editorial remarks introducing *Maus* suggest otherwise. Critics have often discussed the supposed narrowing of distinctions between high and low art in postmodern culture. The sketch of comics history accompanying *Maus* suggests that the division remains stark—that *Maus* has leapt across rather than bridged the gap between the arts. The editors' prefatory note to *Maus* distinguishes between "mere" comic books and *Maus* with the following history of the form:

> Comic panels have existed since the end of the nineteenth century, beginning with Richard F. Outcault's *The Yellow Kid* in 1895. By the 1920s panels had evolved into strips—George Herriman's *Krazy Kat* was the most famous—and by the end of the 1930s these strips had grown into comic books, most successfully with the Superman series produced by Jerry Siegel and Joe Schuster [sic]. It would take the cultural transformations of the 1960s, however, for this trend [. . .] to achieve literary form. As opposed to simple entertainment, literature involves, on a genuinely cultural level, both expression and reflection, comprising the beliefs and practices of a people (Baym 2007, 3090).

The misspelling of Joe Shuster's name is only one of several errors suggesting that comic books remain *terra incognita* for literary critics (in the next paragraph, Bill Griffith, author of *Zippy*, is misidentified as "Bill Griffin"). Errors of fact are pervasive in this summary, beginning with the stature accorded Outcault's *The Yellow Kid*, which was by no means the originator of the comic panel. The paragraph anxiously distinguishes between makers of "literature" and producers of "simple entertainment" (intimations of the assembly line in the editor's characterization of Siegel and Shuster are presumably deliberate). The editors construct an evolutionary narrative that sees *Maus* as the culmination of a long formal development, and implicitly defend the anthology for declining to include, for instance, excerpts from *Krazy Kat*. But in so doing they retreat into abstraction.

What is "literary form," and in what sense is it missing from, for instance, Winsor McCay's *Little Nemo in Slumberland*? What is the precise relation between "literary form" and "the cultural transformations of the 1960s"? What is a "genuinely cultural level"? On what basis can one deny to *Krazy Kat* and *Little Nemo* "expression and reflection"? The editors' fuzzy valorization of "literature" seems to reflect anxiety in the face of eroding distinctions between high and low, and their evocation of comic book history seems designed not to precipitate further study of the form but rather to preempt it, or at least to restrict it to works post-*Maus*. *The Norton Anthology of American Literature* thus strikingly dramatizes the costs of canonization.

AMERICAN MOUSE

Although *Maus* was roundly celebrated in newspaper reviews, it is unlikely it would appear in the Norton anthologies had academics ignored it. But literary critics took an early interest in *Maus*. In 1989, Joseph Witek defended a dissertation on historical narrative in alternative comics; it was published in 1990 with the title *Comic Books as History: The Narrative Art of Jack Jackson, Art Spiegelman, and Harvey Pekar*. Articles on *Maus* began appearing in academic journals in 1992, soon after the 1991 publication of the second volume. Academic attention has endured—indeed, intensified—since the early 1990s. The MLA Bibliography currently lists sixteen texts published between 2006 and 2008, and there is no reason to suppose the spigot will close in 2010. Comics published since *Maus*, especially Marjane Satrapi's *Persepolis*, now compete for literary critics' attention, but no other graphic novel has amassed such a substantial critical literature.

Criticism on *Maus* focuses on several related topics. As one might expect, critics have been fascinated with its unprecedented representation of the Holocaust—and have also consistently been interested in *Maus*'s treatment of gender, especially through its construction of Spiegelman's mother, Anja. Above all, critics have debated Spiegelman's use of the beast allegory—that is, the text's representation of Jews as mice, Germans as cats, and so on. This last aspect of *Maus*, the most ostentatious of its many provocations, continues to preoccupy critics. Criticism has been less interested in *Maus* as a work of specifically American literature, no doubt because almost the entirety of the retrospective action takes place in Europe. Yet understanding *Maus* as an American text is crucial if one wants to understand the history of the representational codes—in particular, the funny-animal allegory—that *Maus* both deploys and subverts.

Maus is by any measure a significant work of Holocaust literature, and readings of it have correspondingly contributed in important ways to Holocaust studies.[5] Major scholars have related *Maus* to a larger theoretical discussion about Holocaust representation—this one centers around two questions: one of them ethical, one of them epistemological. In what circumstances and with what representational means, scholars wonder, can one represent the Holocaust without further victimizing its victims? And how, given the enormity of the Holocaust and its devastating implications for Western culture and metaphysics, can one hope to comprehend it at all?

Many of these scholars use as a point of departure Theodor Adorno's famous apothegm that "to write poetry after Auschwitz is barbaric." Although not in itself a proscription against representations of the Holocaust, it has often been interpreted in this light, and the misinterpretation has led to a productive discussion about the ethics of representations of trauma. Spiegelman has succinctly phrased the problem in his critique of Spielberg's *Schindler's List* (which, in his view, was an ethical failure owing to the ways it delineated the Holocaust): one must find a way to avoid "Holocaust re-creation for the sake of audience recreation" (Qtd. in Mintz 2001, 146). As this formulation suggests, the central problem in representing the Holocaust is the possibility that the audience will respond with aesthetic pleasure (even the pleasure of horror), a perverse exploitation of the suffering and deaths of millions.

Critics addressing these questions observe that *Maus* makes no claim to represent the Holocaust in its totality. The work continually emphasizes that the Holocaust eludes understanding. In *Maus II*, for instance, Spiegelman asserts that "I can't even make any sense out of my relationship with my father . . . How am I supposed to make any sense out of **Auschwitz**? . . . of the **Holocaust**?" (II:14): attempts to "make any sense" of Auschwitz, *Maus* implies, are doomed to fail.[6] Moreover, Vladek's account is idiosyncratic, not emblematic: it is his particular memory of Auschwitz that the work documents. And because this memory is filtered through Art Spiegelman's own textual and visual representations—a process of translation the work continually emphasizes—the reader's perception of the Holocaust is still more profoundly mediated. The provisional character of *Maus*'s representations of the Holocaust, always implicit, becomes explicit in several instances.

In one sequence, often commented upon in criticism, Spiegelman dramatizes a conversation he had with his father Vladek. Asked about an orchestra that played for inmates entering or leaving the camps, Vladek professes to have no memory of it: "I remember only marching, not any orchestras . . . / From the gate guards took us over to the workshop. How could it be there an orchestra?" "I dunno," Art replies, "but it's very well documented . . . " (II:54). The panels accompanying this exchange show two views of the camp gates, one with the orchestra visible as marching inmates approach it, one with the orchestra almost entirely concealed behind the marchers as they pass by; the panels suggest a way of reconciling official history and private memory while calling attention to the disparities between them.

As critics interested in representations of gender have noted, Spiegelman further emphasizes the incomplete character of his Holocaust representations by focusing on the death of his mother Anja (for analyses of gender in *Maus*, see especially Miller 2003 and Hirsch 1992–93). She survived the horrors of Auschwitz but committed suicide, for reasons that *Maus* can only speculate on, in 1968. She haunts the present action. In the course of the first volume, Art discovers that she wrote her own account of the war, and Vladek suggests that she did so on Art's behalf: "'I wish my son, when he grows up, he will be interested by this'" (I:159), Vladek says, quoting her. But Vladek recalls this wish even as he tells Art that, grieving from her death, he destroyed "These notebooks, and other really nice things of mother" (I:158).

The destruction of these notebooks—an act that drives Art to accuse Vladek of murder—means that Art is necessarily reliant on his father's account of the war. The destruction prevents him from having access to a perspective complementing, complicating, perhaps even contradicting his father's narrative—and it denies him a communion, however attenuated, with his dead mother. Anja's absence from the present action is therefore critical. It emphasizes again that Vladek's narrative is an incomplete account of the Spiegelmans' wartime experience. And because Vladek destroyed Anja's testimony—in a brutally ironic echo of the death-camp crematoria,

Fig. 13.1 Representing a "mixed-species" family in the context of the beast allegory. Spiegelman 1991a, 131. From *Maus II: A Survivor's Tale/And Here My Troubles Began* by Art Spiegelman, copyright c 1986, 1989, 1990, 1991 by Art Spiegelman. Used by permission of Pantheon Books, a division of Random House, Inc.

he burned her notebooks—her absence complicates his own claims on the reader's sympathy.

But the conscription of the comic-book funny-animal tradition in the service of Holocaust narrative is the aspect of *Maus* that has received most critical attention. *Maus*'s audacious allegory was debated among comics insiders some time before literary critics discovered the books: already in 1986 the querulous comic-book writer Harvey Pekar complained that Spiegelman stigmatized the Poles by representing them as pigs (reminded about Pekar's "unhappiness" with the representation of Poles, Spiegelman said, "And I'm unhappy that so many readers thought it was OK to use vermin for Jews but not pigs for Poles" [Qtd. in Bolhafner 1991, 96]). Critics more sensitive—or sympathetic—to the work have perceived the beast allegory as self-consuming: as *Maus* unfolds it reveals both the artifice and the inadequacy of the allegory.

Although I shall presently argue that Spiegelman already points to this artifice in the first chapters of *Maus I*, it reaches a level of patent absurdity in the last pages of *Maus II*. When Vladek has escaped Auschwitz and is gradually making his way back to Sosnowiec, he stays with a Jewish man and his German wife, relatives of his traveling companion Shivek. The beast allegory states that this couple is mixed-species, and Spiegelman accordingly represents the man as a mouse and the woman as a cat. The couple's two children, however, are scandals to the allegory—Spiegelman represents them as strange hybrids of cat and mouse.

The sheer impossibility of such "mousecats" makes the insufficiency of the beast metaphor plain (on the same page, the British appear for the first time in *Maus*, represented, ludicrously, as fish—presumably cold ones). Linking the Jew to animals of various kinds, such as snakes or vampire bats, was a staple of the Nazis' (and others') anti-Semitic caricature. Edited by Julius Streicher, the Nazi journal *Der Stürmer* made broad use of beast allegory. *Van den vos Reynaerde* (an animated film produced but not distributed in war-time Holland) represented the Jew as a rhinoceros. Perhaps most famously, Fritz Hippler's *Der Ewige Jude* (*The Eternal Jew*) likened the Jewish diaspora to the migration of rats. Spiegelman has asserted that he was writing "alongside" Hitler in order to explode him. Thus one of *Maus*'s cardinal ambitions is to disclose the inadequacy of its governing metaphor.

Although the beast allegory works brilliantly in *Maus* in part because the Nazis' anti-Semitic caricature routinely likened European Jews to animals, Spiegelman was first inspired to use it when he detected the racial subtexts of American cartoons. In 1985, Spiegelman stated:

A few years ago I was looking at a lot of animated cartoons from the 1920s and 30s, and I was struck by the fact that, in many of them, there was virtually no difference between the way mice and black people were drawn. This got me thinking about drawing a comic strip that used mice in a metaphor for the black experience in America. Well, two minutes into it, I realized that I didn't know the first thing about being black, but I was Jewish, and I was very aware of the experiences of my parents in World War II, so that pushed me in that direction (Qtd. in Tucker 1985).

Spiegelman has reiterated this sketch of the metaphor's American roots elsewhere, most recently in *Portrait of the Artist as a Young #@§*!*. Here he tells the anecdote in comic-strip form, introducing the account with an image that evokes both Mickey Mouse and a child in blackface—his mouse/muse—as the "birth of a notion" (alluding to D. W. Griffith's infamous 1915 Ku Klux Klan epic, *Birth of a Nation*).

Fig. 13.2 Spiegelman alludes to D. W. Griffith's film *Birth of a Nation* (1915) as he introduces the story of *Maus*'s conception. Spiegelman 2008, 12. From *Breakdowns: Portrait of the Artist as a Young %@?*!* by Art Spiegelman, copyright c 1972, 1973, 1974, 1975, 1976, 1977, 2005, 2006, 2007, and 2008 by Art Spiegelman. Used by permission of Pantheon Books, a division of Random House, Inc.

Fig. 13.3 The association of minstrelsy and funny-animal cartoons. Spiegelman 2008, 13. From *Breakdowns: Portrait of the Artist as a Young %@?*!* by Art Spiegelman, copyright c 1972, 1973, 1974, 1975, 1976, 1977, 2005, 2006, 2007, and 2008 by Art Spiegelman. Used by permission of Pantheon Books, a division of Random House, Inc.

Spiegelman notes that Ken Jacobs, an instructor in film history at Harpur College, juxtaposed minstrel shows with early American cartoons, pointing out that the animals and the minstrels were scarcely distinguishable.

Defending the legitimacy of Jacobs's association of minstrelsy and funny-animal cartoons is beyond the scope of this essay. But a gesture towards racial caricature in various American cartoons may be instructive: the [Jim] crows of Disney's *Dumbo* and the apes of Disney's *The Jungle Book* are striking examples linking the funny animal to racial caricature. Already in early twentieth-century animation, filmmakers used beast allegories in the arsenal of political caricature: in 1919, for instance, Henry Ford produced a cartoon short defending "American" values against "Bolsheviki" agitators from the IWW, agitators represented in the cartoon as a grotesque rat infiltrating a wholesome American barn.[7] As I have suggested elsewhere, critics have not attended adequately to *Maus*'s origins in American cartoons (Loman 2006). One hopes that Spiegelman's own repeated insistence on its American roots will spur scholarship—to date the metaphor's roots in popular American culture have been almost entirely overlooked.

A recent article in *American Literary History* suggests the importance of such a focus. In "Plots Against America: Neoliberalism and Antiracism" (2006), Walter Benn Michaels marshals Philip Roth's *The Plot Against America* and Spiegelman's *Maus* as evidence supporting his claim that analyses of racial and sexual identities have replaced class critique in postmodern culture. Michaels complains that Roth's "counterfactual" novel, *The Plot Against America*, substitutes Jews for African-Americans as victims of American racism—a circumstance that effaces the brutal realities of an American history that includes slavery and Jim Crow—and he notes that *Maus* likewise "imagine[s] an America divided not into blacks and whites but into Jews and non-Jews." Michaels states:

> *Maus* [. . .] famously [depicts] its Jews as mice, its Germans as cats, its Poles as pigs, and so on, with Americans as dogs. The picture this gives of nationality in Europe is [. . .] a plausible one, but the picture of America is at least as counterfactual as Roth's. In Spiegelman's America, every immigrant group [. . .] has been assimilated, with the exception of the Jews! Everyone else is dogs (blacks are black dogs); Jews are still mice. It's as if not just the Holocaust itself but the racial system that produced it was an American rather than a European phenomenon. And, of course, this Americanizing of the Holocaust is not just a fictional [sic] event. Why is there a federally funded US Holocaust Museum on the Mall in Washington, DC? In what sense [. . .] is the Holocaust part of American history? (Michaels 2006, 289).

Even were one to overlook Michaels's too narrow definition of American history, his argument would still be surprisingly crude. One can say, flatly, that *Maus*'s picture of nationality in Europe is—by design—*not* plausible. As Michael Rothberg notes, Michaels ignores *Maus*'s "putting into question of the adequacy of those [racial] codes" (Rothberg 2006, 304) that inform racist discourse. The burden of *Maus* is that this kind of symbolism, with its essentialist implications, is morally repugnant; Spiegelman adopts it in order to parody and explode it.

However, Michaels's insistence on the American contexts of *Maus* is not in itself wrong-headed. The first decade and a half of *Maus* criticism has focused minutely on the work's European contexts, while taking America as a stable, even banal, haven from the nightmares of World War II Europe. There is some legitimacy to such readings of *Maus*'s America: where Vladek's narrative focuses on political upheaval, the present action focuses on the tensions of domestic life; Spiegelman's post-9/11 *In the Shadow of No Towers* makes the anxieties of the American scene palpable in a way that *Maus* does not.

Still, it is wrong to imagine, as Michaels does, that *Maus* offers a "counterfactual" America that ignores the history of anti-black racism; to the contrary, it specifically shows that Vladek, an immigrant who had never seen a black person prior to arriving in America, has adopted anti-black racism as part of his Americanization and in defiance of his own experience of European anti-Semitism. "It's not even to compare, the shvartsers and the Jews!" (II:99), he grumbles. Can there be a clearer invitation to defy Vladek, to compare? Such comparisons lead inexorably to the realization that in America, the cat-mouse metaphor also describes white-black relations. In other words, they lead one back to the contexts of Spiegelman's original insight—and coincidentally provide a means of reading American mass culture in relation to an unnervingly similar culture in Nazi Europe.

In considering the disquieting relationship between Nazi and American racial stereotyping in *Maus*, Vladek is the key figure critics must examine. Spiegelman provides no explicit account for Vladek's anti-black racism: its origin is a mystery. In bewildered outrage, Françoise asks Vladek, "How can you, of all people, be such a racist?" (II:98). He declines to answer her, but his narrative as a whole—as translated by his son into comic-book form—may suggest some possibilities.

Although the beast allegory already seems fixed in the prefatory pages of *Maus*, and seems to come under critique only in the second volume, there are nevertheless moments in the first volume when the divisions that structure and give meaning to the beast allegory are invisible or even irrelevant—and two crucial moments when it is extravagantly unstable. The cats—whether representing Germans in general or Nazis in particular—take some time to appear in *Maus*, and this deferral means that in the first third of *Maus I* the beast allegory is incomplete. However, when a Nazi first appears, his representation is momentarily plastic: he is not at first represented as a cat, nor even as an animal. Thus Spiegelman's deconstruction of the beast allegory, although generally held to begin in earnest in *Maus II*, is already well under way in the early pages of *Maus I*.

Chapter 1, which describes Vladek's world in the years before the Nazi invasion of Poland, takes place in a social world made up almost exclusively of mice. Although Vladek does not provide a specific date, his narration begins at some point between 1931 and 1932—thus at the very moment that the Nazis were coming to power in Germany—but the flashbacks in the first chapter make no reference to Nazism whatsoever, focusing instead on Vladek's romantic relationship with Lucia Greenberg and his courtship of his future wife, Anja Zylberberg.

Vladek's references to American mass culture in this chapter mark the first instance where the beast allegory is destabilized. The chapter is named for one of Rudolph Valentino's major films, *The Sheik* (1921)—introducing his reminiscences, Vladek tells Art that "I was at that time, young, and really a nice, handsome boy. // People always told me I looked just like [. . .] Valentino" (I:13). Behind Vladek, and providing the panel's frame (at a skewed angle, however, in relation to the other panels), there is a representation of a poster for *The Sheik* (1921), the film that made Valentino famous. But in the poster, Valentino is represented as a mouse, nonsensical according to the terms of the allegory, since he was not Jewish. We might read the image as Vladek's projection of himself onto the figure of Valentino (and also a projection of Lucia onto Agnes Ayres, the actress who starred alongside Valentino in *The Sheik*): read this way, the ironies of the panel are striking, with the aged, enfeebled Vladek on a stationary bicycle fantasizing about his youthful virility and associating it with American mass culture. But given the subversion of racial categories in *Maus*, it is significant that *The Sheik* is itself preoccupied with cultural and racial masquerade (albeit in profoundly compromised ways): in the film, the Italian-American Valentino plays an Arab; and Agnes Ayres plays an Englishwoman who first appears disguised as an Arab. Thus the allusion to *The Sheik* not only illustrates Vladek's allusion to Valentino, nor only comments, a little sardonically, on Vladek's sexual appeal—it also points to race as a cultural construction.

Maus first represents Nazis in Chapter 2, as Anja and Vladek travel to the sanitarium in Czechoslovakia (the swastika itself first appears earlier on the chapter's title page [I:25]). But this representation is not straightforward.

Fig. 13.4 Vladek and *The Sheik* (1921). Spiegelman 1986, 13. From *Maus I: A Survivor's Tale/My Father Bleeds History* by Art Spiegelman, copyright c 1973, 1980, 1981, 1982, 1984, 1985, 1986 by Art Spiegelman. Used by permission of Pantheon Books, a division of Random House, Inc.

The four chilling panels on 33 emblematize the genocidal tendency of Nazi anti-Semitism. The first shows two Nazis blockading a Jewish store; the second shows them humiliating a Jewish couple; the third shows them beating Jewish victims; and the fourth shows a (deserted) town that declares itself "Jew Free."

Because it so clearly anatomizes the progress of anti-Semitism from marginalization to intimidation to extirpation, this is a key page in *Maus*. However, in a sense the images are also illusory as they represent reports circulating among European Jews in the late 1930s. Although the reports are accurate—and even understate the threat that Nazism poses to Jews—the Nazis represented in these panels are nevertheless figures of the imagination, and the recurring swastika emphasizes that the panels represent the fears of European Jews confronted with the rise of Nazism but as yet acquainted with it only through its symbols and reputation.[8]

Fig. 13.5 A variety of animals populate the sanitarium in Czechoslovakia. Spiegelman 1986, 34. From *Maus I: A Survivor's Tale/My Father Bleeds History* by Art Spiegelman, copyright c 1973, 1980, 1981, 1982, 1984, 1985, 1986 by Art Spiegelman. Used by permission of Pantheon Books, a division of Random House, Inc.

Fig. 13.6 In the café where Vladek and Anja dance, a (German) cat peacefully dines with a (French) frog. Spiegelman 1986, 35. From *Maus I: A Survivor's Tale/My Father Bleeds History* by Art Spiegelman, copyright c 1973, 1980, 1981, 1982, 1984, 1985, 1986 by Art Spiegelman. Used by permission of Pantheon Books, a division of Random House, Inc.

While the chapter primarily shows the gathering cloud of Nazism, it also offers a glimpse of a fragile but nonetheless real alternative. The gardens of the sanitarium in Czechoslovakia are utopian in their cosmopolitanism. Vladek declares that "People came from all over the world with different sicknesses" (I:34); Vladek and Anja wander through the gardens of the sanitarium in the

Fig. 13.7 Pigs and mice mingle in the dance hall. Spiegelman 1986, 13. From *Maus I: A Survivor's Tale/My Father Bleeds History* by Art Spiegelman, copyright c 1973, 1980, 1981, 1982, 1984, 1985, 1986 by Art Spiegelman. Used by permission of Pantheon Books, a division of Random House, Inc.

company of a veritable bestiary (one discerns even a giraffe and elephant). Spiegelman's Eden is therefore defined by its cultural variety. Crucially, the sanitarium sequence is the first to introduce an actual German (rather than the specters conjured on the foregoing pages). In the café where Vladek and Anja dance, Spiegelman represents a (German) cat peacefully dining with a (French) frog. This benign first appearance echoes the introduction of Poles in Chapter 1. When Lucia and Vladek are in the Czestochowa dance hall, at least one of the figures dancing in the background is a pig, although the musicians are mice and so are some of the dancers.

In the panels that follow the introduction of the German cat, Spiegelman again emphasizes cosmopolitan harmony: in the next-to-last panel of the page, the three principal kinds of animal in *Maus*—cats, mice, and pigs—are

Fig. 13.8 A Nazi soldier, prone and dying, refuses to conform to the cat-mouse allegory. Spiegelman 1986, 48. From *Maus I: A Survivor's Tale/My Father Bleeds History* by Art Spiegelman, copyright c 1973, 1980, 1981, 1982, 1984, 1985, 1986 by Art Spiegelman. Used by permission of Pantheon Books, a division of Random House, Inc.

all represented as dancing couples. For all intents and purposes the beast allegory is meaningless here, because the power relations that structure the allegory do not obtain. The dance halls of Czestochowa and Czechoslovakia thus rob the beast allegory of its force, serving as a harmonious alternative to the divisive racial theories of Nazism.

When Nazis enter the narrative directly in Chapter 3, the antagonism implicit in the beast allegory finally coheres; paradoxically, this entrance simultaneously suggests the limits of the allegory. Entrenched at the Polish front, Vladek is reluctant to discharge his weapon: "Why," he wonders, "should I kill anyone?" (I:48). Seeing a Nazi advancing in camouflage, however, he shoots and kills him. This death is the first of many in *Maus*, and it is highly significant that Vladek is the one to cause it. According to the logic of the beast allegory, the death is impossible: mice cannot kill cats. However, Jews can kill Germans. The first death in *Maus*, in other words, confounds the narrative's central allegory.

But *Maus* further disrupts the allegory by introducing the Nazi neither as human nor as cat: camouflaged, the Nazi seems to Vladek to be a moving tree: "I must be seeing things," he thinks. "How can a tree run?" (I:48). Although the Nazi's camouflage accounts for this trick of perception, the moment has significant implications in a narrative that already masks human beings as animals. The second volume of *Maus* famously begins with a page of Art's sketchbook that testifies to his struggle to represent his wife Françoise: he experiments with drawings of her as moose, mouse, poodle, frog, and rabbit.

Fig. 13.9 Only when Vladek finds the dead Nazi's body later does it appear recognizably feline. Spiegelman 1986, 50. From *Maus I: A Survivor's Tale/My Father Bleeds History* by Art Spiegelman, copyright c 1973, 1980, 1981, 1982, 1984, 1985, 1986 by Art Spiegelman. Used by permission of Pantheon Books, a division of Random House, Inc.

The first Nazi to appear in *Maus* is more radically polymorphous still, flora rather than fauna. The page's final panel, which shows the Nazi prone and dying, still refuses to conform to the cat-mouse allegory. Vladek states, "It held up a hand to show it was hurt. To surrender. / But I kept shooting and shooting, until finally the tree stopped moving. Who knows; otherwise he could have shot me!" (I:48).

Crucially, Vladek continues to refer to the Nazi as a tree; only in the pronominal shift of the last clause does he acknowledge he was shooting at a human being. The accompanying image likewise preserves this representational openness. The figure is wearing a recognizable Nazi uniform underneath the camouflage, but the helmet casts the face into shadow, and only the eyes and the lower jaw are visible. The Nazi is not yet a cat. His face is, perhaps, a death's head. Only once Vladek finds the body—two pages later— does the dead Nazi become recognizably feline.

The Nazi becomes fixed in the beast allegory because Vladek casts aside his earlier reluctance to kill and instead expresses satisfaction at the sight of the body: he congratulates himself for having done "something" to resist the Nazis (I:50). At this moment—and even as he registers the dead man's name—he dehumanizes him, just as the Nazis dehumanized the Jews in stigmatizing them as sub-human. From this moment forward, Nazis are the prime perpetrators of violence. Still, although Vladek's testimony provides unambiguous evidence of Nazism's monstrosity, Vladek remains the narrative's first killer. Spiegelman structures *Maus* so that violence is not perpetrated by Germans and Poles alone; the narrative's central figure, whose humanity we embrace even with—indeed because of—his many flaws, is himself corrupted by the violence of war. Under its pressure, Vladek rejects the utopianism of the dance halls, predisposing him, perhaps, to accept the anti-black stereotypes he mutters so outrageously in *Maus*'s second volume.

To understand Vladek's anti-black racism in relation to this moment at the Polish border—that is, to perceive his hostility to American "shvartsers" as the persistence of an ideology that he internalizes in wartime Europe—is to see the funny-animal allegory come full circle. Spiegelman's understanding of the racial dimensions of such allegories derived, he notes, from his viewing of American cartoons, but when he discovered its twin in Nazi anti-Semitic caricature, he crossed the Atlantic. Vladek's anti-black racism, so plainly an echo of the Nazi anti-Semitism that had such catastrophic effects on his own life, represents a tragic homecoming. There is a terrible irony in *Maus*: Spiegelman discovered a way to allegorize his father's experience after perceiving the racial subtexts of American cartoons, and his father subscribed to the prejudices that animated those cartoons. But this irony is visible only to those readers alert to the histories of American comics and cartooning from which Spiegelman draws his inspiration.

NOTES

1. What my transcription renders as "§" is instead a spiral icon, which is not only at the heart of the veiled expletive, but is a major symbol in the work that follows. The standard keyboard has no key to accommodate this new character. Perhaps Spiegelman is pointing to the particularity of graphic narrative, tacitly rebuking those critics who subject his work to elaborate prose analyses that never capture the quiddity of comic books.

2. These numbers derive from a search of the MLA Bibliography on August 1, 2008: they do not reflect the absolute numbers of academic articles on these works. Moore's *From Hell* and *Lost Girls* (collaborations with Eddie Campbell and Melinda Gebbie, respectively) have also generated scholarship, as have Miller's other works, but even so, Spiegelman criticism outpaces criticism of their work. The same search found twenty-four

entries for Robert Crumb, twenty-three for Marjane Satrapi, eleven for Harvey Pekar, ten for George Herriman, eight for Winsor McCay, five apiece for Chris Ware and Lynda Barry, two apiece for Kim Deitch, Adrian Tomine, and Alison Bechdel, and—astonishingly—only one for Joe Sacco. This catalog does not distinguish between the kinds of text in the entries, including interviews and other works on the borders of formal literary criticism. Nevertheless it suggests an overall trend in criticism.

3. The only other Norton anthology to include comics is *The Norton Anthology of Children's Literature* (2005). The passage on comics is prefaced with the following comment: "Including a section on 'comics' in an anthology such as this might seem to be a descent into the trivial. Comics, after all, are not respectable: they are crude, simple-minded, and ephemeral. They [. . .] may be fun, but they are not art: they are read by people who don't or can't read 'proper' books" (Zipes 2005, 1099). This is intended to be ironic, but the assumptions articulated persist, as is implied in the calculation that they need rebuttal. Until recently, one would have had to strike a similar rhetorical posture to defend the study of children's literature. Given the intensifying academic interest in the graphic novel, is it conceivable that Norton might publish a graphic-novel anthology?

4. Her metaphor of the hybrid may be misleading in any case. It suggests that the "genetic code" of two related but distinct "species" of discourse have combined and generated an offspring that unites qualities of both (but is infertile)—*Maus* as discursive liger. I am not convinced that such a biological metaphor is apt, especially since Hutcheon herself suggests that literature and history are not different categories of discourse (in which case *Maus* is not a hybrid at all).

5. The literature discussing *Maus*'s treatment of the Holocaust is vast. See the following essays and studies in particular: Doherty 1996, Hartman 1996, Hirsch 1992–1993, Hirsch 2001, Huyssen 2000, LaCapra 1998, Rothberg 1994, and Young 1998. Of these, Young's article is the best acquainted with Spiegelman's other works, supplementing its reading of *Maus* with the best critical analysis to date of the pieces in *Breakdowns*.

6. For all direct quotations from *Maus*, I have adopted the following (somewhat eccentric) format: I have indicated all Spiegelman's emphases in the text with bold text; where the same character speaks in separate speech balloons within a panel, I have used a single '/' to denote the break, and when the same character speaks in separate panels, I have used a double '//' to denote the break. Although this format is strange to the eyes, it has the virtue of being faithful to the text and attentive to the nuances of panel arrangement.

7. "Uncle Sam and the Bolsheviki-I.W.W. Rat" (ca. 1919). DVD. *Treasures III: Social Issues in American Film, 1900–1934* (Washington, D.C.: National Film Preservation Foundation, 2007). The cartoon climaxes when Uncle Sam brains the rat with a shovel: "Bolshivists," he declares in a speech balloon (the film is silent), "are the rats of civilization." Given Ford's anti-Semitism and his association of Communists with Jews, one may safely infer that this cartoon not only associates Bolsheviks with rats, but (implicitly) links Jews with rats as well; in other words, it anticipates Nazi anti-Semitic caricature by more than a decade.

8. My understanding of these panels has been significantly influenced by discussions with my colleague Nancy Pedri, to whom I extend my thanks.

WORKS CITED

Baetens, Jan. N.d. New=Old, Old=New: Digital and Other Comics Following Scott McCloud and Chris Ware. *Altx Online Network*. www.altx.com/ebr/ebr11/11ware.htm [accessed 2 Aug. 2008].

Baym, Nina, gen. ed. 2007. *The Norton Anthology of American Literature*. 7th ed. New York: W. W. Norton.

Bolhafner, J. Stephen. 1991. Art for Art's Sake: Spiegelman Speaks on *RAW*'s Past, Present, and Future. *The Comics Journal* 145: 96.

Chametzky, Jules, John Felstiner, Hilene Flanzbaum, and Kathryn Hellerstein, eds. 2001. *Jewish American Literature: A Norton Anthology*. New York: W. W. Norton.

Chute, Hillary. 2006. "The Shadow of a Past Time": History and Graphic Representation in *Maus*. *Twentieth Century Literature* 52(2): 199–230.

Doherty, Thomas. 1996. Art Spiegelman's *Maus*: Graphic Art and the Holocaust. *American Literature: A Journal of Literary History, Criticism, and Bibliography* 68(1): 69–84.

Geyh, Paula, Fred G. Leebron, and Andrew Levy, eds. 1997. *Postmodern American Fiction: A Norton Anthology*. New York: W. W. Norton.

Groensteen, Thierry. 2007. *The System of Comics*. Trans. Bart Beaty and Nick Nguyen. Jackson, MS: University Press of Mississippi.

Hartman, Geoffrey. 1996. *The Longest Shadow: In the Aftermath of the Holocaust*. Bloomington: Indiana University Press.

Hirsch, Marianne. 1992–93. Family Pictures: *Maus*, Mourning, and Post-Memory. *Discourse: Journal for Theoretical Studies in Media and Culture* 15(2): 3–29.

———. 2001. Surviving Images: Holocaust Photographs and the Work of Postmemory. *Yale Journal of Criticism: Interpretation in the Humanities* 14(1): 5–37.

Hutcheon, Linda. 1988. *A Poetics of Postmodernism: History, Theory, Fiction*. New York: Routledge.

———. 1999. Literature Meets History: Counter-Discursive "Comix." *Anglia* 117: 4–14.

Huyssen, Andreas. 2000. Of Mice and Mimesis: Reading Spiegelman with Adorno. *New German Critique: An Interdisciplinary Journal of German Studies* 81: 65–82.

LaCapra, Dominick. 1998. *History and Memory after Auschwitz*. Ithaca, NY: Cornell University Press.

Loman, Andrew. 2006. Well Intended Liberal Slop. *Journal of American Studies* 40(3): 551–71.

Michaels, Walter Benn. 2006. Plots Against America: Neoliberalism and Antiracism. *American Literary History* 18(2): 288–302.

Miller, Nancy K. 2003. Cartoons of the Self: Portrait of the Artist as a Young Murderer: Art Spiegelman's *Maus*. In *Considering Maus: Approaches to Art Spiegelman's "Survivor's Tale" of the Holocaust*, ed. Deborah R. Geis, 44–59. Tuscaloosa, AL: University of Alabama Press.

Mintz, Alan. 2001. *Popular Culture and the Shaping of Holocaust Memory in America*. Seattle: University of Washington Press.

Pekar, Harvey. 1986. *Maus* and Other Topics. *The Comics Journal* 113: 54–57.

Rothberg, Michael. 1994. "We Were Talking Jewish": Art Spiegelman's *Maus* as "Holocaust" Production. *Contemporary Literature* 35(4): 661–687.

———. 2006. Against Zero-Sum Logic: A Response to Walter Benn Michaels. *American Literary History* 18(2): 303–311.

Spiegelman, Art. 1986. *Maus I: My Father Bleeds History*. New York: Pantheon.

———. 1991a. *Maus II: And Here My Troubles Began*. New York: Pantheon.

———. 1991b. A Problem of Taxonomy. *The New York Times*, 29 Dec. http://query.nytimes .com/gst/fullpage.html?res=9E0CE7D81526EF31BC4A52DFB76F958A&scp=28&sq=%22 art%20spiegelman%22%201991&st=cse [accessed 8 Aug. 2008].

———. 2004. *In the Shadow of No Towers*. New York: Pantheon.

———. 2008. *Breakdowns* and *Portrait of the Artist as a Young %@§*!*. New York: Pantheon.

Tucker, Ken. 1985. Cats, Mice and History—the Avant-Garde of the Comic Strip. *The New York Times*, 26 May. http://query.nytimes.com/gst/fullpage.html?res=9905E4DB1639F 935A15756C0A963948260&scp=1&sq=cats,%20mice%20and%20history&st=cse [accessed 8 Aug. 2008].

Witek, Joseph. 2004. Imagetext, or, Why Art Spiegelman Doesn't Draw Comics. *ImageTexT: Interdisciplinary Comics Studies* 1(1). http://www.english.ufl.edu/imagetext/ archives/v1_1/witek/index.shtml [accessed 8 Aug. 2008].

Young, James E. 1998. The Holocaust as Vicarious Past: Art Spiegelman's *Maus* and the Afterimages of History. *Critical Inquiry* 24(3): 666–699.

Zipes, Jack, gen. ed. 2005. *The Norton Anthology of Children's Literature*. New York: W. W. Norton.

Interview

—SCOTT McCLOUD

Scott McCloud was born in Boston in 1960. The major work of his early career was the Eclipse-published superhero drama *Zot!* (1984–1991), but international fame and academic attention has focused on McCloud's graphic-novel-length comics essay *Understanding Comics: The Invisible Art* (1993). McCloud used *Understanding Comics* to outline the formal grammar of meaning-making in comics, to offer a history of the medium and to discuss key compositional features including color, time, and framing. *Understanding Comics* was ambitious and brave, and few comic texts have been as ubiquitous in the last twenty years—or as controversial.

McCloud attracted striking praise, and the ideas in *Understanding Comics* continue to be taught, contested, and defended by McCloud's peers in the academy and the comics industry. McCloud returned to the format of the book-length sequential art essay in two successors to *Understanding Comics*. *Reinventing Comics* (2000) offered twelve potential revolutions lying ahead in comics' (then) future, while *Making Comics* (2006) concentrated on the formal elements and mechanics of comics creation.

Those latter two texts in McCloud's trilogy of comics on comics stress the potential of computers and information technology for the production and distribution of sequential art. This has been part of McCloud's comics production practice as well as a theoretical interest, and in 1998 he used computers to generate the art for his graphic novel *The New Adventures of Abraham Lincoln*, an exploration of racism, iconography, and the abuse of myth-making in United States politics. McCloud's website features many online comics of various genres, and evidences the range and accessibility he argues for in translating comics onto the Internet: (http://www.scottmccloud.com/com ics/comics.html).

The following is a summary of an interview conducted by telephone on April 7, 2008.

Paul Williams: In terms of thinking about the status of comics outside the comic community—and I've been rereading some of your old comics for this interview—in *Understanding Comics*, you talk about some of the prejudices surrounding comics, you mention "comic book talk" (McCloud 1994, 3) and the sort of pejorative associations of comics. How far do you think that has changed, now, in 2008? If you do think there's a wider change in how the reading public has seen comics, where are the most important points?

Scott McCloud: There are regions of society where the status of comics has gone relatively unchanged in twenty years, and other regions where those prejudices have evaporated. In institutions of higher learning comics are half-way there. In the publishing world there has been very significant progress, so that aspects of publishing see comics as very important. The library system in North America has embraced the genre, and they do see it as a genre. This has caused a tremendous surge in circulation, and I know one public library that now has eight times as many comics on its shelves.

You don't see so many simplistic headlines equating comics with children's literature anymore, but that attitude hasn't completely gone away. Around five years ago in Texas, I was called as a witness to a case being defended by the Comic Book Legal Defense Fund, where an adult comic shop owner had sold a comic to an adult reader who had asked for that comic by name. The prosecutor equated comics with children's literature, successfully in this case—so I failed as a defense witness! So there's still a vulnerability to comics. But the people highest up the socio-cultural ladder, the people I call the taste-makers, have come around to the graphic novel with such gusto and wide-spread affection they have been culturally established. Of course we could be about to have the backlash, with hipsters in New York about to start claiming they never read comics anymore.

PW: It's all about the hipsters, isn't it?

SM: Well, not always, but it can be: the earthquake that causes the tsunami.

PW: Do you think, in relation to the hard-fought status of comics amongst taste-makers, that the gains can be taken for granted now, or do you think in twenty years' time we could be back where we were in the early 1980s?

SM: That depends on the quality of the work and the ability to get it out to readers, and there have been terrible setbacks in the latter but I see at least another ten years of creative work. Working with young comic creators, I see a tremendous improvement in storytelling and in coherence. Technique and creativity have all improved. Comics have often lurched forward in stages. If you look at *Watchmen*, *The Dark Knight Returns*, and *Maus*, I'm sure that Alan Moore, Frank Miller, and Art Spiegelman all thought that others would try to be more creative after these works, but what you got were a lot of gritty superhero comics that aped the surface qualities of the first two and didn't touch the latter. We now know that in fact ideas were being swallowed and metabolized by the next generation.

Chris Ware could not turn around and draw *Jimmy Corrigan* in twelve months after reading *Raw*, the comics anthology edited by Spiegelman and Françoise Mouly. There is a certain amount of time it takes for influence to manifest itself. We're starting to see the influence of Craig Thompson's *Blankets* on the next generation of comic creators . . . We can now see those derivative superhero comics that came after *Dark Knight* and *Watchmen* as undigested lumps on the surface of comics while the profound changes were coming underneath.

PW: You mention Chris Ware. It seems like there are certain comic creators at the moment, comic creators whom I am tempted to call celebrities. First of all, do you agree with that, and is that double-edged? Does it mean more people are reading comics to find out who are these people and why are they saying such nice things about them, but does it also mean that celebrity status gets in the way of people looking at these comics in new and exciting ways? I guess *Maus* would be an example of that: so much is written about Art Spiegelman, is it difficult for people to discover that comic on their own, to come at things with a fresh pair of eyes?

SM: I think what you are talking about, the cult of celebrity, depends a lot on the celebrity concerned. I think at best it means those creators have managed to acquire opportunities to tell their next story, and at worst it can lead down sidepaths that are distractions. I think comics has produced creators who are somewhat allergic to the cult of celebrity, who shun the limelight, and those that do, adopt it with great style. I'm thinking of Neil Gaiman, for example, or Paul Pope, who has just designed a range of clothes for Donna Karan, very colorful, with comic panels on them. I'm sure that someone like Neil Gaiman puts all this aside when he sits down to write his next book.

PW: We seem to be seeing at the moment a spate of returning to the archive, deluxe editions of the last hundred years of comic art, and particularly comic strip art. Is this symptomatic of an anxiety about the future of comics, or does it actually just reinforce this idea of maturity, of a medium that is capable of appreciating its predecessors and seminal figures?

SM: The latter—this is just shoring up the houses. It is a prerequisite of any medium built to last that it has some kind of institutional memory, and in many ways it was the lack of it that was remarkable. Take Charlie Chaplin films: you'd be shocked if they didn't exist any more. That doesn't necessarily mean you expect them to be available in your local video store, but that they were out there in some form or other. How could they not be? Do you think they'll ever be a day when you can't buy a copy of *Moby Dick*?

PW: I know you're very interested in online comics; the people we have been discussing are very well known for being graphic novelists, and also I think for producing quite hefty tomes. Do you think that can work with online comics—can there be a symbiotic relationship between these glossy expensive hardback editions and something that exists only in digital form? Can they work together or are they two different opportunities for the future of comics?

SM: That's a huge topic, and a difficult question to answer since it means unlocking about a thousand other questions . . . my goal was to make the web a viable environment for long-form works—and I failed! The web still favors short-term work. The reading experience is inferior to print, you can proceed less quickly than is the case with print, so there is still unfinished business. The web is maturing nicely for short-term work, for humor and light entertainment, but the online graphic novel genre is less mature.

PW: You can easily see ways in which they could inform each other; do you know the work of Tom Gauld? He is often published in *The Guardian*, which is a very prestigious British newspaper—a taste-makers' newspaper—and his web presence is a stepping stone for people interested in what they see in the *Guardian* to get more without necessarily going into a comic shop.

SM: Clearly there's a synergy. From the beginning, from the early 1990s onwards, it was a no-brainer that the web would contribute to communicating and publishing comics. It has transformed the community of comics and it has transformed the way information about comics is disseminated. But in terms of work produced for the web, those efforts have only been half successful.

PW: At least (and you might think different) there isn't, as in the music industry, a vile antipathy for the web and its encroachment into musicians and royalties and the future of music. It seems some other media, and comics

I think might be one of them, at least still keep an open mind, but maybe you think differently.

SM: The web means that there are thousands of comics out there, many more comics than are in print! In that sense it represents comics' long tail. You say the music industry is hostile towards the web, but how do we define it? Music executives might have antipathy, but everyone else is looking . . .

PW: . . . at how to exploit it . . .

SM: So how do we define industry? Musicians on MySpace might not be making any money, but the opportunities offered by the web might operate in the same way for comics. The communicating and promoting that I already mentioned is step one. Step two is about delivering a product online, and step three is about adapting the form to the medium of the web.

PW: It is a future that really is limitless and any attempts to predict it will inevitably be pleasurably exploded.

SM: Well, the basic principles were called as early as sixty years ago. Vannevar Bush during the Eisenhower administration thought we'd all be sitting down to desks and machines with all the world's information on them. That was how we would live in the future. He was asking "how can we facilitate this transition?"—he knew it was going to happen. He was dead right about where we ended up.

Now, he thought these machines would be the size of steamer trunks and we would be reading microfilm, but he was not trying to predict the actual technology itself but the shape of the technology's trajectory. Back in the early 1990s and the debut of the web I was interested in the same predictions, and I see no reason to back off from my basic position. I see no reason why our medium should be shackled to paper. Comics on the web would mean costs lowered, speed raised, and ubiquity more closely addressed.

It's like a leaf. It would be hopeless and futile to try and guess how many chaotic vectors and factors will affect a leaf that has fallen from the tree. There is no way to predict the chaotic process of air molecules, whether the leaf will float or turn. You *do* know that at the end of the process it will go down. You can compare this to comics in different media: we can predict the general destination, just not the process.

PW: It is a fascinating time to be interested in comics. As we were saying, if you're interested in comics from the archive, comics from one hundred years ago, this is the best time—not twenty years ago, not thirty years. If you're a Herriman fan or a Kelly fan you're actually going to get your hands on this stuff!

SM: It takes a little while but we have generational continuity now. Usually the comics world pulls itself out of the sea, and comics walk erect for a while before the comet hits and there's another mass extinction. And it takes another ten to fifteen years before it pulls itself out of the sea again. But now, since the early 1980s and the growth of comic book stores, there has been continuity: people like Spiegelman and Crumb are still working, continuing to pass down their learning to a younger generation. Their longevity will inspire us to reach further than they have done already.

PW: I've got to say that's a great model of comics history: catastrophism . . . The first time I read *Understanding Comics* I saw the Scott McCloud character as a transparent vehicle for you to get your ideas across in comic form. Reading it again makes me think that this is using the techniques of fiction, and the narrator, if you like, is a fictional construct, lines on paper, by no means your stand-in, but actually a self-conscious device to engage and to probe and to entertain the reader.

SM: Well, there's certainly a narrative quality and an emotional arc in order to generate interest, and achieve specific goals. I wanted to inspire people, and there is some sense of a dramatic arc. You may want to read Dylan Horrocks's essay, "Inventing Comics" (2001)—he takes me gently to task for my sleight of hand in claiming to analyze comics but actually inventing the history of comics I discuss. Horrocks suggests I am proposing an entirely different sense of a medium to the one that exists, as if I am busy with plaster of paris creating a counterfeit sphinx and lopping off its nose to make it look old!

I think that the definition of comics in *Understanding Comics* was already being used. In 1993 I could have pulled out pieces of cloth and nailed them to the wall and got another comic professional to look at them and they would have identified a narrative connection. A sequence 1, 2, 3 implies a change going on. This is fundamental to the medium.

In that book I was proposing a way of looking at the medium but I was not erasing others. If you are rummaging through a discount bin, my avatar won't jump out at you if you think that a collection of single panel cartoons like *The Far Side* or a stapled magazine are comics. They might be another definition of comics—in some ways they are comics, Dylan Horrocks says. But I think it is constructive to look at comics in the way I did in *Understanding Comics*, which excluded single-panel works but drew the borders of the map so large it incorporated all sorts of things people hadn't thought of as comics. The definition I used was not that particular about period or place, so that the old nineteenth-century European broadsheets that Kunzle talks about were fundamentally comics.

PW: I actually think that is the germ of the book that is most useful, the idea that this is sequential art, art in sequence, and it is interesting and informative to start from that premise and go from there. In some ways we could compare *Understanding Comics* to a whodunit—that is the body that starts the rest of the investigation.

SM: In using such an expansive definition my primary purpose was not just to take the reader backward and highjack high art. My intention was to draw a more expansive map, so that everything from stained glass, to sculpture, to painting, to photography, to scrolls might be a viable option for comics artists. Why should comics be restricted to paper? That's one of my . . . what's the opposite of regret?

PW: Sense of satisfaction?

SM: I guess regret doesn't have a perfect antonym. Well, what I was most satisfied about in *Understanding Comics* was that I drew a definition of comics that never mentioned paper. At the same time in the early 1990s I was working on the book the World Wide Web as we know it was being launched. So as my definition walked out the door the web walked in at the same moment.

PW: You're been very important in terms of creators and creator's rights—I remember coming into comics in the 1980s and into the early 1990s that was a very hot topic, but it seems the last ten years, on things like letters pages and fans forums, the issue of creator's rights isn't being discussed that much. Is this a symbol that things are heading in the right direction, that they have momentum that won't be stopped in terms of the recognition of creators?

SM: Well, I think comics go through cycles of revolution and complacency and this is a period of complacency! There are plenty of sharks looking to acquire young artists' properties, I have heard from some of the young artists and a few of the sharks. There are lots of artists self-publishing on the web who have signed nothing except the contract with their server. Control and ownership is simply not an issue for them. That doesn't mean that if they're making $5 and someone offers them $50 to sign their rights away forever they won't take it!

But a recent effort by a large newspaper syndicate to move into online comics had to offer artists a very liberal deal. Siegel getting the rights to Superman back recently, sadly posthumously, had enormous symbolic value and sent ripples through the industry (see Cieply 2008). This was comics' "original sin" (that was what some creators called it) and this victory called a note of finality, if not finality in actuality. This "original sin" goes back to before The Creator's Bill of Rights—it goes back to Neal Adams in the 1970s.

WORKS CITED

Cieply, Michael. 2008. Ruling Gives Heirs a Share of Superman Copyright. *The New York Times*. http://www.nytimes.com/2008/03/29/business/media/29comics.html?_r=3&oref=slogin&oref=slogin&oref=slogin [accessed 8 Apr. 2008].

Horrocks, Dylan. 2001. Inventing Comics: Scott McCloud's Definition of Comics. *Hicksville: The Website of Dylan Horrocks*. http://www.hicksville.co.nz/Inventing%20Comics.htm [accessed 8 Apr. 2008]. Originally published in *Comics Journal*.

McCloud, Scott. 1994. *Understanding Comics*. New York: HarperPerennial. Originally published in 1993.

Contributors

David M. Ball is an Assistant Professor of English at Dickinson College where he teaches courses in multicultural and multidisciplinary American modernism and the graphic novel. His essays and reviews have appeared or are forthcoming in *Modern Fiction Studies, ESQ: A Journal of the American Renaissance, South Atlantic Review, Critical Matrix,* and *College Literature.* He is currently working on two book manuscripts, a co-edited volume of critical essays titled *The Comics of Chris Ware: Drawing Is a Way of Thinking,* from the University Press of Mississippi in 2010, and a study of the rhetoric of failure in American literature from 1850 to the present.

Ian Gordon is an Associate Professor in History and American Studies Convenor at the National University of Singapore. His books include *Comic Strips and Consumer Culture* (1998) and *Film and Comic Books* (2007). His article "Nostalgia, Myth, and Ideology: Visions of Superman at the End of the American Century" is reprinted in the Michael Ryan-edited anthology, *Cultural Studies* (2008).

Andrew Loman, Assistant Professor at Memorial University of Newfoundland, is the author of *"Somewhat on the Community-System": Fourierism in the Works of Nathaniel Hawthorne* (Routledge, 2005) and essays in the *Journal of American Studies* and the *Emerson Society Quarterly*; his short fiction has appeared in the Canadian literary quarterly *Exile.* He is currently researching a book about his father, a survivor of concentration camps in WWII Indonesia.

Andrea A. Lunsford is the Louise Hewlett Nixon Professor of English and Humanities and Director of the Program in Writing and Rhetoric at Stanford University. She has designed and taught undergraduate and graduate courses in writing history and theory, rhetoric, literacy studies, and women's writing and is the author or co-author of many books and articles, including *The Everyday Writer, Essays on Classical Rhetoric and Modern Discourse, Singular*

Texts/Plural Authors: Perspectives on Collaborative Writing, Reclaiming Rhetorica: Women in the History of Rhetoric, Everything's an Argument, Exploring Borderlands: Composition and Postcolonial Studies, and *Writing Matters: Rhetoric in Private and Public Lives.*

James Lyons is Senior Lecturer in Film Studies at the University of Exeter. He is author of *Selling Seattle* (2004), and *Miami Vice* (2010), and co-editor of *Quality Popular Television* (with Mark Jancovich, 2003), and *Multimedia Histories* (with John Plunkett, 2007). He was a founding member of the editorial board for *Scope: An Online Journal of Film Studies.*

Ana Merino is associate professor at The University of Iowa. She has published a scholarly book on comics titled *El Comic Hispanico* (Cátedra, 2003), a critical monograph on Chris Ware (Sinsentido 2005), five books of poetry and one work of fiction. She was awarded the Diario de Avisos Award for best critical short article about comics for the Spanish literary magazine *Leer.* Merino is a member of the Board of Directors for the Center for Cartoon Studies and a member of the executive committee of International Comic Art Forum. Merino's articles on comics have appeared in *Leer, DDLV, The Comics Journal, International Journal of Comic Art,* and *Hispanic Issues.* She has served as curator for three comics exhibitions and is the author of the bilingual catalogue *Fantagraphics creadores del canon* (2003).

Graham J. Murphy has published in *Queer Universes: Sexualities in Science Fiction, The Routledge Companion to Science Fiction, Fifty Key Figures in Science Fiction, Science Fiction Studies, Extrapolation, Foundation, ImageTexT: Interdisciplinary Comics Studies,* and a variety of other venues. He co-authored *Ursula K. Le Guin: A Critical Companion* (Greenwood) and has co-edited *Beyond Cyberpunk: New Critical Perspectives* (Routledge). His current research explores the critical intersections of post/human subjectivities and insect ontologies in speculative fictions. He teaches with Trent University's Cultural Studies Department and its Department of English Literature as well as Seneca College of Applied Arts and Technology.

Chris Murray lectures in English and Film Studies at the University of Dundee. He is a central member of the Scottish Word and Image Group (SWIG), which organizes annual conferences on aspects of word and image study. He also organizes an annual comics conference in Dundee as part of the Dundee Literary Festival. His book on superheroes and propaganda will be published by Hampton Press in 2010. Other publications include papers in *Comics and Culture* (Museum of Tusculaneum/University of Copenhagen Press, 2000), *The Scottish Society of Art History Journal* (2006), *Sub/versions: Genre, Cultural Status and Critique* (Cambridge Scholars Publishing, 2008), as well as several papers in *The International Journal of Comic Art*. He has contributed sections on comics to *Encyclopedia Britannica*, *The Blackwell Encyclopedia of Cultural Theory*, and *The Greenwood Encyclopedia of Comics and Graphic Novels*. He is co-editor, along with Julia Round, of the journal *Studies in Comics*, published by Intellect.

Adam Rosenblatt is a PhD candidate in Modern Thought and Literature at Stanford University. He is writing a dissertation about the forensic investigations of human rights violations, including the ethical treatment of dead bodies. He has also published articles about Argentinean comics and handcrafted mini-comics.

Julia Round (MA, PhD) lectures in Media and Communication at Bournemouth University, UK, and edits the academic journal *Studies in Comics*. She has published and presented work internationally on cross-media adaptation, the "graphic novel" redefinition, the application of literary criticism and terminology to comics, and the presence of gothic and fantastic motifs and themes in this medium. Further details are at www.juliaround.com.

Joe Sutliff Sanders is an assistant professor in the English Department at California State University—San Bernardino. His articles have appeared in *The Journal of the Fantastic In the Arts*, *The Children's Literature Association Quarterly*, *Foundation*, *The Sandman Papers*, and *The Lion and the Unicorn*. He reviews graphic novels for the international journal *Teacher Librarian*.

Stephen Weiner, Director of the Maynard Public Library in Maynard, Massachusetts, holds an M.A. in Children's Literature as well as an M.L.I.S., and has been a pioneering advocate for the inclusion of graphic novels in libraries and other educational settings. He has been writing about comics art since 1992, and his reviews and articles have appeared in numerous publications. He is also a sought-after speaker and has spoken at academic and library conferences at the regional, state, and national level since 1998. His books include *Bring an Author to Your Library* (1993), *100 Graphic Novels for Public Libraries* (1996), *The 101 Best Graphic Novels* (2001), *Faster than a Speeding Bullet: the Rise of the Graphic Novel* (2003), and *The 101 Best Graphic Novels—2nd Edition*

(2005). In addition, he is co-author of *The Will Eisner Companion* (2004), *Using Graphic Novels in the Classroom including Bone by Jeff Smith: A Guide for Teachers and Librarians* (2005), and *Hellboy: The Companion* (2008).

Paul Williams is Teaching Fellow in Critical Theory, Twentieth-Century and Contemporary Literature at the University of Exeter. His work is concerned with how the idea of race and the assumptions of colonialism resurface in the representation of modern and future war, with several articles and chapters ranging across Vietnam War films, the nuclear criticism of the 1980s, and the relationship between hip-hop culture and the War on Terror. He is currently writing a book exploring how cultural texts have understood nuclear weapons as emblematic of "white" Western culture.

Index